THE Illustrated
Cairo
Genizah

Nick Posegay &
Melonie Schmierer-Lee

GORGIAS PRESS

2024

Gorgias Press LLC, 954 River Road, Piscataway, NJ, 08854, USA

www.gorgiaspress.com

2024

ISBN 978-1-4632-4772-0

Library of Congress Cataloging-in-Publication Data

A Cataloging-in-Publication Record is available from the Library of Congress.
Printed in China.

For Alex, Travis, and Sophia

Table of Contents

Acknowledgements

We have wanted to make this book for many years. Promoting public knowledge of the Cairo Genizah has been part of the Genizah Research Unit's mission since 1974, but it took a remarkable confluence of events – the 50th anniversary of the GRU, three public exhibitions, a wildly successful programme of show-and-tell manuscript tours, and a modestly successful Instagram page – for all the pieces to fall into place. It also could not have happened without financial support from Cambridge University Library, the Second Joseph Aaron Littman Foundation, the Isaac Newton Trust, and the Leverhulme Trust project, "Interfaith Exchange in the Intellectual History of Middle Eastern Languages." Thank you to the Syndics of Cambridge University Library for permitting us to publish the images within.

One of the inspirations for this book was the Genizah Research Unit's Instagram page (@CambridgeGRU) that Nick began in 2021. Many of the fragments and discussions that ended up in this book came from there, and we would be remiss if we did not thank all of its readers for their support. In particular, thank you to Edson De Faria, Lucy De Los Reyes, Haim Gottschalk, Daniel Newman, Amanda Posegay, Kristine Rose-Beers, David Selis, and Noah van Renswoude. Special thanks to Sarah Sykes for the time she spent identifying and fetching images to share. The other inspiration was the GRU's recent public educational programming: show-and-tell visits under the auspices of the Littman Genizah Educational Programme, and a series of major exhibitions, *Discarded History* (Cambridge, 2017), *Ghost Words* (Cambridge, 2021), and *The Golden Age of the Jews of Al-Andalus* (Madrid, 2023–24).

Thank you to our friends and colleagues who helped with brainstorming and fact-checking, including Catherine Ansorge, Dotan Arad, Estara Arrant, Frank Bowles, Orietta Da Rold, Magdalen Connolly, Alan Elbaum, Huw Jones, Geoffrey Khan, George Kiraz, Julia Krivoruchko, José (Pepe) Martínez Delgado, Ann McCoy, Marc Michaels, Blazej Mikula, Seth Musser, Suzanne Paul, Maciej Pawlikowski, David Posegay, Noah van Renswoude, Zvi Stampfer, Nadia Vidro, and Peggy Xu. Thank you to Amir Ashur, Kim Phillips, and Rabbi Aubrey Hersh for their helpful comments on drafts of our chapters. Further thanks to our incredible graphic designer, Andy Harvey, and his team at H2 Associates – they did a fantastic job turning our plain text into an absolute work of art. Thank you to Sophia Johnson and Travis Lee for offering moral support and acting as sounding boards for our more outlandish ideas, whether they really wanted to or not.

Finally, thank you to the Head of the Genizah Research Unit, Ben Outhwaite, the single person without whom this book would not exist. Thank you for approving our foolhardy scheme, thank you for navigating the labyrinths of university administration, thank you for teaching us the deep lore of the GRU, and thank you for working around the clock with us to ensure this book was finished in a timely manner. We could not have done it without you.

Nick Posegay
Melonie Schmierer-Lee
Cambridge University Library
April 2024

The Ben Ezra Synagogue based on 1970s photograph, illustration by Melonie Schmierer-Lee.

Introduction

This is the first illustrated volume intended to provide an introduction to the Cairo Genizah that is accessible to everyone, even those who have never heard of it before. Within these pages, you'll tour ancient artefacts that are entirely unique in world history – manuscripts that have redefined our understanding of the Middle East, the Mediterranean world, and most of all, the history of Judaism. Among them are some of the world's oldest Bibles, the official records of long-defeated empires, and works of literature once thought lost to the ages. You'll see the writings of some of the most famous names in history, people like Avicenna, Origen, Augustine, Galen, Saladin, Joseph Karo, and Moses Maimonides. You'll read about the daily travails of ordinary people in the Middle Ages – residents of Egypt, Iberia, India, Byzantium, Iraq, and Palestine – through the personal letters that they sent to their loved ones. You'll begin to understand the evidence for how modern legal, economic, and religious systems are built on foundations that are more than 1000 years old. All of these things and more survived to the present day because of the Cairo Genizah, a medieval repository of worn-out manuscripts created by the Jews of Cairo.

This book is also a celebration of 127 years of Cairo Genizah research in Cambridge, and it marks 50 years since the founding of Cambridge University Library's Taylor-Schechter Genizah Research Unit. We, the authors, are researchers at the University of Cambridge with a combined 25 years of experience in studying Cairo Genizah manuscripts – and a drive to share that research with a wide audience. We developed this book alongside the Genizah Research Unit's ongoing public tours, special exhibitions, and social media programming. You're more than welcome to visit us at Cambridge University Library to see the manuscripts yourself, but if you can't make the trip, then this book is the next best thing.

What is the Cairo Genizah?

To explain exactly what the Cairo Genizah is, we should first ask, "What is a genizah?" The word *genizah* is Hebrew, from an ancient root meaning 'hidden' or 'stored up', thought to be related to the Persian word *ganza*, 'treasury'. A genizah is a hidden space where Jewish communities deposit worn-out texts that are too old or damaged for continued use. Their main purpose is to prevent items that contain the sacred name of God from being destroyed like other rubbish. Many *genizot* (plural of genizah) are cupboards in synagogues, where they act as temporary storage spaces before the texts can be given proper burials in the ground.

The term 'Cairo Genizah' refers to the corpus of manuscripts that Egyptian Jewish communities deposited into various genizot between the 11th and 19th centuries CE. The vast majority of these manuscripts come from the genizah chamber of the Ben Ezra Synagogue in Fustat, the old city of what is now modern Cairo. Others come from the Karaite Dar Simha synagogue and the Basatin Cemetery on the edge of Cairo. Today, they are held primarily in European and American libraries, with approximately two-thirds in Cambridge University Library (~200,000 fragments), and other major collections in the Jewish Theological Seminary of America (~31,000), the Russian National Library (~15,000), Oxford's Bodleian Library (~12,000), Manchester's John Rylands Library (~11,000), and the British Library (~6,000).

For the communities that produced the Cairo Genizah, it seems that almost every scrap of paper with Hebrew letters was considered sacred enough to deposit into a genizah. Some of them may even have deposited all papers with writing on them – including those with no Hebrew – rather than throwing them away. The result is that the Cairo Genizah holds not just Jewish religious texts like Bibles and Torah scrolls, but also thousands of personal letters, government documents, business contracts, receipts, notes, drawings, and literary works in Hebrew, Aramaic, Arabic, Judaeo-Arabic, Ladino, Yiddish, Judaeo-Italian, Judaeo-Persian, Greek, Syriac, Coptic, Turkish, Georgian, Latin, and French.

This book will take you on a tour of these manuscripts. All of them were – almost by definition – thrown away, often after long lives of use and reuse, so many are badly torn, scraped, rubbed, faded, or stained. As well as wear-and-tear from use, most of them are also about 900 years old, and they have not always been kept in the best conditions. Nevertheless, even for the most badly damaged fragments, their very presence in the Cairo Genizah tells us a story about what people were reading, writing, and doing in Egypt during the Middle Ages.

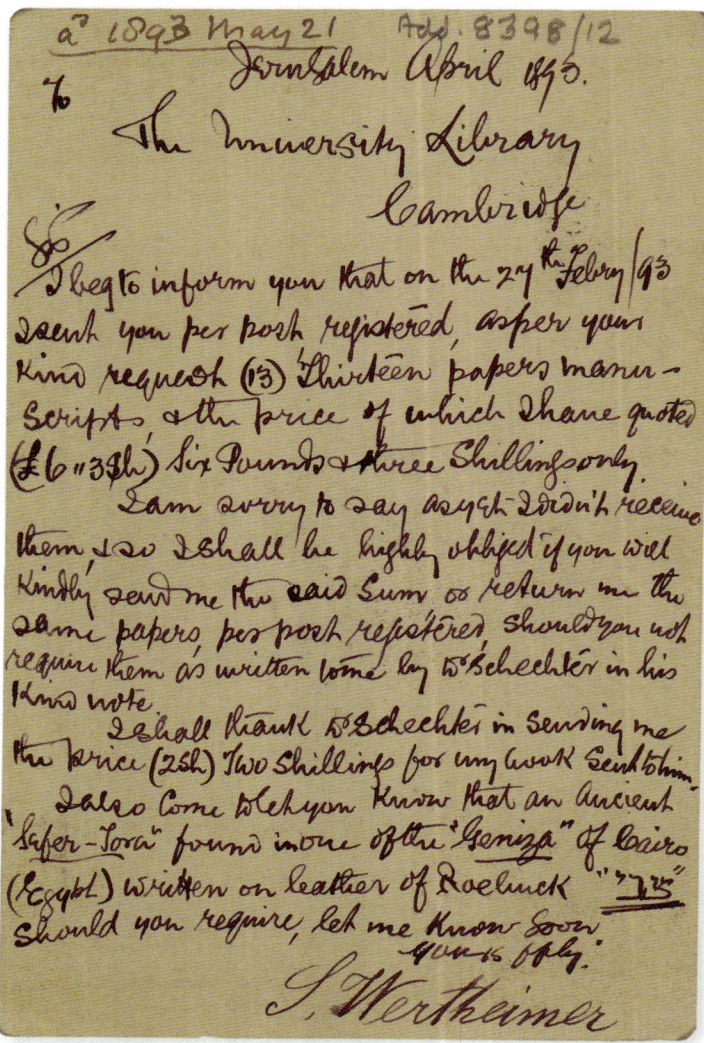

CUL Add.8398/12. Letter from Solomon Wertheimer to Cambridge University Library, April 1893.

The 'Discovery' of the Manuscripts

The first Genizah fragments came to Cambridge University Library in the early 1890s. A Hungarian rare books dealer, Rabbi Solomon Aaron Wertheimer, posted bundles of manuscripts to Cambridge from Jerusalem. The Library purchased some as part of an initiative to bolster their Hebrew collections, but others failed to generate much interest, and Wertheimer sent plaintive letters to the Library asking either for payment or the return of the unwanted manuscripts. In one note from 1893, he mentioned an ancient Torah scroll that was acquired from a synagogue storage room – a genizah – in Cairo.

Cambridge's resident Hebrew specialist, Solomon Schechter, routinely checked Wertheimer's manuscript offerings. Schechter was born into a Hasidic family in the Moldavian town of Focşani in 1847, and was recognised as an intellectual prodigy as a child. After studying in Vienna and Berlin, he came to London at the invitation of the Jewish scholar and educator, Claude

Solomon Schechter in his doctoral robes, ca. 1900.

Portraits of Agnes Smith Lewis and Margaret Dunlop Gibson, by John Peddie, oil on canvas. Westminster College, Cambridge.

Montefiore, who saw his potential as a leading Jewish thinker. By all accounts, he took to England and its people with great enthusiasm, and quickly became proficient in English.[1] Cambridge recognised the value of Schechter's scholarship and appointed him Lecturer in Talmudics in 1890. He was only the second Jewish person to teach at the University. The study of Jewish law had previously been taught for centuries by and for Christian clergymen.

Something of an outsider in Cambridge society, Schechter found kindred spirits among other unorthodox scholars. Two adventurous and fabulously wealthy Scottish sister scholars – Agnes Lewis and Margaret Gibson – had settled together in Cambridge after the untimely deaths of their husbands. As devout Presbyterians, the twins were interested in the origins of the biblical text, and began

to visit monasteries in the hopes of discovering early biblical manuscripts. They were especially familiar with St. Catherine's Monastery in the Sinai, where – after being hauled up over the walls in a basket – they befriended its Orthodox monks by conversing in fluent Greek. The monks gave them permission to inspect the oldest manuscripts in the monastic library, where they found an early Syriac version of the Gospels.[2] This discovery established their scholarly reputations in Cambridge, but as women they could not be admitted to the University.

During their 1896 expedition to St. Catherine's, the sisters purchased a bundle of Hebrew and Aramaic manuscripts from a local dealer. When they returned to Cambridge, they invited Schechter to examine them. Agnes described the dramatic events:[3]

---

1   N. Bentwich, *Solomon Schechter: A Biography* (Philadelphia: The Jewish Publication Society of America, 1940), 64.

2   M. Gibson, *How the Codex was Found: A Narrative of Two Visits to Sinai, From Mrs. Lewis's Journals, 1892–1893* (Cambridge, 1893).

3   A. Smith Lewis, *In the Shadow of Sinai: A Story of Travel and Research from 1895 to 1897* (Cambridge, 1898).

…we resolved on asking our friend Dr Solomon Schechter, Reader in Talmudic to the University, to examine them. Accordingly, on May 13th, I met him by chance on King's Parade, and told him that we had a number of things at home which awaited his inspection. He must have gone to our house immediately, for I returned after doing a little shopping and found him in the dining-room with our two bundles of fragments on the table. He held up a large vellum leaf saying, "This is part of the Jerusalem Talmud, which is very rare; may I take it away?" "Certainly," I replied. Then he held up a dirty scrap of paper. "This, too, is very interesting; may I take it away and identify it?" "Certainly." "May I publish it?" I replied, "Mrs Gibson and I will only be too happy if you find that it is worth publishing."

A few hours later, a letter arrived:

Schechter's message announced the identification of a text that had not been seen for a thousand years: the original Hebrew of the apocryphal book of Ben Sira (known in Christian circles as Ecclesiasticus). The discovery became national news. Schechter's rivals in Oxford identified more pages of the book among manuscripts they had collected in Egypt, and a race was on: who would succeed in tracking down their source, and whatever else might remain there?

Schechter approached his friend, Charles Taylor, for advice in securing University travel funding. Taylor, a mathematician, Hebraicist, and Master of St John's College, advised him not to delay and offered his own money to fund an expedition. Schechter set off for Egypt in the winter of 1896, hoping to find more leaves of Ben Sira and other rare works. On his return, he described his 'pilgrimage' to the Genizah in an article for *The Times*,

Schechter's note to Agnes Lewis, dated 13 May, 1896.

Entrance to the Ben Ezra Synagogue's genizah chamber, ca. 1900.

titled "A Hoard of Hebrew Manuscripts."[4] He began by introducing the concept of a genizah to the British public:

> The Genizah of the old Jewish community… represents a combination of sacred lumber-room and secular record office.

He then explained that before arriving in Egypt, he worried that much of its history had been lost:

> I felt reassured after a brief interview with the Rev. Aaron Bensimon, the Grand Rabbi of Cairo, to whom I had an introduction from the Chief Rabbi, the Very Rev. Dr. Hermann Adler. From him I soon learnt that Old Cairo would be the proper field of my activity, a place old enough to enjoy the respect even of a resident of Cambridge.

The rabbi took him to the Ben Ezra synagogue:

> We left our carriage somewhere in the neighbourhood of the "Fortress of Babylon," whence the Rabbi directed his steps to the so-called Synagogue of Ezra the Scribe.

And he was shown the genizah chamber:

> The Genizah, which probably always formed an integral part of the synagogue, is now situated at the end of the gallery, presenting the appearance of a sort of windowless and doorless room of fair dimensions. The entrance is on the west side, through a big, shapeless hole reached by a ladder. After showing me over the place and the neighbouring buildings, or rather ruins, the Rabbi introduced me to the beadles of the synagogue, who are at the same time the keepers of the Genizah, and authorised me to take from it what, and as much as, I liked. Now, as a matter of fact, I liked all. Still, some discretion was necessary… One can hardly realise the confusion in a genuine old Genizah until one has seen it. It is a battlefield of books, and the literary production of many centuries had their share in the battle, and their *disjecta membra* are now strewn over its area. Some of the belligerents have perished outright, and are literally ground to dust in the terrible struggle for space…

---

4   *The Times*, "A Hoard of Hebrew MSS," issued 3 August 1897 (London).

Not all of the 'belligerents' interested Schechter, and – much to the chagrin of the present authors – he weeded out the later printed material:

> Most of my time in Cairo was spent in getting rid of these *parvenus*, whilst every piece of paper or parchment that had any claim to a respectable age was packed in bags and conveyed to the forwarding agent to be shipped to England. The task was by no means easy, the Genizah being very dark, and emitting clouds of dust when its contents were stirred, as if protesting against the disturbance of its inmates. The protest is the less to be ignored as the dust settles in one's throat, and threatens suffocation.

He was also opposed to some of the customs of the local Jews who cared for the synagogue:

> I was thus compelled to accept the aid offered me by the keepers of the place, who had some experience in such work from their connexion with former acquisitions (perhaps they were rather depredations) from the Genizah. Of course, they declined to be paid for their services in hard cash of so many piastres per diem. This was a vulgar way of doing business to which no self-respecting keeper of a real Genizah would degrade himself. The keepers insisted the more on *bakhshish*, which, besides being a more dignified kind of remuneration, has the advantage of being expected also for services not rendered.

Schechter then offered the public an overview of the collected manuscripts, noting Bibles with a new system of punctuation, historical Jewish prayer books with "psalmists hitherto unknown," and old rabbinic works "long ago given up as lost for ever." He also described the exceptionally rich documents of daily life:

> All sorts and conditions of men and situations are represented in them: the happy young married couple by their marriage contract; the marriage that failed by its letter of divorce; the slave by his deed of emancipation; the Court of justice by its legal decisions; the heads of the schools by their learned epistles; the newly appointed "Prince of the Exile" by the description of his installation; the rich trader by his correspondence with his agents in Malabar; the gentleman-beggar by his letters of recommendation to the great ones in Israel; the fanatics by their thundering excommunications; the meek man by his mild apologies; the fool by his amulet; the medical man by his prescriptions; and the patient by his will.

Exterior of the Ben Ezra Synagogue in 2017.

The Ben Ezra Synagogue

The Ben Ezra synagogue was constructed in the 1040s CE, likely on the foundations of an older synagogue that was destroyed on the orders of the oppressive caliph, al-Hakim. Over its lifetime, it has been associated with various figures from Jewish tradition, including Moses, Jeremiah, Elijah, and Ezra. It is known today as 'Ben Ezra' because it once housed a Torah scroll rumoured to have been written by the ancient biblical scribe, Ezra. However, in the Middle Ages it was known as Kanisat al-Yerushalmiyyin ('the Synagogue of the Jerusalemites') or Kanisat al-Shamiyyin ('the Synagogue of the Palestinians'), and later on, Kanisat Eliyahu ('the Synagogue of Elijah').

As the largest and most ancient synagogue in Fustat, it was the seat of the religious court (the 'Bet Din'), a hub for social welfare, and a place of study. In the 10th and 11th centuries, the wealthiest members of the Jewish community lived nearby, and some bequeathed their houses to the synagogue's charitable foundation to help fund communal needs. In the 12th century, however, more prosperous Jews gravitated to Cairo – the Fatimid and Ayyubid capital north of Fustat – and from the latter part of the 13th century onwards the area around the synagogue mainly housed the poor and destitute. Visitors to Fustat in the 15th century described the synagogue in poor condition, damaged by fire. Although daily services stopped, its venerable history still attracted pilgrims from Cairo and further afield for weekly or monthly services.

Access to the synagogue's genizah chamber was through a hatch in the second-floor women's gallery (men and women worshipped separately). The chamber was no secret, but for many years, local custom held that it was guarded by a serpent. Some 19th-century scholars did receive permission to remove sacks of manuscripts from the chamber, and those manuscripts made their way to libraries and private collections all over Europe, including Cambridge – though few European researchers knew of their origins or realised their significance.

Periodic efforts were made to renovate the decaying building until 1889. After the roof collapsed, the entire structure was demolished and rebuilt to the same specifications. The contents of the genizah chamber were removed during demolition, but most of them were replaced after construction ended in 1892. It was this newly rebuilt synagogue that Schechter visited in 1897. In the 1990s, the building benefited from another major restoration project. It is no longer a functioning synagogue, but a historical monument open to the public.

In closing, Schechter proved himself master of the understatement:

> All these treasures are now stored up in the Library of the University of Cambridge, where they are undergoing the slow process of a thorough examination. The results of this examination will certainly prove interesting alike to the theologian and the historian.

In candid letters sent from Cairo, Schechter described more of what had gone on behind the scenes. He told his wife, Mathilde, about how he befriended the local Chief Rabbi after taking him to see the Giza pyramids:[5]

> I flirted with him for hours, and am now taking Arabic lessons three times a week. You see how practical your old man is… The Rabbi is very kind to me and kisses me on my mouth, which is not very pleasant… I am just back from the Geniza and brought two big sacks with fragments. I must have a bath at once. You have no idea of the dirt.

---

5   Bentwich, 129.

To Francis Jenkinson, Cambridge's University Librarian, Schechter wrote about the practical aspects of gathering the manuscripts:[6]

> I am now here since three weeks. After making the acquaintance of the Chief Rabbi here and the president of the Jewish community I set to work on the "Genizas" where I spend the most of my time in the dust of centuries. The beadel & other infernal scoundrels are helping me to clear away the rubbish and the printed matter. I have constantly to bakeshish them, but still they are stealing many good things and sell them to the dealers in antiquities. I cannot possibly prevent it, but I found out the said dealers and bought from them the fragments which have interest for me. In the Genizah itself which is dark dusty and full of all possible insects there is no opportunity of examining the content of MSS. My policy is to take as much as I can (for which I have the full permission of the authorities). I have till now thirteen large bags of fragments, of which though not examined, I am sure, contain many most important things.

Schechter then set out his plan to give the manuscripts a permanent home in Cambridge University Library:

> Now I have a great request… I do not consider it desirable to the MSS here and am anxious to send the first lot home to England. Will you give them a place in the University Library till I return. The MSS will probably belong soon to your Library. I want only to hear first whether you and the Syndics will agree to certain conditions which I have to make. Money plays no important part in these conditions and I am sure you will find them very fair and just.

Agnes and Margaret had arrived in Cairo soon after Schechter and came to see the synagogue. As a custodian slipped through the hole into the genizah chamber, Agnes listened in astonishment to the sound of manuscripts crunching beneath his feet. She was concerned for Schechter's wellbeing, and wrote to his wife back in Cambridge:[7]

> Schechter has found a few good things among heaps of what I won't say is rubbish, but unimportant stuff. He has been choked with dust and bad air and has worked like a horse. He wishes he had a respirator…

Schechter arranged for a licence to export the fragments from Egypt's highest authority at the time – the British colonial consul general, Lord Cromer – and sent them ahead to England by steamer and train. Schechter himself travelled back separately aboard a ship where he met the famed archaeologist Flinders Petrie There was a hairy moment when the ship ran aground on rocks near Marseilles, but a tugboat took all passengers to safety.

On 15 December, 1898, the University Orator in the Cambridge Senate House conveyed the University's official thanks to the Jewish community of Cairo for the gift of the Genizah Collection. The text was sent to Cairo in Latin and Hebrew versions. An English edition appeared in the *Jewish Chronicle* of 30 December, 1898:[8]

> To the Heads of the Jewish Community in Cairo:
>
> We offer you our thanks, not only on account of the singular goodwill with which you received our Reader in Rabbinic, but also on account of the conspicuous liberality with which you permitted him to return to us laden with so many fragments of books from your Treasury. In the faithful preservation of books, the saying, "the written word remains", seems to have been as a law to you… By the generous gift of your ancient books to our envoy you have not only increased your own ancient renown but have even made a considerable addition to the history of your ancient literature. Even from our islands so far to the West, some light will doubtless be shed upon your literature…

---

6   Schechter's letter to Francis Jenkinson, dated 12th January 1897: Cambridge University Library Add.6463(e)3416. For more on the working relationship between Jenkinson and Schechter, see S. Reif, "Jenkinson and Schechter at Cambridge: an expanded and updated assessment," *Jewish Historical Studies*, Vol. 32 (1990–1992), 279–316.

7   Bentwich, 130.

8   The full Hebrew and English text appears here: https://www.lib.cam.ac.uk/genizah-fragments/posts/we-offer-you-our-thanks-cambridges-letter-egypts-jewish-community.

The Cairo Genizah in Cambridge

Schechter donated the entire 'hoard' of Genizah fragments to Cambridge University Library in 1898. The terms of the donation required the University to preserve the manuscripts and draw up a catalogue list within ten years. This proved to be a rather ambitious commitment. The University Library granted Schechter the use of a dedicated room to sort the collection with a small team of assistants,[9] which soon became known as the 'Cairo Room'. Some fragments were given identifying classmark numbers and organised into categories, such as 'Bible', 'Commentary', 'Mishnah', 'Talmud', or 'Document'. Many were steamed, flattened, and put between large panes of glass, but the task must have seemed neverending. Schechter had left money in Egypt with instructions to buy any other fragments that came to light, and more kept arriving.

Cambridge's Cairo Genizah collections would eventually be counted at almost 200,000 fragments, but it is likely that some of the fragments later sent to Cambridge came from sources other than the Ben Ezra Synagogue.

In 1902, after 4 years of productive work, Schechter heeded a personal spiritual call and left Cambridge to revive Conservative Judaism in the United States. He took some Genizah fragments with him, continuing research in his new post as president of the Jewish Theological Seminary of America until his death in 1915. Schechter's successor in Cambridge, Ernest Worman, continued in a similarly productive vein between 1906 and 1909, drawing up handlists for thousands of fragments, only to be struck down by a sudden illness ('galloping

Schechter at work in the 'Cairo Room', 1898.

9   The University Library relocated to its current building in 1934. The library of Schechter's day is the university administrative building now known as the 'Old Schools'.

consumption') at the age of 38.[10] The still unclassified fragments – more than three quarters of the collection – survived the threats of war and librarians inclined towards decluttering, but progress stalled for decades. Jenkinson's successor as University Librarian, Alwyn Faber Scholfield, later despaired of the collection, writing: "They might from their size and condition be fairly described as a dust heap… [and] seem (to an ignorant person) to be a hopeless case."[11]

Most of the unsorted fragments remained in their shipping crates until the 1950s, when the historian Shelomo Dov Goitein arrived in Cambridge seeking manuscripts relating to the economic history of the medieval Mediterranean world. After Goitein examined the fragments conserved in glass, the University Librarian offered to show him the crates of unsorted material (marked 'Rubbish') in the Library's attic. His discoveries among these boxes spurred the Library to re-invest in the collection. In 1965, Henry Knopf – a

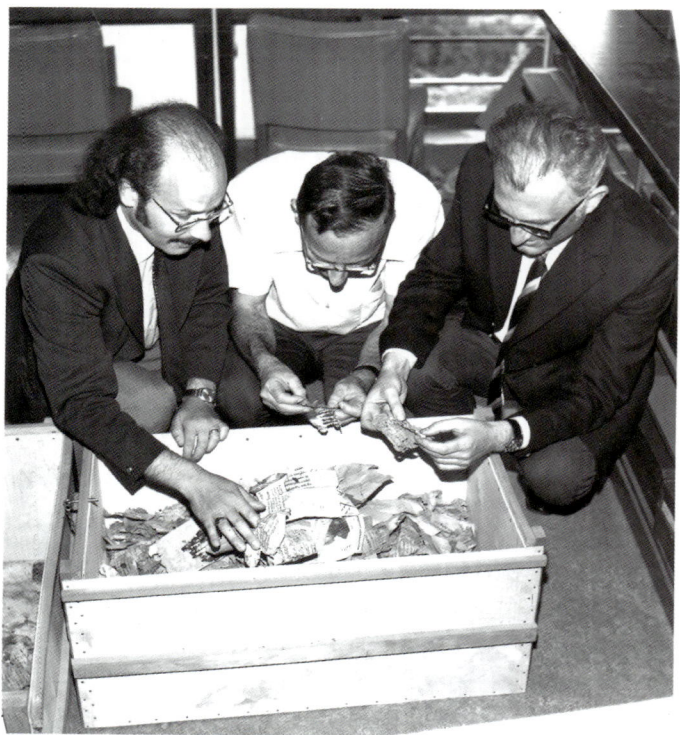

Stefan Reif, Israel Yeivin, and Ezra Fleischer examine a crate of unconserved fragments (1970s).

Conservators at work in the 1970s: Mrs Susan Fitzgeorge removing creases from manuscripts, and Mrs E. Burton sewing manuscripts into Melinex pockets.

10   Nick Posegay, "Ernest James Worman and the Victorian Genizah: A Salt-Miner's Tale of Romance, Tax Evasion, and Sudden Death," in N. Posegay, M. Connolly and B. Outhwaite (eds) *From the Battlefield of Books: Essays Celebrating 50 Years of the Taylor-Schechter Genizah Research Unit* (Leiden: Brill, 2024).

11   Adina Hoffman and Peter Cole, *Sacred Trash: The Lost and Found World of the Cairo Geniza* (New York: Nextbook, Schocken, 2011), 195.

Conservator cleaning a paper fragment from the Mosseri Collection, 2016.

curator of Hebrew printing – was reassigned to have special responsibility for the Genizah, and conservation work slowly restarted. Then in 1973, Stefan Reif took over from Knopf as Assistant Under-Librarian "responsible for the cataloguing and arrangement" of the collection. In February the following year, Reif established the Genizah Research Unit (GRU), and a comprehensive programme to facilitate research and improve access to the collection began.

By 1983, the entire collection – including 150,000 fragments that had been stored in the attic – had been cleaned, flattened, and sewn into pockets of 'Melinex' archival polyester to be bound into folders of varying size. Manuscript conservation techniques have advanced considerably since then.[12] Today, University Library conservators are highly skilled in the care of Genizah material and tailor individual treatments for each fragment's unique situation. Many manuscripts

have flaky ink that must be consolidated to prevent it falling off the page. Dirt is carefully removed using soft brushes – sometimes under microscope – and creases are gently relaxed with small amounts of deionised water before being flattened under weights. Conservators can also repair tears using wheat starch paste or remoistenable tissue, but the aim is not to return a manuscript to its original condition, only to stabilise it so it can be studied without incurring further damage.

Thanks to a generous donation from Dov Friedberg, the Friedberg Geniza Project sponsored the digitisation of the Cambridge Genizah collections between 2009 and 2012, and now nearly all Genizah collections around the world have been photographed. The images – available to browse online – have transformed Genizah research. Manuscripts torn apart and housed on different continents are now regularly reunited in digital format.

---

12   It is, for example, no longer best practice to iron medieval parchment, but given the costs of conservation work today, it
     is something of a relief that most of it was done at pace in the 1970s and 1980s.

How to Read this Book

This book is not a work of traditional academic research, nor is it targeted at Genizah specialists, although it does contain considerable academic and specialist research. It is also not a catalogue of Genizah fragments, but it does attempt to represent the diverse contents of Cambridge University Library's Genizah collections. Every page features images of one or more Genizah fragments that we think are particularly interesting, whether because they're visually distinct, historically significant, widely known, or just help us tell a good story. We've divided them into 12 thematic chapters that demonstrate the major social, historical, and artistic trends that we find throughout the ten centuries of the Cairo Genizah. You can read them in any order, but if this is your first introduction to the Genizah, we recommend you start with Chapter I.

Each chapter has between 20 and 30 manuscript entries. For each one, we have written a title and short description alongside an image from Cambridge University Library's digital archive. Below the description is the date of the fragment (estimated to the best of our knowledge). Next to each image, in red text, there is also a small identification number. This is the fragment's 'classmark', the number assigned to it by Cambridge University Library to identify it in archives and academic publications. Additional information about any manuscript can be found by entering its classmark in the Cambridge University Digital Library (CUDL) database. CUDL (pronounced 'cuddle') is an online repository for accessing the digitised archival materials at the University of Cambridge. There you can find further descriptions, measurements, and high-resolution, zoomable, downloadable images of every manuscript. To access the CUDL database, visit cudl.lib.cam.ac.uk and search for the classmark you want to see.

The classmarks in this book come in five different formats: T-S, Add., Or., L-G, and Mosseri. Each represents a different manuscript collection at Cambridge University Library:

1) The Taylor-Schechter Collection

With almost 200,000 fragments, the Taylor-Schechter Collection is the largest collection of Genizah manuscripts in the world. It is named after Solomon Schechter, the Cambridge Reader responsible for bringing most of the manuscripts to Cambridge, and Charles Taylor, the Master of St. John's College who bankrolled Schechter's efforts. A large majority of the fragments in this book come from this collection. The Taylor-Schechter (T-S) manuscripts are further organised based on their contents and when they were conserved in Cambridge. Some of the most common sub-collections in this book are the New Series (T-S NS), the Additional Series (T-S AS), the Arabic Series (T-S Ar), and the Miscellaneous Series (T-S Misc).

2) The CUL Additional Collection

The Additional Collection contains certain Genizah fragments that the University Library purchased from Jewish manuscript dealers (particularly Rabbi Solomon Wertheimer) in the early 1890s. We don't always know exactly how these dealers acquired their manuscripts. We think that most of them came from the Cairo Genizah, but it is possible that some were from other Jewish communities in Egypt and Palestine. Classmarks from this collection start with Add.

3) The CUL Oriental Collection

Some other Genizah fragments that Cambridge University Library purchased in the 1890s were only assigned classmarks in the 1950s. These were added to the 'Oriental' Collection, now referred to as the Or. Collection. The classmarks of Genizah fragments from this collection mainly begin with Or.1080 or Or.1081.

4) The Lewis-Gibson Collection

The Lewis-Gibson Collection contains over 1700 manuscripts that Agnes Lewis and Margaret Gibson collected during their travels in Egypt and Palestine at the end of the 19th century. They bequeathed this collection to Westminster College in Cambridge, where it became known as the 'Westminster Collection'. In 2013, Cambridge University Library partnered with Oxford's Bodleian Library to purchase the Westminster Collection for £1.2 million. Together, the two libraries conserved the manuscripts to a modern standard and renamed the collection after Lewis and Gibson. Classmarks from this collection begin with L-G.

5) The Mosseri Collection

The Mosseri Collection contains more than 7000 fragments that Jacques (Jack) Mosseri collected in Cairo between 1909 and 1912. Mosseri was an Egyptian Jew who scoured the local synagogues for manuscripts that collectors like Schechter missed in the 1890s. In 2006, the Mosseri collection came to Cambridge University Library for a 20-year period of conservation and study. Classmarks from this collection begin with 'Mosseri'.

After studying in Cambridge, Jacques Mosseri returned to Egypt and collected manuscripts that had been buried in the synagogue grounds and in nearby cemeteries. His plan to open a museum celebrating Jewish life in Egypt was thwarted by his death in 1934.

Unconserved fragments from the Mosseri Collection, ca. 2006.

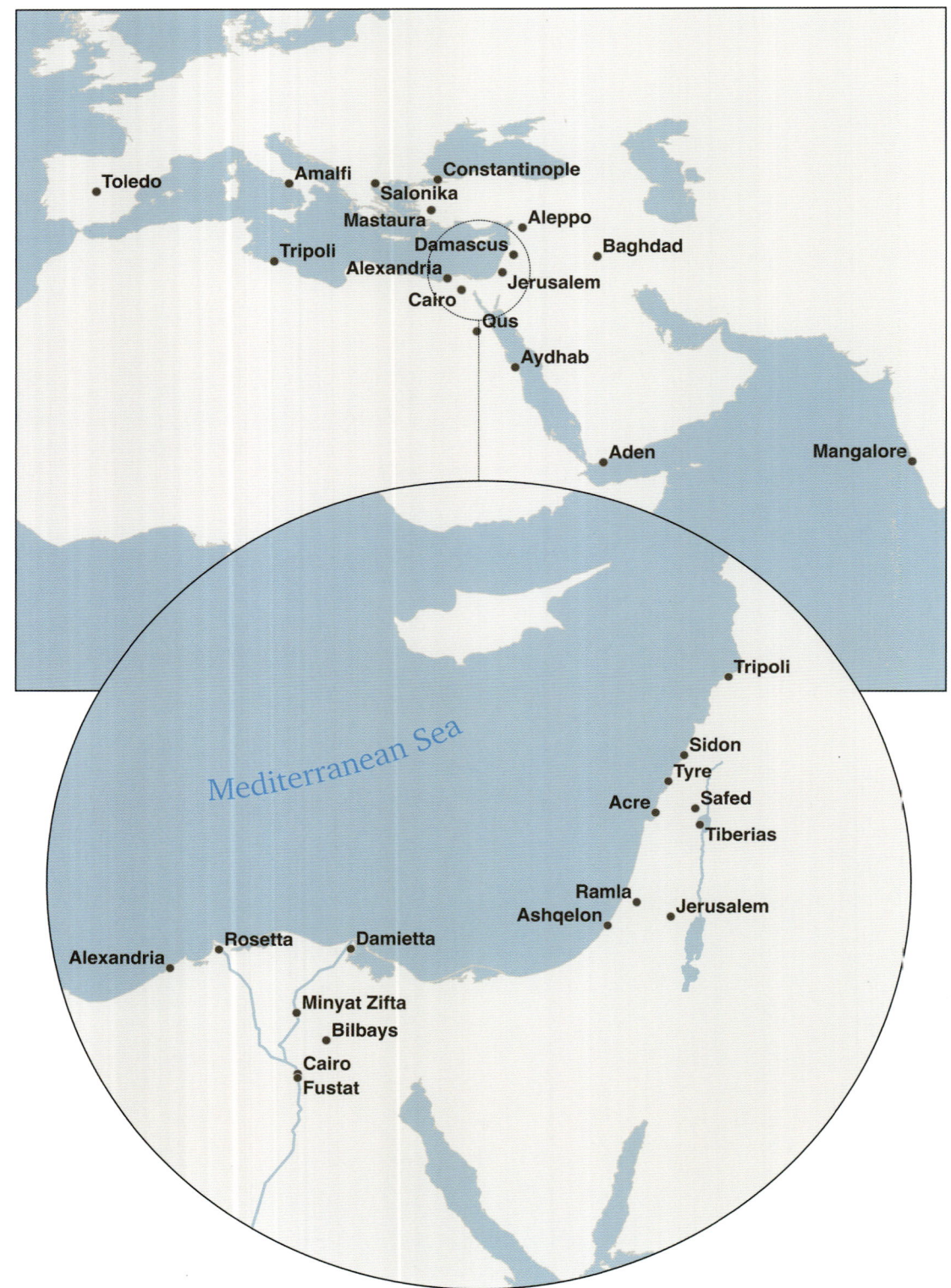

Collection Highlights

The Cairo Genizah has become famous for many great discoveries over the last 125 years. In 1896, Solomon Schechter identified the lost Hebrew work of Ben Sira in fragments collected by the travelling scholars Agnes Lewis and Margaret Gibson. He set off to Cairo in search of the rest of it, but found much more than he ever anticipated. Schechter's "hoard" contained manuscripts of lost Greek translations of the Bible, surviving on parchment that had been washed clean and recycled already in the early Middle Ages. Scholars at Cambridge scoured the collection for unique Bible texts and other copies of the formative works of Judaism. The early 1900s brought historians' interest – most notably Jacob Mann – into how the documents could illuminate Jewish society in the Middle Ages. Though he'd left for America, Schechter continued delving and, in 1910, revealed what would turn out to be the first copies of Dead Sea Scrolls texts in the Genizah – unearthed fifty years before the famous finds at Qumran. In the 1950s, one of the most celebrated names in Genizah research, Shelomo Dov Goitein, made his first visit to Cambridge to examine the manuscripts. His discoveries among the documentary fragments shed light on almost every aspect of social and economic life in the Middle Ages. His enormous masterwork, *A Mediterranean Society*, is still an essential work for the history of the medieval world. Goitein was an academic powerhouse, not only identifying new autograph fragments of Moses Maimonides (in fact, we are still finding new autographs in the 2020s!) and his brother, but establishing a whole new field of study in the forgotten medieval Jewish trade with India. His efforts encouraged the Library to complete the conservation of the collection, large parts of which were still in the original boxes that Schechter had used to ship it from Egypt, and ultimately led to the founding of the Taylor-Schechter Genizah Research Unit under Stefan Reif in 1974. The 1980s and 90s saw important discoveries in the history of the Hebrew language, Karaite contributions to medieval Judaism, and Arabic documentary culture. The last few decades have seen increasing interest in the Genizah as a source of evidence for interactions between Jews, Muslims, and Christians in Europe, the Middle East, and North Africa, and have placed the collection at the heart of world history.

We at the Genizah Research Unit have spent the last 50 years working to document and share these discoveries with the wider public. In this chapter, we've selected some of the Cambridge collection's most famous and historically significant manuscripts – those one-of-a-kind items that can only be found in the Cairo Genizah.

The Lost Hebrew Book of Ben Sira

This fragment comes from the book of Ben Sira in Hebrew. In 1896, Solomon Schechter identified the long-lost Hebrew text of Ben Sira (known as Ecclesiasticus or Sirach in the Christian tradition, where it circulated mainly in Greek, Latin and Syriac versions) when Agnes Lewis and Margaret Gibson showed him this manuscript that they'd purchased from a dealer in Cairo. Almost immediately, he set off for Egypt looking for more pieces of the book, returning to Cambridge in 1897 with over 100,000 fragments from the Cairo Genizah. Six different copies of the book of Ben Sira have since been identified in the collection.[1]

Ca. 10th century

Or.1102

Q: What is the Wisdom of Ben Sira?

The book of Ben Sira is a work of proverbial wisdom – similar to the books of Proverbs and Ecclesiastes – written at the beginning of the 2nd century BCE. Its author – either Shim'on ben Yeshua' ben Eliezer ben Sira or Yeshua' ben Eliezer ben Sira, depending on which version you read – presented an ordered view of the universe in which destiny for both the created order and mankind is fixed and regular. Despite the regularity of life and the inevitability of death, Ben Sira believed that God's work is good and He would ensure prosperity for those that trust in Him. Doubts about the sanctity of this book led Jewish authorities to exclude it from their canon. Eventually, the original Hebrew text was lost, and the book was preserved only in translation, as Catholic and Eastern Orthodox Christians considered it part of their Bibles. By the 19th century, the nature of the book's original language had become enmeshed with the rancorous scholarly tussle over the true age of the Bible's composition. Solomon Schechter had long had an interest in trying to establish the original Hebrew text of the book, and had scoured rabbinic sources for quotations from the work. This manuscript, however, finally, and completely unexpectedly, gave him the original Hebrew text. Had Agnes and Margaret not shown it to him, he might never have travelled to Cairo, and this unique collection might have been lost to future generations.

In the mid-20th century, fragments of Ben Sira in Hebrew were found among the Dead Sea Scrolls, confirming that the medieval copies in the Cairo Genizah descended from truly ancient originals. The Genizah fragments also tell us how medieval readers used Ben Sira. Although some rabbis disapproved of it – even stating that it was forbidden to read (Talmud tractate Sanhedrin 100b) – their frequent references imply it was a popular text that Jewish scholars regularly studied. This is confirmed by the presence of the book in the Cairo Genizah in no fewer than six versions. Moreover, in the first leaf spotted by Schechter, the scribe added marginal notes with corrections from another copy. They even wrote, on a separate leaf, a note in Persian saying that the manuscript they'd been copying from had come to an end and they were switching to a second. Scribes seem to have regarded Ben Sira highly enough to copy it carefully and record its textual variants.

St Augustine's Sermons

One of several fragments in the collection from what was once a large, finely produced Latin edition of St Augustine's sermons. The surviving portions include his *Sermon on the Mount*, *Sermon Against the Arians*, and a sermon for Easter Sunday, all several centuries older than any other copies in the world. In the 9th or 10th century, a Hebrew scribe erased the Latin text and reused the parchment as a 'palimpsest' to write lists of masoretic notes on the Hebrew Bible.[2]

Undertext: Ca. 6th century

Overtext: Ca. 9th–10th century

Add.4320c

Three Ancient Versions of the Bible in Palimpsest

These pages all come from a single book of Hebrew liturgical poetry (*piyyutim*) by the renowned Late Antique Jewish poet, Yannai. In the 9th or 10th century, a Jewish scribe recycled several pieces of parchment to make it. However, the parchment had already been used to record early translations of the Bible, which the scribe erased to make space for the Hebrew text. Manuscripts that have been recycled in this way are called 'palimpsests'. Each of these fragments preserves a different ancient Bible translation, most likely copied at Christian monasteries in Palestine. Multi-spectral imaging (photos taken using all parts of the light spectrum) can help to reveal the original texts on the parchment.

Origen's Hexapla

The undertext on this page is one of only two surviving manuscripts of the famed Hexapla, a six-column edition of the Hebrew and Greek Bibles by the Church Father, Origen (d. 253 CE). Each column contains a different version: Hebrew, Hebrew in Greek characters, the Greek translation by Aquila, the Greek translation by Symmachus, the Septuagint, and the Greek translation by Theodotion. This fragment preserves two and a half columns of Psalm 21.[3] The Tetragrammaton (the traditionally unpronounceable Hebrew name of God) is written using the Greek letters *pi-iota-pi-iota* (πιπι), chosen because they visually resemble the Hebrew characters of the Tetragrammaton (יהוה).

Undertext: Ca. 6th–7th century
Overtext: Ca. 9th–10th century

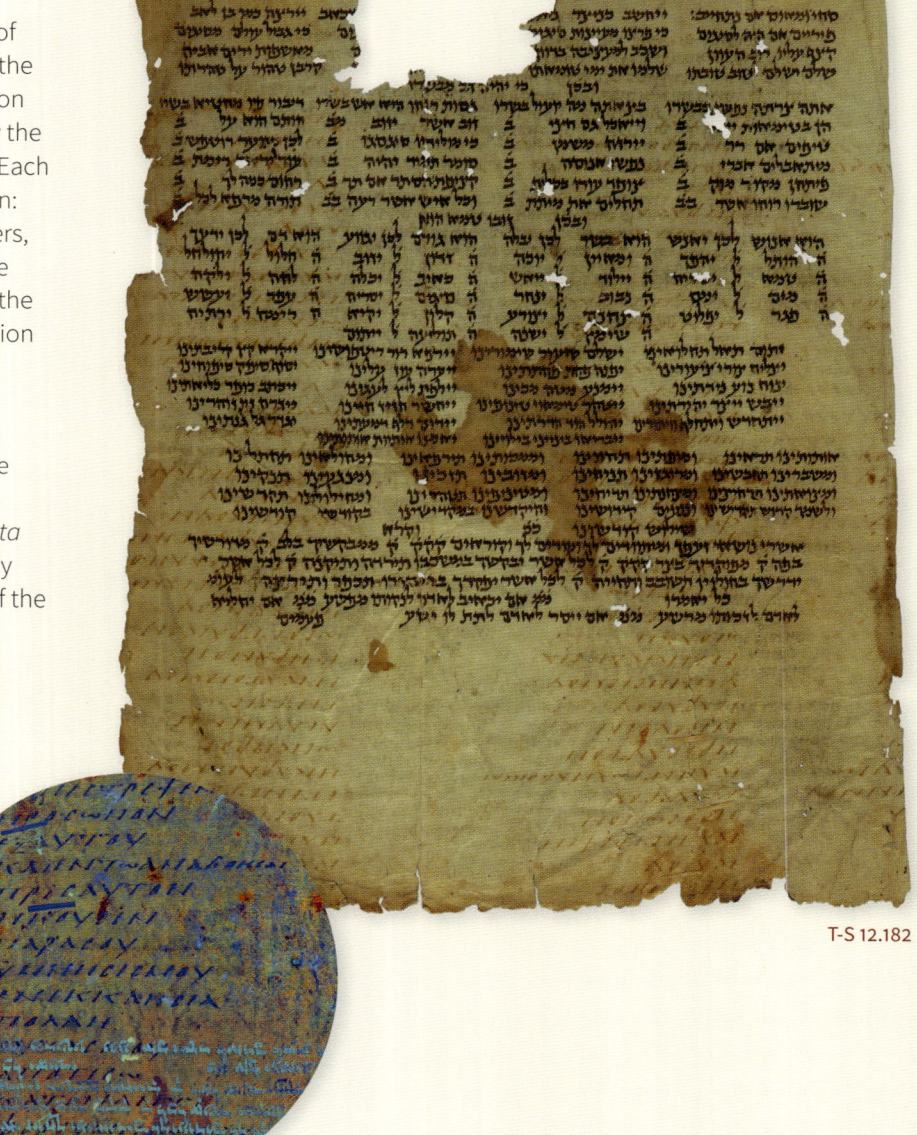

T-S 12.182

T-S 12.184

Aquila's Translation of Kings

The undertext on this page is a 5th- or 6th-century copy of Aquila of Sinope's 2nd-century Greek translation of the biblical book of Kings (specifically 1 Kings 21). It is the oldest manuscript known from the Cairo Genizah and was one of the first published when Cambridge scholars began to study the collection in the late 1890s.[4]

Undertext: Ca. 5th–6th century
Overtext: Ca. 9th–10th century

The New Testament in Christian Palestinian Aramaic

The undertext here is the New Testament Gospel of John 14–15 in Christian Palestinian Aramaic, a dialect of Aramaic used by Christians in Palestine after the 5th century CE. The language is similar to Jewish Palestinian Aramaic, but the script resembles Syriac, more commonly known from Syriac Christians in Syria and Iraq.

Undertext: Ca. 7th–8th century
Overtext: Ca. 9th–10th century

T-S 16.98

Papyrus Codex of Hebrew Poetry

This 8th-century papyrus manuscript comes from an ancient book of liturgical poetry by the fifth-century Jewish *paytan*, Joseph ben Nissan. It is special in a number of ways: it's the only papyrus item in the Cairo Genizah collection, it's the only known papyrus book in Hebrew, and as an 8th-century manuscript, it's one of the oldest Hebrew books in the world. It was also originally bound in an unusual, old-fashioned way – a single gathering, a method thought to have died out in the 5th century. These fragments arrived in Cambridge still bound together in a booklet, but in the 1950s (as was the practice at the time), Cambridge conservators took them apart to preserve the delicate material and encase them in glass.[5]

Ca. 8th century

T-S 6H13

Palestinian Talmud over an Old Georgian Bible

Palimpsest of the Palestinian Talmud (Bava Qama 9) overwritten on an Old Georgian translation of the biblical book of Jeremiah (Chapter 12). Analysis of the Georgian script style suggests it was originally copied in the 8th century, most likely at a Christian monastery in Palestine. The parchment was then recycled by a Jewish scribe around the 10th century.[6]

Undertext: Ca. 8th century
Overtext: Ca. 10th century

T-S 12.183

Q: What is a palimpsest?

Before the invention of paper, parchment made from sheep and goat skin was the main writing material. It was expensive, often in short supply, and had to be reused where possible. A 'palimpsest' is a recycled manuscript that has been cleaned by washing or scraping and reused to write a new text. The term comes from the Greek *palímpsestos*, meaning 'scratched or scraped again'. Because new parchment was so expensive to produce, manuscript owners often sold their parchment texts to be recycled in this way. Their original 'undertexts' – sometimes hundreds of years earlier than the newer 'overtexts' – can preserve ancient works that otherwise would have been lost.

Mosseri VIII.479

A Gaonic Seal

This fragment is so fragile that no visitors are currently allowed to see it. Nehemiah ben Kohen Sedeq composed this letter in the court of the great Jewish academy of Pumbeditha (modern Fallujah) in Iraq. Nehemiah was trying to stabilise his position as the gaon ('head') of the academy, and in his letter he requests that the Egyptian Jewish community support his claim to the gaonate. Attached to the bottom is a crumbling clay impression (known as a 'bulla') of his seal, the only gaonic bulla known to survive. Jews and Christians were generally forbidden from using seals like this, so Nehemiah must have had special permission from the caliph. It says 'Nehemiah Gaon son of a gaon, may he live'. And he did, for around 8 more years.

960 CE

Detail of Mosseri VIII.479

Haggadah with an Extra Question

Although the Passover liturgy has its origins at least as early as the Second Temple Period, the text of the Haggadah has evolved over time and was still subject to revision in the early Middle Ages. Nowadays, the youngest child at a Passover Seder asks four questions about the meal, but this manuscript preserves a fifth question from the ancient Palestinian rite, which reflects the centrality of the Jerusalem Temple in their collective memory: "Why is it that on all other nights we eat meat either roasted, marinated, or cooked, but on this night it is entirely roasted?" The answer: "On all other nights, we eat meat that is roasted, stewed, or boiled, while tonight we used to eat only roast meat in the Temple."

Ca. 10th century

T-S H2.152

T-S 10K6

The Damascus Document

This is a medieval copy of the 'Damascus Document', famously one of the Dead Sea Scrolls discovered at Qumran in 1947. Solomon Schechter recovered this copy 50 years earlier from the Cairo Genizah, identifying it as a foundational document of a Jewish sect from the Second Temple Period. He published it in 1910, referring to it as a 'Zadokite' (from the Hebrew word for 'righteousness' – *sedeq*) work, though not many scholars shared his view that it was an ancient text and not a medieval composition. Long after his death, the discovery of the Damascus Document among the Dead Sea Scrolls confirmed that Schechter had been correct, though the Qumran community that produced the document did not actually call themselves Zadokites. Scholars are still unsure how a copy of the Damascus Document came to rest in the Cairo Genizah – and why Jewish scribes continued to transmit it for over a thousand years.[7]

Ca. 10th century

The Aramaic Levi Document

Also known as the Testament of Levi, this apocryphal text dates back to the 2nd century BCE. It is perhaps best known as one of the Dead Sea Scrolls found at Qumran in 1947, but this copy was made around the 10th century and was identified about 50 years before the scrolls. Additional fragments have since been found in the Genizah collections of Oxford's Bodleian Library and Manchester's John Rylands Library.[8]

Ca. 10th century

T-S 16.94

A Crusader Note?

This is the ownership page from a commentary on Isaiah by the famous 10th-century rabbi, Saʿadyah Gaon (d. 942). It says that in 1030–31 CE, Josiah he-Haver ben Aaron purchased this book in the city of Acre. This was the year that Josiah was ordained into the Jerusalem Academy (perhaps it was a celebratory gift to himself?). At the bottom of the page, in tiny, upside-down Carolingian letters, is another note, this one identifying the book in Latin: *[inter]p[re]tacio esaye prophete* 'commentary on the prophet Isaiah'. Most likely, a European invader seized this book during the First Crusade's sack of Jerusalem in 1099, and – not knowing how to read Hebrew or Arabic – incorrectly held it like a Latin book while writing the note. In addition to taking prisoners, Crusaders seized many valuable manuscripts from cities in Palestine and ransomed both people and books back to the Jewish community in Egypt.

1030–31 CE

T-S 12.722

Poem by the Wife of Dunash ibn Labrat

A Hebrew poem composed by the wife of Dunash ibn Labrat (d. 990), the only medieval Hebrew poem believed to have been written by a woman. While don't know her name, she apparently wrote this to her husband in the 10th century:

Will her love remember his graceful doe / her only son in her arms as he parted? / On her left hand he placed a ring from his right, / on his wrist she placed her bracelet. / As a keepsake she took his mantle from him, / and he in turn took hers from her. / Would he settle, now, in the land of Spain, / if its prince gave him half his kingdom?

Dunash, himself a well-known poet in Spain, replied:

Were you seeking the day of my death when you wrote: / 'Have you betrayed and abandoned your vows?' / Could I betray a woman so wise / given by God as the bride of my youth? / Had my heart ever thought to leave you / I would have torn it into pieces. / For those who betray their beloved companion, / God brings down with the trials of foes. / Lions soon will devour his flesh, / and vultures will consume his blood. / Who resembles the stars of dawn [...]

[Translation by Peter Cole]

Despite these honeyed words, we know from another fragment that Dunash eventually betrayed and divorced his wife.[9]

Ca. 11th–13th century

T-S NS 143.46

Karaite Transcriptions of Biblical Hebrew in Arabic Script

These two manuscripts, which date to about the 11th century, were both copied by Karaite Jewish scribes. They represent a unique historical phenomenon by which some Karaites transcribed the text of the Hebrew Bible into Arabic script, probably as a way to more precisely record how they believed the sacred text should be pronounced. The Karaites of Cairo had their own distinct community based around the Dar Simha Synagogue, but we know that they had close relations with the Rabbanite community of the Ben Ezra Synagogue.

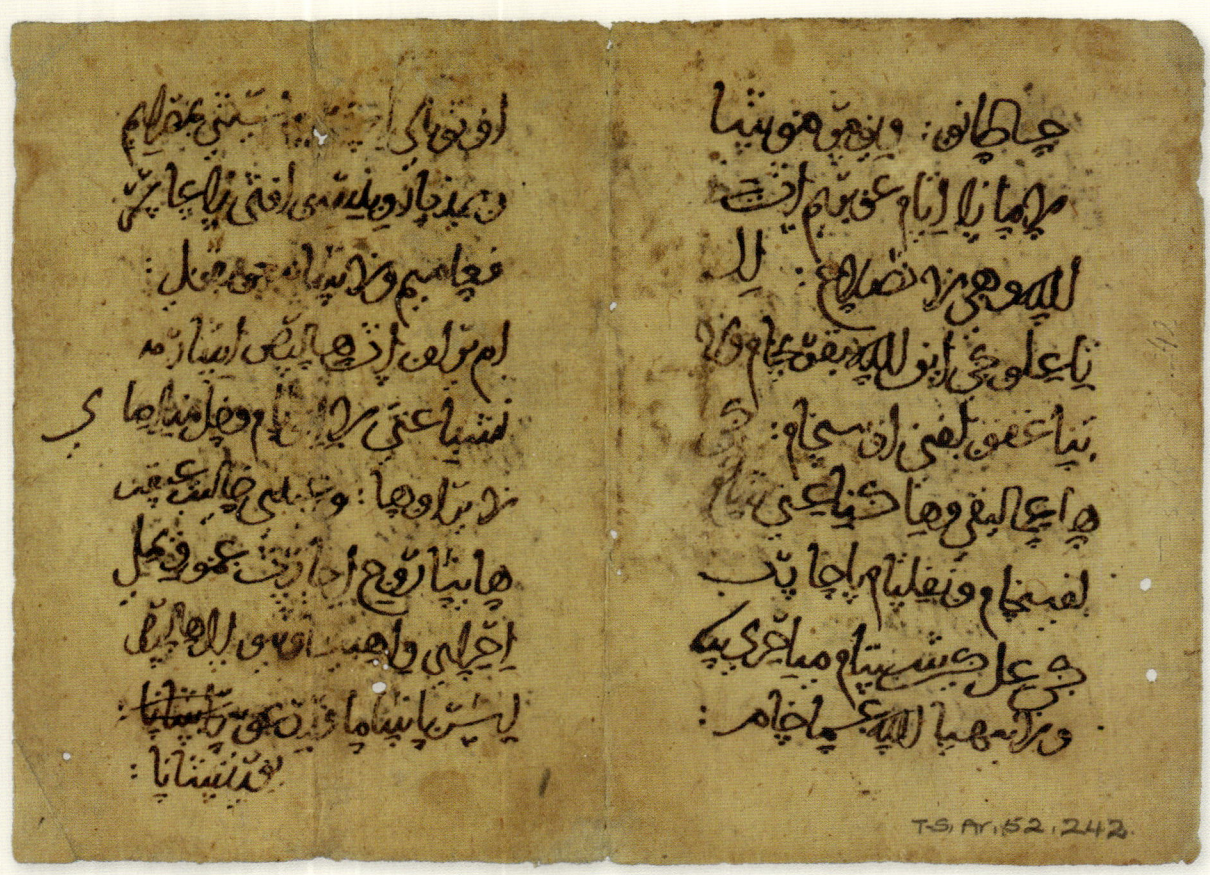

T-S Ar.52.242

Two pages from the biblical book of Numbers written in Hebrew using Arabic script. The language is Hebrew, simply transliterated into a different alphabet, but still with Hebrew vowel signs. Medieval Karaites produced many transliterations of Biblical Hebrew with Arabic characters, although their reasons for doing so are still debated. Some scholars think it was a way for them to signal their unique religious identity in contrast to Rabbanite Jews. This Bible and others like it provide invaluable evidence of how Jews pronounced Hebrew in the Middle Ages.[10]

Ca. 11th century

This is the Hebrew text of Ezekiel, again transcribed in Arabic script by a Karaite scribe. These manuscripts are often notable for resembling contemporary Qur'ans more than Hebrew Bibles (☞ Chapter VII). For instance, the scribe here marked Hebrew vowels on the Arabic consonants using signs in red ink.

Ca. 11th century

T-S Ar.52.172

Q: Who are the Karaites?

The Karaites are a Jewish group that object to the rabbinic interpretation of the Torah as found in the Mishnah and Talmud – that is, the rabbinic Oral Torah. They thus rejected the authority of Rabbinic law, believing that every person should interpret the Bible for themselves. Karaites celebrate the Jewish festivals at different times, follow different dietary rules, and observe the Sabbath differently, adhering to a more literal understanding of the Hebrew Bible. Karaism was the main Jewish rival to Rabbinic Judaism in the Middle Ages, and debates between Rabbanite and Karaite leaders could reach vitriolic boiling points. Rabbis repeatedly warned their followers against being seduced by the Karaite movement. In Egypt, however, at least during the 10th–12th centuries, there appears to have been less tension between the two communities, and they even occasionally married each other (☞ Chapter VIIIb). When asked, Moses Maimonides ruled that Karaites should be regarded as Jews.

T-S Ar.51.62

Qur'an in Hebrew Script

The righthand side of this manuscript is the beginning of the Qur'an (Sura 1:1 through 2:10), the holy book of Islam, copied in Arabic using Hebrew script. It is followed by omens for undertaking a journey, likely meant as protection for a traveller. The reverse has the name of the manuscript's apparent Jewish owner – a man called Samuel ben Judah – written in a different hand. This fragment and others like it show that the Jews of Egypt had access to Islamic religious texts and engaged with Muslim beliefs for a variety of reasons.[11]

Ca. 11th–13th century

Verses Set to Music

Musical notation arranged with the lyrics of Hebrew liturgical poetry, written in the 12th century by Obadiah the Proselyte. Formerly a Norman-Italian priest, Obadiah converted to Judaism in 1102 CE and used 'Lombardic neumatic notation' to create the earliest known records of Hebrew liturgical music. These records utilise formulas derived from Gregorian chant, which Obadiah knew from his time as a priest. Obadiah's own memoirs of his life and conversion are also preserved in the Genizah.[12]

Ca. 1102–1150 CE

T-S K5.41

Autographs by Moses Maimonides

Moses Maimonides is the most famous Jewish figure known from the Genizah. He was born in Cordoba in 1138 in what was then known as al-Andalus, part of southern Spain ruled by the Muslim Almoravid dynasty. In 1148, the Almohad dynasty conquered Cordoba, and Maimonides fled to Morocco, then Palestine, and finally to Egypt in 1168. There he became the chief Rav ('legal authority') of the Egyptian Jewish community until his death in 1204, even serving two stints as 'Head of the Jews'. In addition to being a community leader, he was also a philosopher, a scholar, and a physician to the court of the Ayyubid Sultan, Salah al-Din (Saladin).

Around 60 manuscripts that Maimonides personally penned have survived in the Cairo Genizah, often identifiable by the long looping form of the Hebrew letter 'heh' (ה) that he used at the ends of words. Such manuscripts are known today as 'autographs'.

Signed Ransom Receipt

This Judaeo-Arabic receipt was written and signed by Maimonides. It's thought that he issued it to a donor who gave money to pay for the ransom of Jewish captives after a Crusader attack on the Egyptian city of Bilbays. In the middle of the first line here, he writes his full name as "Moses bir[abbi] Maymun" (Moses, son of the scholar Maymun). 'Maimonides' is a Greek form of his Hebrew name.

1170 CE

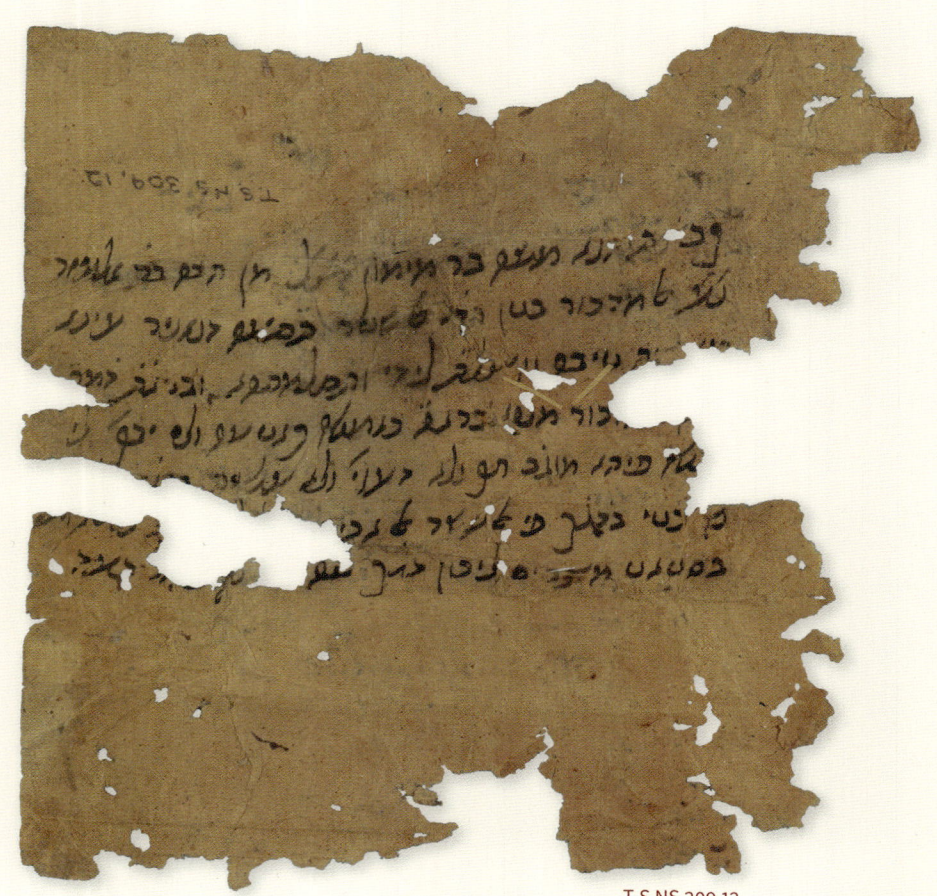

T-S NS 309.12

Draft Poem from *The Guide for the Perplexed*

Maimonides was one of the foremost thinkers of the Middle Ages, and the beginning of his greatest philosophical treatise, *The Guide for the Perplexed*, contains a three-line poem he composed for it. This is a draft of that poem inscribed by Maimonides himself, possibly the first time it was ever written down. On the back, the scribe Solomon ben Yefet – a well known copyist of Maimonides' works – wrote the opening of *The Guide for the Perplexed* (which Maimonides crafted in the form of a letter to a student). Maimonides' poem reads:

My knowledge goes forth to point out the way, to pave straight its road

Lo, everyone who goes astray in the field of Torah, come and follow its path

The unclean and the fool shall not pass over it; it shall be called the 'Way of Holiness' [13]

Ca. 1185–1190 CE

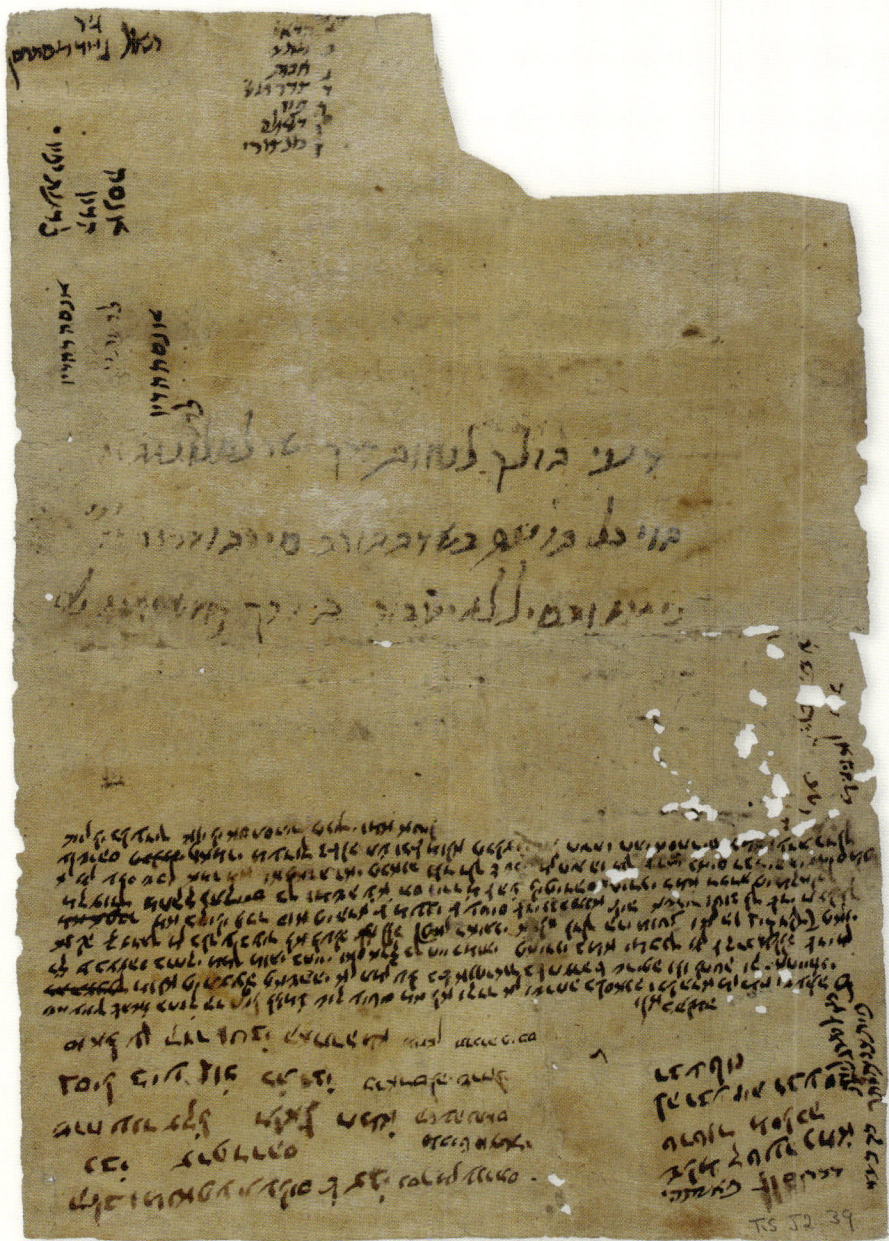

T-S J2.39

Edited Draft of *The Guide for the Perplexed*

Draft copy of *The Guide for the Perplexed*, the most famous Jewish philosophical work, again written in the hand of its original author, Moses Maimonides. You can see where he had trouble with his pen and places where he crossed out and reconsidered words.

Ca. 1185–1190 CE

T-S 10Ka4.1

T-S NS 163.57

Romance Glossary

This is a Judaeo-Arabic glossary of basic vocabulary (foods, colours, etc.) in a medieval Romance language related to Spanish. Maimonides wrote this personally, filling in Romance words below their Judaeo-Arabic equivalents. For example, in the top row of the second column from the left, Maimonides translates the Arabic *lahm* 'meat' as *carne*. But even some simple words are missing their translations. The Arabic word *jibn* 'cheese' appears on the back of this page, but the expected translation *queso* is nowhere to be found. The missing entries may imply that Maimonides did not have a strong command of this Romance language. Despite being a 'Spaniard', his native tongue, after all, was Arabic.[14]

Ca. 1170–1204 CE

Petition to Sultan Saladin

All citizens of Egypt had a right to petition the Islamic government to seek justice from the ruler. In this Arabic petition, a Jew named 'Abd al-Baqi complains that the government forced him to work as a tax collector, an occupation which had taken him away from home and made him unpopular among his friends and family. He requests that "the Conqueror of the Worshippers of the Cross," Sultan Salah al-Din – better known as Saladin – release him from this duty. On the back, Saladin's secretaries recorded his decision: since 'Abd al-Baqi has experience as a tax collector, he cannot avoid this service. After the case was dealt with, the large piece of paper was put to another use. An essay on how to calculate leap years in the Hebrew calendar fills all the remaining blank space on the page.

1169–1193 CE

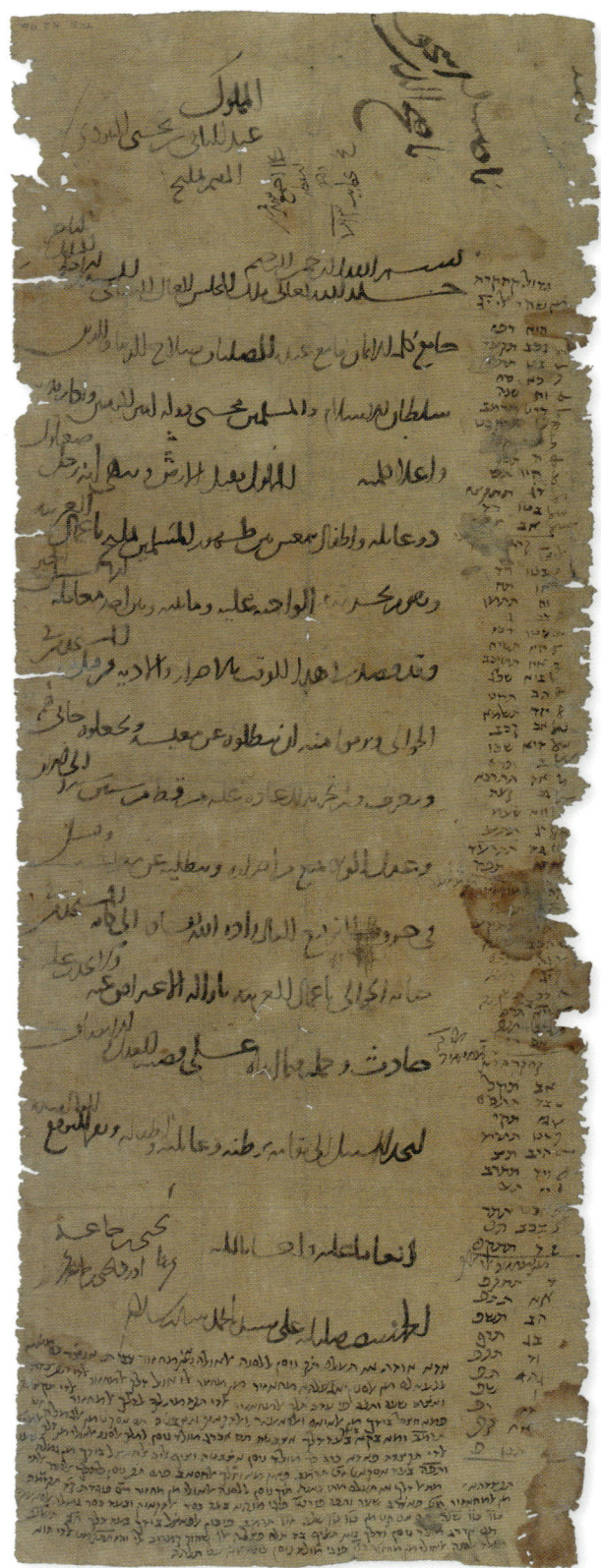

T-S K2.96

Copy of the Aleppo Codex

This small personal Bible bears witness to a part of the famous 'Aleppo Codex' that is now lost. At the end of the book of Numbers, the scribe added a note explaining that the text was copied from "the Codex of the Taj which is in the Synagogue of the Jerusalemites in Fustat." The 'Taj' (the Persian word for 'crown') was the name given to the copy of the Bible known today as the Aleppo Codex. It was copied in the 10th century, redeemed from Crusaders after the capture of Jerusalem, and brought to Fustat. In the 12th century, Maimonides praised the manuscript for its accuracy. More recently, it was kept in a synagogue in Aleppo, Syria (hence the name), but it was damaged during riots in 1947 and most of the Torah, including this portion of Numbers, was lost.

Ca. 12th–13th century

T–S Misc.24.137.3

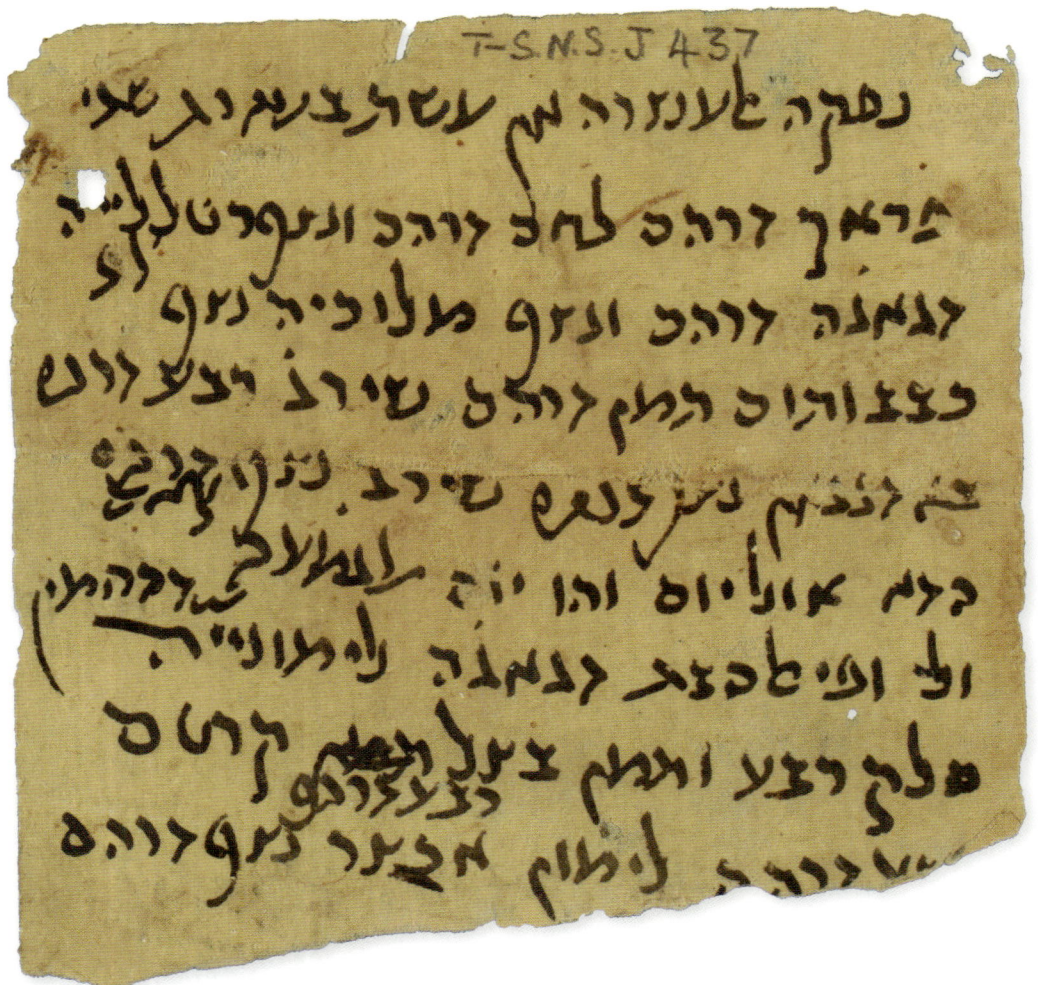

T-S NS J437

Shopping List for Shavuot

The Cairo Genizah preserves everyday notes as well as great works of sacred literature. This is a shopping list, revealing the careful planning and budgeting needed to celebrate the festival of Shavuot in style. It includes (for Friday): little chickens, meat, a pound of fat tail, a hen, garden mallow, cubeb, garlic, two measures of sesame oil, and eggplants. Then (for Saturday): a lemon hen, chard, onions, safflower, and green lemons. The budget for these purchases was 10 dirhams – a significant portion of a government official's monthly income. The menu planner was Solomon ben Elijah, the clerk of Fustat's Rabbinical Court (Bet Din) during the time of Abraham Maimonides.

13th century

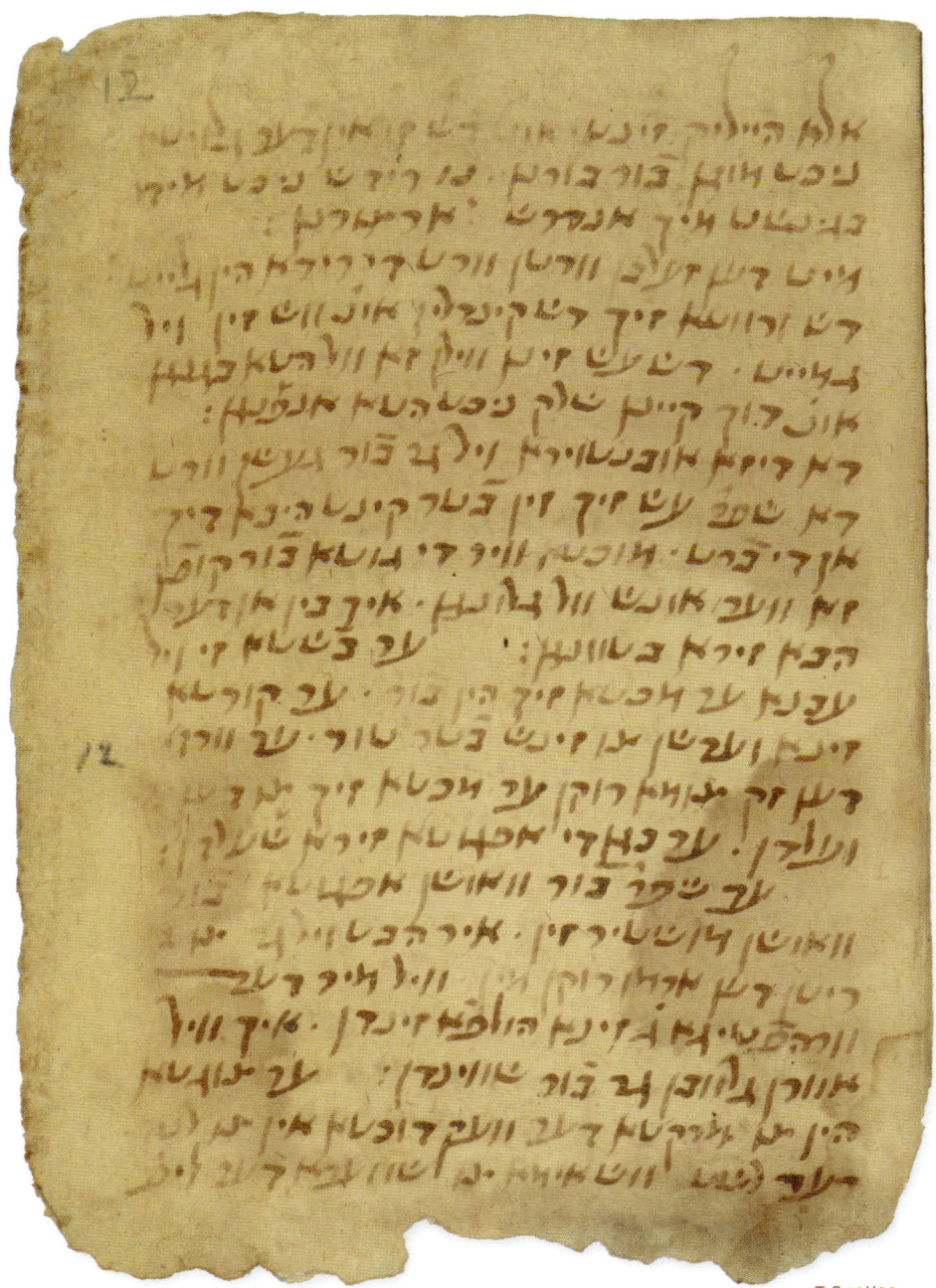

T-S 10K22

The Cambridge Yiddish Codex

This is the earliest known collection of texts in Yiddish, a form of German used by Central and Eastern European Jews. Yiddish is typically written in Hebrew characters, and here you see them in a distinctive Ashkenazi cursive script. The texts in this book include homilies, literary fables, poetry, and a Yiddish-Hebrew glossary of the gemstones said to be on the breastplate of the Israelite high priest. Most importantly, it preserves a lost poem of the German epic tradition (in its Yiddish version), *Dukus Horant* 'Duke Horant'. Although this manuscript is known as the 'Yiddish Codex' (which is just a fancy word for 'book'), it is actually a gathering of separate leaves put together in a modern library binding.

1382 CE

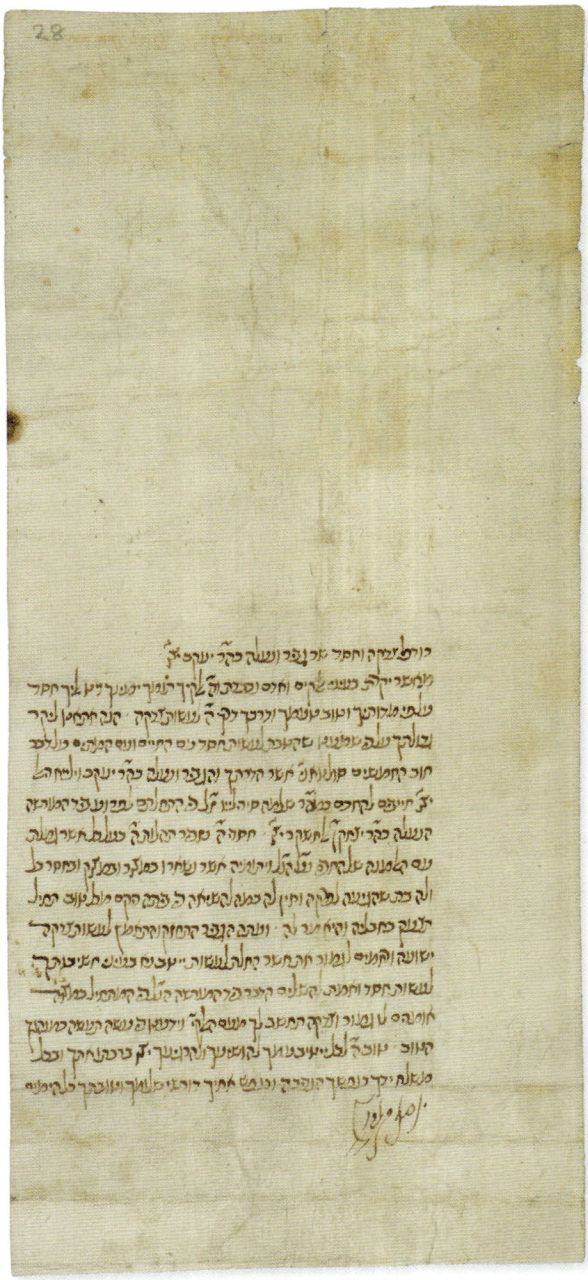

T-S 13J24.28

A Gentle Nudge from Joseph Karo

Letter sent by the famed legal scholar, Joseph Karo (d. 1575), during his time as the head of the Jewish community in Safed, Palestine. A man has died and the recipient of the letter owes money to his widow. Karo tactfully mentions the debtor's virtue, honesty, and good judgement, nudging him to repay the money that is owed. The paper was imported from Europe, and a scribe probably wrote the main text, but Karo's elegant signature can be seen below the last line.

Ca. 1546–1575 CE

Isaac Luria's Lonely Pepper Club

Isaac Luria, also known as 'the Ari' (d. 1572), is the founding father of Lurianic Kabbalah, the leading school of Jewish esotericism. He famously spent years in seclusion, meditating on the banks of the Nile and saying as little as possible. There are few traces of Luria's time in Egypt preserved in the Genizah, and all attest to his commercial rather than spiritual practices. This modest letter on local paper, which he wrote and signed himself (see his elaborate signature at bottom left), was carried by a messenger from Alexandria, where Luria was waiting for goods to arrive, probably to Luria's business associate in Rosetta, Moses Benjamin. Luria was trying to trace money and a missing consignment: "Up to now I've received not a thing. And the season of heat has passed, and the might of the rains has arrived." From other Genizah fragments we learn that Luria traded pepper and other spices to generate income.[15]

Ca. 1552–1572 CE

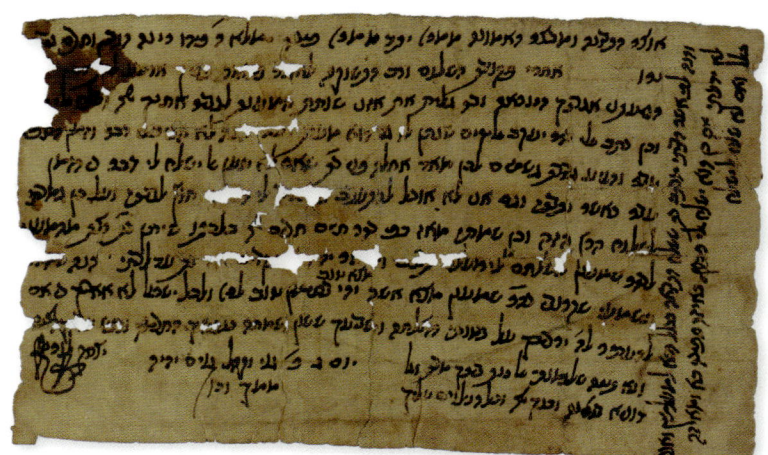

Mosseri III.232

Minute Genizah Fragments

There are hundreds of thousands of manuscript fragments from the Cairo Genizah, and some of them are too small to get their own identifying classmarks. Instead, they are gathered together and conserved with a single classmark at the end of folders. In Cambridge, we refer to these as 'minute fragments', each being only a few centimetres long. Now that the collection has been digitised, scholars are gradually able to recombine some of these fragments into larger manuscript images.

Ca. 10th–19th century

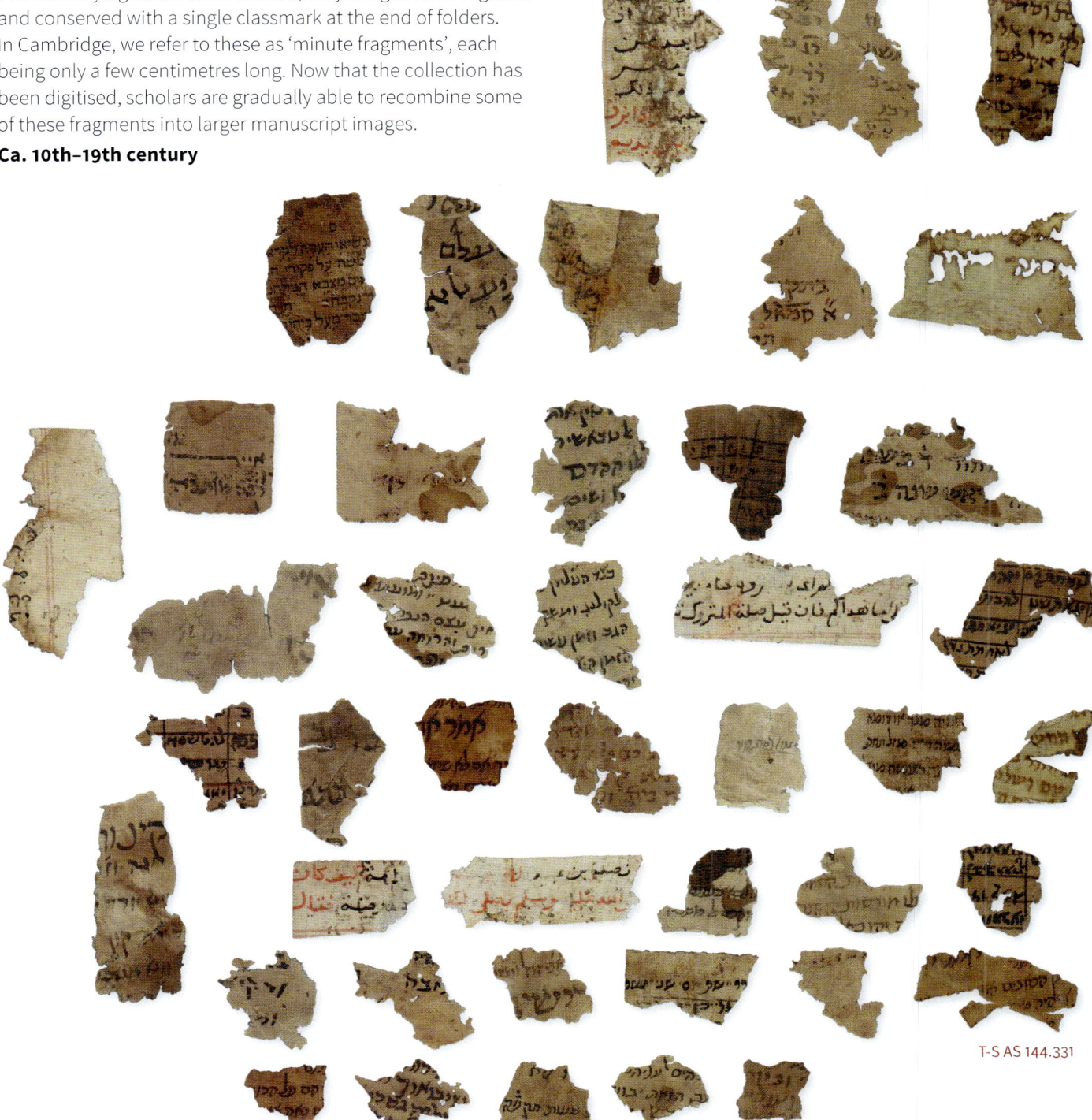

T-S AS 144.331

Notes to Chapter I

1 Solomon Schechter, 'Genizah Specimens: Ecclesiasticus', *Jewish Quarterly Review* 10, no. 2 (1898): 197–206; Rebecca J.W. Jefferson, 'Dangerous Liaisons in Cairo: Reginald Q. Henriques and the Taylor-Schechter Genizah Manuscript Collection', *Judaica Librarianship* 20, no. 1 (2017): 21–51.

2 H. A. G. Houghton, 'New Identifications Among the Sixth-Century Fragments of Augustine in Cambridge University Library', *Sacris Erudiri* 58 (2019): 171–79.

3 Ben Kantor. 'The Oldest Fragment of Origen's Hexapla: T-S 12.182.' *Fragment of the Month (March),* Cambridge University Library: Genizah Research Unit (2019).

4 Francis Crawford Burkitt, *Fragments of the Books of Kings, According to the Translation of Aquila from a MS Formerly in the Geniza at Cairo* (Cambridge: Cambridge University Press, 1897).

5 Rebecca J.W. Jefferson, 'T-S 6H9–21: The Papyrus Codex Rebound', *Fragment of the Month (July)*, Cambridge University Library: Genizah Research Unit, 2009.

6 Robert P. Blake, 'Catalogue of the Georgian Manuscripts in the Cambridge University Library', *The Harvard Theological Review* 25, no. 3 (1932): 209–211.

7 Solomon Schechter, *Fragments of a Zadokite Work, Documents of Jewish Sectaries 1* (Cambridge: Cambridge University Press, 1910).

8 H.L. Pass and J. Arendzen, 'Fragments of an Aramaic Text of the Testament of Levi', *Jewish Quarterly Review* 12 (1900): 651–56; James Kugel, 'How Old Is the "Aramaic Levi Document"?', *Dead Sea Discoveries* 14, no. 3 (2007): 291–312.

9 Adina Hoffman and Peter Cole, *Sacred Trash: The Lost and Found World of the Cairo Geniza* (New York: Nextbook, Schocken, 2011), 179–180.

10 Geoffrey Khan, *Karaite Bible Manuscripts from the Cairo Genizah*, Cambridge University Library Genizah Series 9 (Cambridge; New York: Cambridge University Library; Cambridge University Press, 1990); Geoffrey Khan, 'Medieval Karaite Transcriptions of Hebrew into Arabic Script', in *Israel Oriental Studies*, ed. Joel Kraemer, XII (Leiden: E.J. Brill, 1992), 157–76.

11 Aleida Paudice, 'On Three Extant Sources of the Qur'an Transcribed in Hebrew', *European Journal of Jewish Studies* 2, no. 2 (1 December 2008): 213–57.

12 Some fragments of the autobiographical 'Scroll of Obadiah' are T-S Misc.35.31, T-S 8.271, and T-S 10K21. For more on Obadiah, see our *Genizah Fragments* interview with Gary Rendsburg: https://www.lib.cam.ac.uk/genizah-fragments/posts/qa-wednesday-monk-jew-1102-obadiah-proselyte-gary-rendsburg.

13 Maimonides, *The Guide of the Perplexed*, ed. and trans. S. Pines (Chicago, 1963), 2. Solomon ben Yefet is also the scribe who copied the Mishneh Torah found in Oxford's MS Huntington 80.

14 J. Martínez Delgado, A. Montaner Frutos, & A. Ashur 'Un nuevo autógrafo de Maimónides: un glosario judeo-árabe con glosas romances (T-S NS 163.57),' *Sefarad*, 83(1), (2023), 7–77. https://doi.org/10.3989/sefarad.023-001.

15 B. Outhwaite 'Lionising Luria: Mosseri III.232.' *Fragment of the Month (March)*, Cambridge University Library, Genizah Research Unit (2024).

II.

Bible & Judaism

We expect to find biblical scrolls, books, and other sacred Jewish texts in a typical genizah, and we do find them in the Cairo Genizah, in vast quantities. There are around 25,000 fragments from Bible manuscripts in the collection, including large, finely-produced 'codices' (i.e. 'books'), sections of Torah scrolls, small books and pamphlets for personal use, and leaves from later printed editions. Recitation of the Bible in the synagogue was in Hebrew, with a traditional translation (the Targum) in Aramaic, but medieval Jews used Arabic and other translations as well, especially for personal study. There are also thousands of pages from the Talmud and Mishnah – the great works of Rabbinic Jewish law – and an estimated 50,000 fragments of liturgical poetry.

The history of the Jews in Egypt is a long and venerable one. There are archaeological traces of a Judean garrison stationed at Elephantine as far back as the 7th century BCE, and under later Greek, Roman, and Byzantine rule, Jews settled in Egypt in significant numbers. Egyptian Jews traditionally accepted the leadership of the Gaon (head) of the Palestinian academy, and followed the ancient Palestinian rite for their services, but this changed as Jews from Iraq, Persia, and North Africa migrated to Egypt and set up their own synagogues that followed Babylonian customs. By the 13th century, Egyptian Jews had largely abandoned the Palestinian rite – it was more important to consolidate the divided Jewish community. The Genizah is our main source for the lost Palestinian traditions. They held an important connection to the destroyed Jerusalem Temple in their communal memory. They emphasised this memory in their Passover seder by including a fifth question that recalled the practice of roasting meat for sacrifices in the Temple. The Babylonian practice of reading the whole of the Torah in one year left little time for much else in the synagogue service, but Palestinian Jews followed a triennial (three-year) reading cycle and supplemented their services with ancient liturgical poems designed to connect the weekly Torah reading with the reading from the Prophets (Haftarah). Palestinian practices extended into the home as well: women maintained a clear right to divorce their husbands in marriage contracts drawn up according to the Palestinian rite (☛ Chapter VIIIb).

T-S NS 3.21

Ancient Torah Scroll

Remnant from what was likely once a scroll of the entire Torah, datable to approximately the 7th century, and possibly even pre-Islamic. It was made in Syria or Palestine. This is one of the oldest Hebrew manuscripts in the collection and is among the oldest Torah scrolls in the world. It is one of the only surviving Bibles from the so-called 'dark age' of Hebrew manuscripts, a period between the latest Dead Sea Scrolls (ca. 100 CE) and the rise of the medieval Bible tradition (ca. 900 CE) when very few Hebrew manuscripts are extant. It thus provides a rare glimpse into the changing scribal traditions for writing the biblical text during the first millennium. Before the 1950s, it was stored in a crate in Cambridge University Library's attic with over 100,000 other Genizah fragments that were, at times, deemed 'rubbish'. To save space, it was once suggested that these crates be cleared out and burned. Thankfully, that did not happen and this fragment is now properly conserved. It has a small difference from the text of the Hebrew Bible today. At Genesis 17:1, the scribe wrote 'year' (*shanah*) instead of 'years' (*shanim*).[1]

Ca. 6th–7th century

Carbon-Dated Scroll Fragment

Genesis 47–50 from a leather fragment of the 'Ashkar-Gilson' scroll – one of the oldest Torah scrolls in the world. You can still see in the bottom right corner where this leaf was sewn to another to make a longer roll. Fragments of this scroll survive in the Cambridge collection and other libraries in Europe and North America. Carbon-14 dating carried out on one of the American pieces suggests it was produced around 700 CE, making it one of the oldest Hebrew manuscripts in the collection. Early medieval scrolls like this are refining our understanding of rabbinic scribal practices in the second half of the first millennium.[2]

Ca. 7th–8th century

T-S AS 37.1

Palestinian Pointed Mishnah

Pages from a copy of the Mishnah (*Bava Batra* and *Sanhedrin*) produced in Palestine sometime in the 9th century. The Mishnah is the first codification of the oral tradition of rabbinic law, transmitted by rabbis known as the *Tannaim* ('repeaters') in the 1st and 2nd centuries CE. Many of the dots and dashes around the words come from the rare Palestinian pointing system – more commonly used to mark accentuation and vowels ('vocalisation') in biblical texts.

Ca. 9th century

T-S E1.107

T-S NS 246.26.2

Early Dated Babylonian Bible

This is the end of the biblical book of Nehemiah, written in Hebrew and vocalised with the Babylonian vowel system. In contrast to the Palestinian and Tiberian systems – which mainly used dots to represent vowel sounds – the Babylonian system also used miniature Hebrew letters for vowels and accents. Like the Palestinian system, the Babylonian vowel signs fell out of favour with the rise of the Tiberian system. This fragment includes a colophon (in the middle of the lefthand page) from a scribe named Joseph ben Nimorad, stating that he copied the book in a town in Iran in the year 903/904 CE. This makes it one of the earliest known dated Hebrew manuscripts. While Joseph was a member of the Jewish diaspora community that lived in Iraq and Iran, eventually someone carried his manuscript to Egypt.

903–904 CE

T-S A42.2

Dated Tiberian Bible

One of the end pages from a parchment Hebrew Bible, containing writing from three different scribes. The main hand (who identified himself as "Semah ben Abraham the Scribe") copied the text of Isaiah 58 (left) and a colophon offset in a box (right) noting the date of the book's completion – 856 years from the destruction of the Temple (= 924–926 CE). This makes it one of the oldest dated Genizah manuscripts. A second hand added another colophon (centre-right, top), and a third added a Judaeo-Arabic note with a snippet of the the 'amidah prayer for an afternoon synagogue service on Shabbat (centre-right, bottom).[3] The biblical text is vocalised and accentuated using the Tiberian (rather than the Palestinian or Babylonian) system. Tiberian pointing became the standard vocalisation system for medieval Bibles and remains in use for Modern Hebrew today.

924–926 CE

Cursed Prayer Book

Parchment Hebrew prayer book according to the Palestinian rite, containing an *'amidah* prayer
to be recited at every weekday synagogue service and some instructions in Judaeo-Arabic. This
leaf includes a curse at the top of the lefthand page: "may the Christians and heretics instantly
perish" (הנצרים והמינים כרגע יאבדו). In modern versions, this wording has been changed to curse
"slanderers" and "enemies" instead.

Ca. 10th–11th century

T-S K27.33b

Work of Two Masoretes

Part of *Okhlah ve-Okhlah*, a famous compendium of masoretic lists relating to the proper reading and scribal transmission of the Hebrew Bible. A second hand has added further masoretic notes perpendicularly in the margins. The main hand is estimated to the 10th or 11th century, but the second hand could be a bit later. Compilations like this one were important tools for masoretic scribes engaged in producing biblical manuscripts, and many show signs of long-term – even multi-generational – use.

Ca. 10th–11th century

T-S D1.89

Q: Who were the Masoretes?

In a time before the printing press, the only way to make a new copy of a Bible was to write it out by hand. Hebrew scribes took extreme care with this work, as a single error introduced by a lapse in attention could drop a word or line, changing the meaning of the sacred text. If such an error wasn't corrected, any future copies made from the defective manuscript would carry the same mistake. The Masoretes (from *masorah*, meaning 'tradition') were a group of Jewish scholars between the 8th and 10th centuries CE who were devoted to preserving the accurate transmission and consistent pronunciation of the Bible. They compiled detailed notes that were designed to be copied alongside the biblical text, marking unusual spellings, unique words, and tips for remembering differences between verses with similar features. Their ultimate aim was to ensure that the Bible passed unchanged from generation to generation.

In order to preserve what they saw as the correct way of reciting the Bible, the Masoretes also introduced the systems of dots and signs that represent vowel sounds in Hebrew text. The Babylonian Masoretes, based mainly in Iraq, created the 'Babylonian' vocalisation signs for this purpose (☞ T-S NS 246.26.2, above). Their system was popular among Jews across Iraq, Iran, and Yemen, as well as the Babylonian diaspora community in Egypt. The primary alternative to the Babylonian system was the 'Tiberian' system, a set of vocalisation points invented by Masoretes at the city of Tiberias in Galilee. Over time, the authoritative status of the Tiberians grew with the reputations of their 'great masters', Aharon ben Asher and Moshe ben Naftali. Most manuscripts in the Cairo Genizah – and nearly all Hebrew scribes today – use the Tiberian system. Some Genizah fragments also preserve a rare third system, known as the Palestinian system (☞ T-S NS 249.5 below), which was less developed than the Tiberian and Babylonian systems. Scholars are still debating the origins and development of the Palestinian vowel signs.

The Scribe Who Wrote the Bible

Codex Leningrad B19a – the earliest complete dated copy of the Hebrew Bible and the basis for today's scholarly printed editions – is not a Cairo Genizah manuscript, but could easily have become one. It was skillfully copied and decorated with elaborate carpet pages by the *sofer* (scribe), Samuel ben Jacob, in Fustat during the early 11th century. After passing through the hands of a succession of careful owners, it eventually attracted the notice of the 19th-century manuscript collector, Abraham Firkovich. The so-called 'Leningrad Codex' is now housed in St Petersburg at the National Library of Russia. Had it fallen apart over the years, it might well have ended up in the Ben Ezra genizah chamber like this page from Exodus, also copied by Samuel ben Jacob. Other Genizah manuscripts reveal his working process (he borrowed an exemplar text from a colleague) and the fees that he commanded for his expert work (the enormous sum of 25 dinars for copying 'eight books of the Prophets and the Writings' in a contract dated 1021 CE).[4]

Ca. 1008–1021

A Tale of Two Prophets

This is the last page of the biblical book of Isaiah (Chapter 66), marked by a later hand which has written 'the end' in Judaeo-Arabic after the final verse in the bottom left. The large illustration resembling a marble column contains a brief introduction to the next book, Jeremiah, noting that the Prophet Jeremiah preached for over 41 years around the time that Nebuchadnezzar 'the wicked' destroyed the Temple. The hand that wrote this note also added marginal annotations in Hebrew concerning the portions of the biblical text to be recited during Shabbat synagogue services.[5]

Ca. 11th century

T-S K10.9

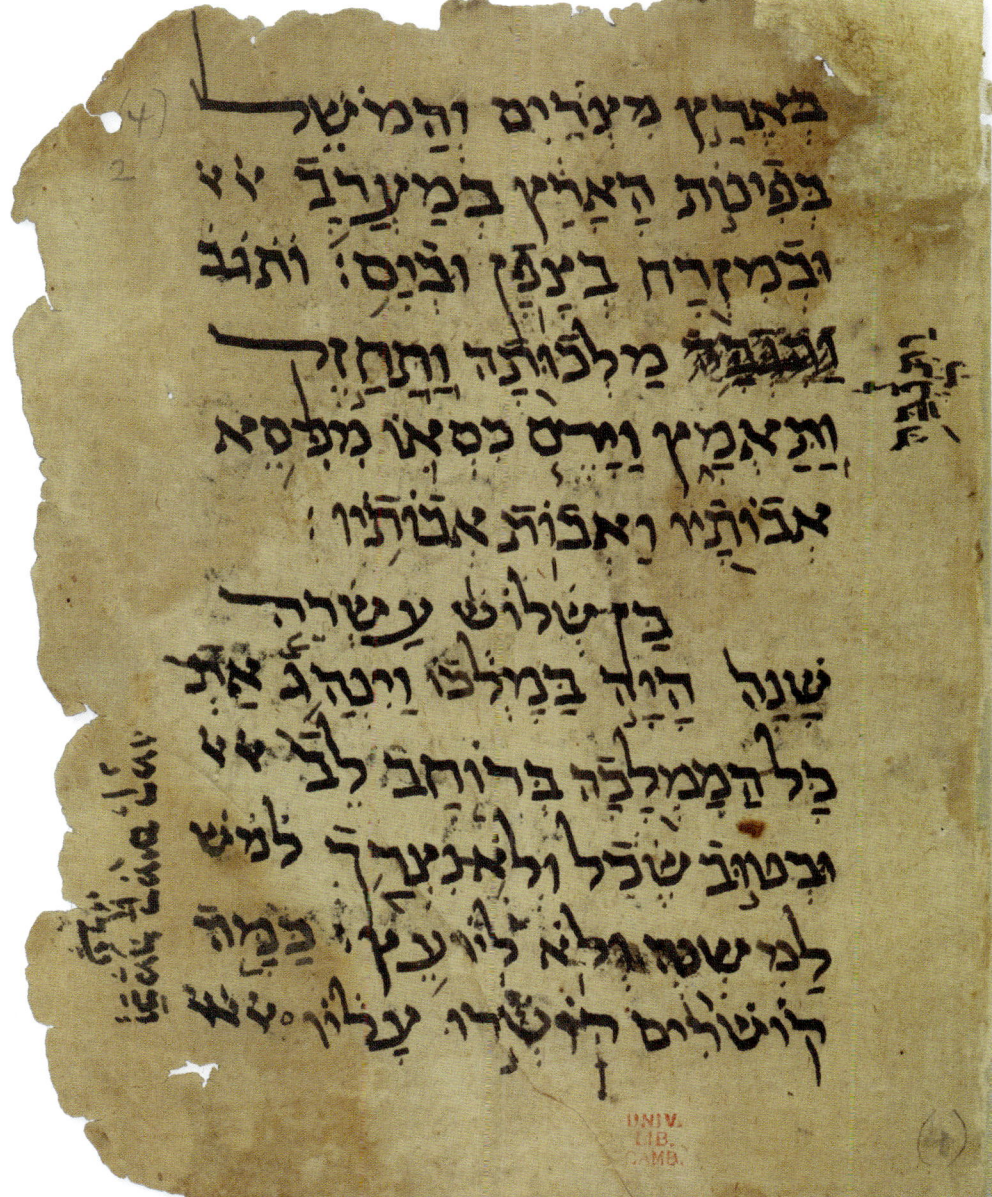

An Anniversary for Giving Thanks

In 1012, a Jewish funeral procession in Fustat provoked violence from a local mob, ending in the arrest and trial of 23 members of the Jewish community. A Muslim judge sentenced the Jews to death for their part in the riot. As was their right, the Jews appealed to the caliph. He investigated the evidence and overturned the judgement, freeing the Jewish prisoners and punishing the Muslim witnesses instead. This remarkable event was celebrated in a poem, written by one of the prisoners who happened to be a liturgical poet, Samuel 'the Third' ben Hosha'nah. Known as the 'Egyptian Scroll', Egyptian Jews read it out in celebration each year. Unexpectedly, the caliph involved was al-Hakim, whose reign is more often associated with harsh persecution of Jewish and Christian populations and the destruction of churches and synagogues.

Ca. 11th century

T-S 8K10

Second Kings with Decorated Masorah

The end of 2 Kings 25, followed by masoretic notes enclosed in decorative borders. High-quality Bibles like this often contained long masoretic notes and lists after each book, sometimes with multiple, ornate pages of notes at the end of the volume (known as the *masorah finalis*).
A parchment book of this scale – with professional Hebrew calligraphy, masorah, and colourful embellishments – would have held considerable financial value over many years. It is likely that its owner placed it in the Genizah only after it had sustained significant wear from continuous use.[6]

Ca. 11th–12th century

T-S K10.5

Genesis 1 with Micrographic Masorah

This large parchment folio comes from the beginning of a Hebrew Bible, including the first chapter of the book of Genesis presented in three columns. The scribe employed 'micrography' – a technique for creating patterns with tiny letters – to decorate the right margin (☛ Chapter X). The micrographic text consists of long strings of masoretic notes. At first glance, it appears that a (later?) scribe filled the bottom margin with further masoretic notes in a geometric pattern, but this is not the case. In fact, someone simply copied the first few verses of Chronicles and the first half of Genesis 1 in more minute writing.[7]

Ca. 11th–13th century

T-S A1.3

Qohelet in Arabic Translation

A small parchment copy of a Judaeo-Arabic translation of the book of Qohelet (Ecclesiastes), copied with near-full Hebrew vocalisation. Likely produced around the 11th century, the writing system preserves features of an Egyptian Arabic dialect spoken at that time. Most Jews in Egypt spoke Arabic as their native language, so translations like this were important for them to learn the Hebrew Bible. The scribe pricked guide-holes in the outer margins and ruled the pages with a straight edge.[8]

Ca. 11th–12th century

T-S Ar.53.12

T-S AS 16.166

Illuminated Esther Scroll

Illuminated parchment scroll of the biblical book of Esther (chapters 5–6). Unlike Torah scrolls, this one is small and was most likely intended for individual reading rather than public recitation.[9]

Ca. 13th century

T-S A36.18

A Holey Scroll

This large parchment scroll of the book of Esther (chapters 5–8) was written by a skilled scribe in the 10th century, making it one of the oldest – if not *the* oldest – Megillat Esther. It suffered wear while rolled up, leaving a repeating pattern of damage.

Ca. 10th century

Shorthand Hebrew Bibles

Sometimes biblical manuscripts are written in abbreviated form. Either each word of the verse is written but abbreviated to just one letter, or, in other cases, each verse is represented simply by its first few words. Some of these manuscripts apparently served as memory aids for people highly familiar with the biblical text. Others are more formal scribal tools, short reference works from which the full masoretic apparatus of the Bible could be reconstructed. These types of shorthand Bibles are known as *serugin*.[10]

T-S NS 249.5

Part of a Bible codex containing Ezekiel 31–36. Most words are abbreviated to just a single letter, usually from the accented syllable, and the scribe added vowel and accent signs from the Palestinian masoretic system. Such a manuscript was most likely the property of a professional scribe, a valuable tool of the trade.

Ca. 9th–10th century

The text of Numbers 30:2-17 abbreviated to just the first few words of each verse. Whoever copied this was obviously in a hurry – you can see their handwriting slip into a more cursive style as they get to the end. Perhaps whoever wrote it was running late on the way to synagogue.

Ca. 11th–13th century

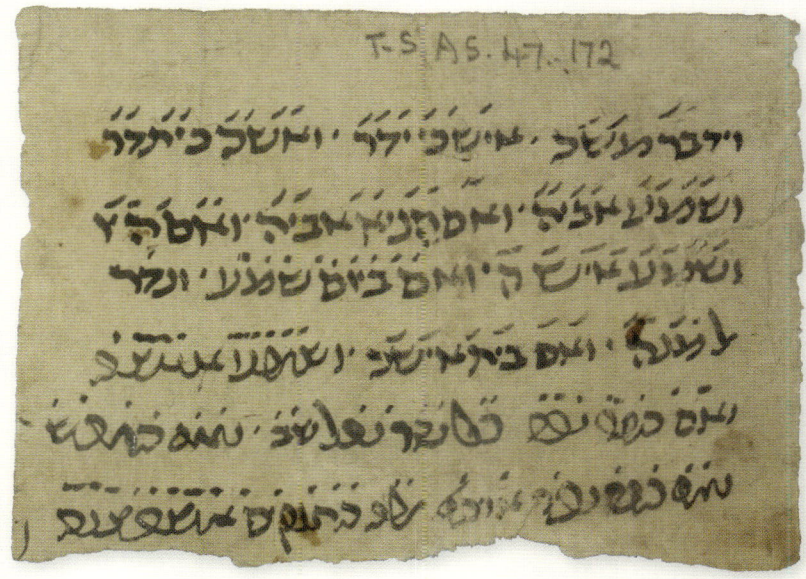

T-S AS 47.172

This scroll was made by glueing two paper leaves together. The text (Esther 6–7) is greatly abbreviated, with some verses reduced to just a single word. Rough dots have been added as decorative borders.

Ca. 12th–13th century

T-S AS 41.207

Autograph Draft of the *Mishneh Torah*

Maimonides' greatest halakhic work was his comprehensive code of Jewish law, the *Mishneh Torah* (*Repetition of the Torah*), which aimed to replace the need to scour the Talmud and all the other sources of Jewish law. He sought to provide a clear, concise guide to every commandment, relieving common people from having to wade through centuries of rabbinic debates. These pages are from Maimonides' own draft of the *Mishneh Torah*. The text is in Hebrew, but a later hand (or perhaps Maimonides himself?) used the top margin for Arabic pen tests.

Ca. 1170–1180 CE

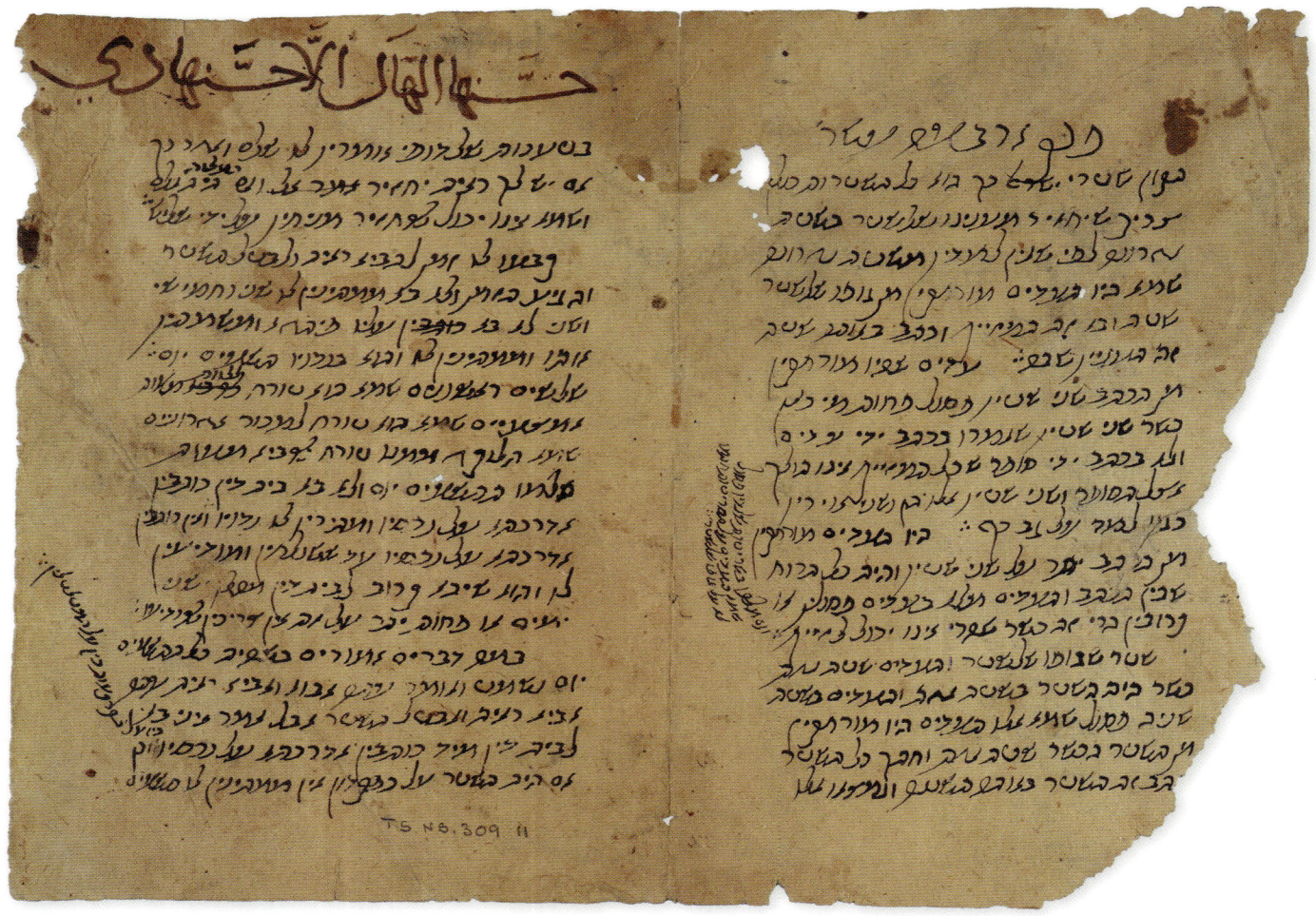

T-S NS 309.11

Or.1080 2.50

Babylonian Talmud in Ashkenazi Style

Parchment copy of the Babylonian Talmud (*Zevahim* 57–59 and 69–70) with extensive marginal writing by later users. The Talmud is the primary collection of Jewish law, compiled in Late Antiquity by authorities at the Jewish academies in Iraq. At least four different scribes had a hand in this manuscript, but the original used a professional 'Ashkenazi' script style, distinguished by its thick horizontal and angled strokes in contrast to thin vertical strokes. Ashkenazi calligraphy was common among Jews of Central and Eastern Europe. The extensive marginal notes in this fragment are a precursor to the format that Hebrew printers would adopt for modern Talmud editions (☞ Chapter XI), which typically include commentaries surrounding the main text.

Ca. 12th–13th century

T-S NS 244.77

Piyyut with Musical Instructions

This paper leaf was torn from a book of Hebrew liturgical poetry, known as *piyyut*. Poets who composed *piyyutim* are known as *paytanim*. The goal of a *paytan* was to produce religious poetry that would be recited or sung during synagogue services. This book includes musical instructions in Judaeo-Arabic alongside the Hebrew poems. Hebrew vowels have been added in red ink to facilitate easier recitation.[11]

Ca. 12th–13th century

Medieval Passover Haggadah

This small paper book is a medieval Haggadah, one of the more common types of manuscript in the collection. A Haggadah is a liturgical text that is read at a Seder meal during the Jewish holiday of Pesach (Passover), meant to tell the biblical story of the Exodus to new generations. Traditionally in Hebrew and Aramaic, many haggadot also include translations into the spoken languages of the Jewish communities that used them. This one – belonging to Egyptian Jews – has a translation in Judaeo-Arabic. Later haggadot tend to be decorated with illustrations of scenes from the Exodus story (☛ Chapter XI), but this one opts for stylish headings in a mix of red, blue, and gold ink.[12]

Ca. 12th–14th century

T-S NS 325.80

The Prayer of Judah ha-Levi

Pages from a book of Hebrew *piyyut* (liturgical poetry) by the famous medieval poet (and physician) Judah ha-Levi. He was born in Toledo in what is now Spain and spent most of his life in the Andalusian kingdoms of the early 12th century. The righthand page has a decorative scribal note in Judaeo-Arabic – known as a colophon – that refers to this poem as the "prayer of Judah ha-Levi." It names the scribe who copied the book as Eliezer ben Nathan.[13]

Ca. 13th century

T-S K6.108

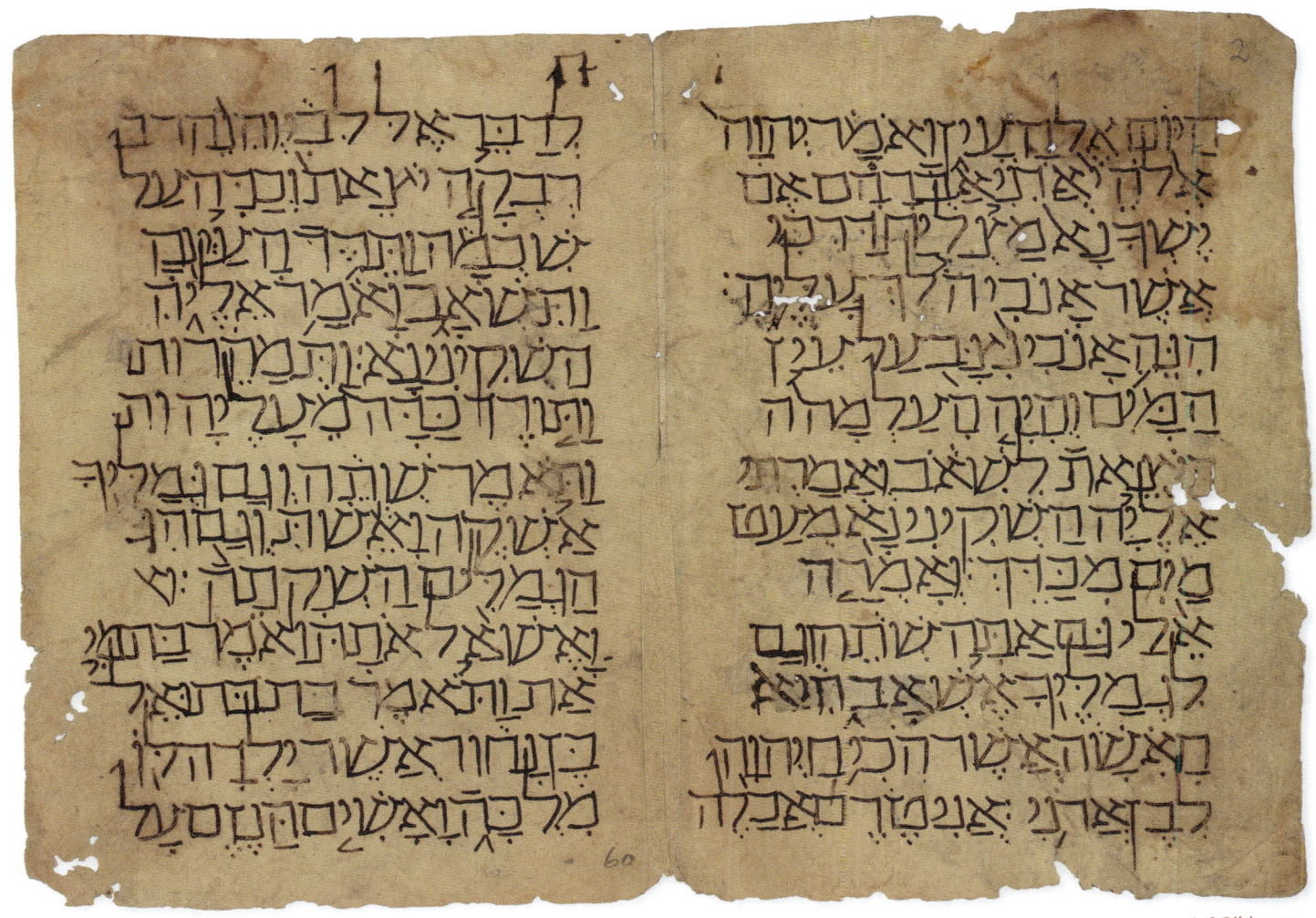

L-G Bible 1.59

Genesis, in a Distinctive Hand

Two pages from a small, paper Hebrew Bible containing Genesis 24. The text is copied in a
rather distinctive Hebrew script that we don't often associate with professional Hebrew scribes.
It was likely made by an individual practising their writing or who simply wanted their own
copy of Genesis. It is part of a tradition of 'common' Bibles – many of them are preserved in
the Genizah – that lack the multiple columns and marginal masoretic notes typical of more
professional, 'model' Bibles.[14]

Ca. 13th–14th century

Trilingual Bible

Written in a Yemeni hand, this book contains the text of Exodus in three languages: Hebrew, Aramaic, and Arabic. Each verse begins with the original Hebrew including vocalisation with Tiberian vowel and accent signs. Next comes Targum Onqelos, the most popular Jewish Aramaic translation of the Bible, vocalised with Babylonian signs. Yemeni Jews continued using the Babylonian vocalisation system even after the Tiberian system replaced it in other regions. Finally, an unvocalised Arabic translation follows Onqelos, transliterated using Hebrew characters.[15]

Ca. 13th–14th century

T-S B1.17

ותתמרו ותכתרו אל עלמא אל מחלוק לל דיא וקלובהם מלאנן

פעאיל חסאן מתל אל רומאן ;

לא יָדַעְתִּי נַפְשִׁי שָׂמַתְנִי

מַרְכְּבוֹת בַת נָדִיב

וכיף אנכשף פי עלם אלה תע עלא אנדהום

צאלחין ולאהנין פאל ⟨...⟩ה קץ אל⟨...⟩

באמרה לם אזיד ארטהום ואיצה לם אפנוהם אא אדבר⟨...⟩

בעטמתי אני אכיר להום ותנעלהום שאמכין ברכאב אל מלך

לאגל זכת צאלחן אגל אדי שאבהין פעאילהום לאברהים

אבוהום ; **שׁוּבִי שׁוּבִי הַשּׁוּלַמִּית**

שׁוּבִי שׁוּבִי וְנֶחֱזֶה בָּךְ מַה

תֶּחֱזוּ בַּשּׁוּלַמִּית כִּמְחֹלַת הַמַּחֲנָיִם

ארנעי לעדי יא כנסת ישראל ארנעי

לירושלם ארנעי לבית תעלים אל שׁועה

Arabic Commentary
on the Song of Songs

Judaeo-Arabic commentary on the Song of
Songs. The biblical verses are copied in Hebrew in red
and green ink, followed by the Arabic commentary
(transcribed in Hebrew characters) in black ink. The two
verses on this page are Song of Songs 6:12 and 6:13.

Ca. 14th–15th century

T-S K10.24

Biblical Commentary by Maimonides' Grandson

This is a copy of a commentary on Genesis that David ha-Nagid (1222–1300 CE), the grandson of Moses Maimonides, composed in the 13th century. The descendants of Maimonides inherited his position as 'Head of the Jews' in Egypt, adopting the title *nagid* ('prince, governor'), for five generations. This manuscript is decoratively inscribed in red to mark the end of a *parashah* (weekly Torah reading).

Ca. 14th–15th century

T-S K6.163

Sefardi Prayer Book

Two pages from a pocket-sized book of Hebrew prayers. Each page is only two inches wide. The Hebrew script is written in a 'Sefardi' style, exemplified by its long, fluid strokes and lack of hard corners. This type of calligraphy developed among Jews living in the Iberian Peninsula. The lefthand page is labelled "The Prayer of Elijah."

Ca. 15th–16th century

Mosseri I.107.1

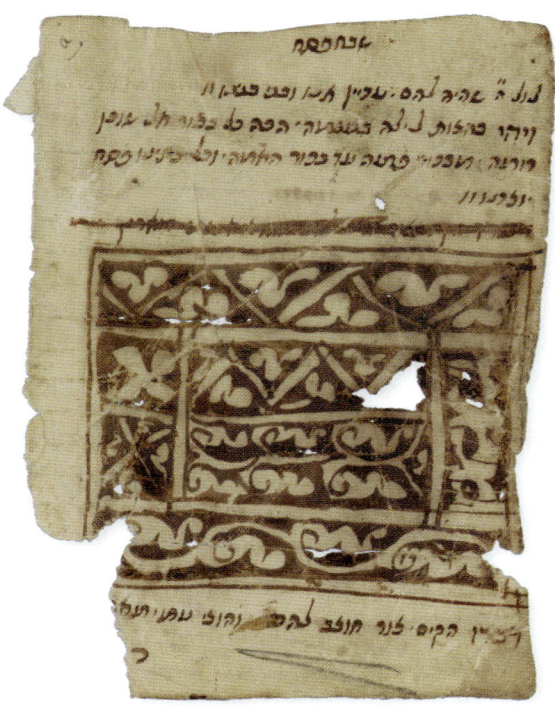

Mosseri V.27.3

A Moroccan Rock Star

This decorated page comes from a work of Hebrew *piyyut* for Passover, composed by the great Moroccan poet and *paytan*, David ben Hasin (1727–1792 CE). Ben Hasin was born in Meknes, but his work was so popular that he toured Morocco to sing for other Jewish communities, even travelling to Gibraltar. After his death, anthologies of his poetry spread across North Africa and the Middle East.[16]

Ca. 18th–19th century

Notes to Chapter II

1   Colette Sirat, *Hebrew Manuscripts of the Middle Ages* (Cambridge, UK: Cambridge University Press, 2002), 27–28; Adina Hoffman and Peter Cole, *Sacred Trash: The Lost and Found World of the Cairo Geniza* (New York: Nextbook, Schocken, 2011), 194–195; Ben Outhwaite, 'Fragments of the earliest complete Torah scroll in the Cairo Genizah?', in Patrick Andrist, Élodie Attia and Marilena Maniaci (eds), *From the Thames to the Euphrates: Intersecting Perspectives on Greek, Latin and Hebrew Bibles* (De Gruyter: Berlin, Boston, 2023), 143–152, https://doi.org/10.1515/9783111019963-009.

2   Malcolm C. Davis and Ben Outhwaite, *Hebrew Bible Manuscripts in the Cairo Genizah Collections* (Cambridge: Cambridge University Library, 2003), volume IV, no. 301 and plate 2; Mordechai Mishor, 'An Ancient Scroll of the Book of Exodus: The Reunion of Two Separate Fragments,' *Israel Museum Studies in Archaeology* 7 (2015): 24–69; Mordechai Veintroub, 'More Fragments of an Early Torah Scroll Come to Light,' *Genizah Fragments*, 2019.

3   Malcolm C. Davis, *Hebrew Bible Manuscripts in the Cambridge Genizah Collections* (Cambridge: Cambridge University Library, 1978), volume I, plates 13–14.

4   Thank you to Kim Phillips for suggesting this fragment for inclusion in this chapter. The contract to copy the Prophets and Writings in 1021 CE is T-S 10J5.15. Samuel also made copies of Bible translations, and leaves from his edition of Saʿadyah Gaon's *Tafsir* (Judaeo-Arabic translation of the Bible) are also preserved in the Genizah at T-S AS 72.79 and T-S Ar.1a.38. For more on Samuel ben Jacob, see Ben Outhwaite, 'Beyond the Leningrad Codex: Samuel b. Jacob in the Cairo Genizah', in N. Vidro, R. Vollandt, E.-M. Wagner and J. Olszowy-Schlanger (eds), *Studies in Semitic Linguistics and Manuscripts* (Uppsala: University of Uppsala Press, 2018), 320–340 and Kim Phillips, 'More Genizah Bible Fragments Written by Samuel b. Jacob', in Nick Posegay, Magdalen M. Connolly, and Ben Outhwaite (eds), *From the Battlefield of Books: Essays Celebrating 50 Years of the Taylor-Schechter Genizah Research Unit* Cambridge Genizah Studies Series 16 (Leiden: Brill, 2024).

5   Malcolm C. Davis, *Hebrew Bible Manuscripts in the Cambridge Genizah Collections* (Cambridge: Cambridge University Library, 1978), volume I. Thank you to Kim Phillips for deciphering the Hebrew notes.

6   Malcolm C. Davis, *Hebrew Bible Manuscripts in the Cambridge Genizah Collections* (Cambridge: Cambridge University Library, 1978), volume I.

7   Malcolm C. Davis, *Hebrew Bible Manuscripts in the Cambridge Genizah Collections* (Cambridge: Cambridge University Library, 1978), volume I. Thank you to Kim Phillips for his help in identifying the marginal texts.

8   Nick Posegay and Estara J Arrant, 'Three Fragments of a Judaeo-Arabic Translation of Ecclesiastes with Full Tiberian Vocalisation', *Intellectual History of the Islamicate World* 9, no. 3 (2021): 259–96.

9   Malcolm C. Davis and Ben Outhwaite, *Hebrew Bible Manuscripts in the Cairo Genizah Collections* (Cambridge: Cambridge University Library, 2003), volume III, no. 3385.

10 See Kim Phillips, 'Abbreviated Bible Manuscripts in the Cairo Genizah', *Textus* 31 (2022): 69–120.

11 Avihai Shivtiel and Friedrich Niessen, *Arabic and Judaeo-Arabic Manuscripts in the Cambridge Genizah Collections: Taylor-Schechter New Series*, Cambridge Genizah Series 14 (Cambridge: Cambridge University Press, 2006), no. 4530.

12 Avihai Shivtiel and Friedrich Niessen, *Arabic and Judaeo-Arabic Manuscripts in the Cambridge Genizah Collections: Taylor-Schechter New Series*, Cambridge Genizah Series 14 (Cambridge: Cambridge University Press, 2006), no. 8095.

13 Identified by the Fleischer Institute for Research of Hebrew Poetry in the Genizah, accessed via the Friedberg Genizah Project.

14 See Colette Sirat, *Hebrew Manuscripts of the Middle Ages* (Cambridge: Cambridge University Press, 2002) and Benjamin Outhwaite, 'The Tiberian Tradition in Common Bibles from the Cairo Genizah', in *Studies in Semitic Vocalisation and Reading Traditions*, ed. Aaron D. Hornkohl and Geoffrey Khan, Cambridge Semitic Languages and Cultures 3 (Cambridge: University of Cambridge & Open Book Publishers, 2020), 405–66.

15 Michael L. Klein, *Targumic Manuscripts in the Cambridge Genizah Collections* (Cambridge: Cambridge University Library, 1992), 4.

16 André E. Elbaz and Ephraim Hazan, 'Three Unknown Pyyutim by David Ben Ḥasin', *Association for Jewish Studies Review* 20, no. 1 (1995): 87–98. Israel Adler, *Catalogue of the Jack Mosseri Collection*, ed. Institute of Microfilmed Hebrew Manuscripts (Jerusalem: Jewish National and University Library, 1990), 124; Lysette Hassine-Mamane, *Le Piyyut de Rabbi David Hassine. Traduction et annotation de quelques poèmes* (Paris: Maisonneuve and Larose, 2000).

III.
Sketches & Illustrations

Not everything is as complicated or momentous as a lost biblical book or an ancient Greek palimpsest. Some Genizah fragments are simply fun to look at. Many are skilled works of art in and of themselves, but others are just simple sketches produced by ordinary folk – even children – who were, at one time, very bored. While they may not be what we expect to find in a storage room meant for holy books, Fustat's Jews nevertheless deposited them in their genizot, and they have survived to reach us today. They are part of what makes the Cairo Genizah such a unique source for studying the everyday lives of people in the Middle Ages.

The use of resources like ink and paper for something as trivial as doodling demonstrates that writing materials were abundant for the people of medieval Egypt. Egyptian society, especially in Jewish communities, was highly literate, and the spread of relatively cheap papermaking techniques to Egypt during the 10th century CE made reading and writing more affordable than ever. Ink could also be made from widely available materials – in particular, we find numerous ink recipes based on charcoal and soot that could be collected from any fire. Pens too were easy to get hold of. The primary writing implement was known as a *qalam* (from the Greek word *calamos*, 'reed'), a hollow reed pen that would draw in a bit of liquid when dipped into an inkpot. Writers had to frequently re-dip their *qalam* when writing, so you can see variations on manuscripts where the ink started to run dry. The nib of a *qalam* would also wear out quickly, so writers would keep a small knife on hand to re-cut and sharpen it. As we see in this chapter, the availability of all these scribal tools meant that some people could use them for (often impromptu) works of art.

Noah's Ark

Drawing of Noah's Ark surrounded by exercises practising the Hebrew alphabet. Many Hebrew language textbooks had illustrations to keep the attention of young children (☛ Chapter IX), but this one appears to be a sketch done by a student.

Ca. 10th–11th century

T-S K5.82

T-S 16.371

Book of Lots

These two drawings of human heads are on the back of a page from a book of lots used to predict the future (☛ Chapter V), but it's not clear what their purpose is. While the book was written in Judaeo-Arabic, there is also a short Arabic-script note in the bottom right corner.

Ca. 10th–11th century

Sunrise Sketches

Prayers in Hebrew to be recited upon waking up, with several sketches, perhaps drawn by the person who used this book to pray. One of them is a scroll labelled *ha-sefer* ('the scroll'). If you look closely in the centre right, you can still see the hair follicles from the animal skin used to make this parchment. This need for animal skin made parchment much more expensive to produce than paper. At the lower right corner of this fragment, there is a patch that looks wet and sticky. It has become 'gelatinised' – an irreversible process where the collagen in the animal skin deteriorated because it was exposed to humidity.[1]

Ca. 10th–11th century

T-S NS 121.12

Picture Purrfect

Of course we have a cat fragment. This drawing appears on the back of a Judaeo-Arabic magical recipe. You can see where the Cambridge University Library conservators have patched a tear with a thin strip of Japanese repair paper.

Ca. 11th–13th century

T-S Ar.44.220

Moon Phase Diagram

This beautiful illustration of the sun and moon appears in an Arabic astrological text. It depicts the changing phases of the moon throughout the lunar cycle. The Islamic and Jewish years are both based on lunar months, so diagrams like this helped to keep calendars straight in the Middle Ages.

Ca. 11th–13th century

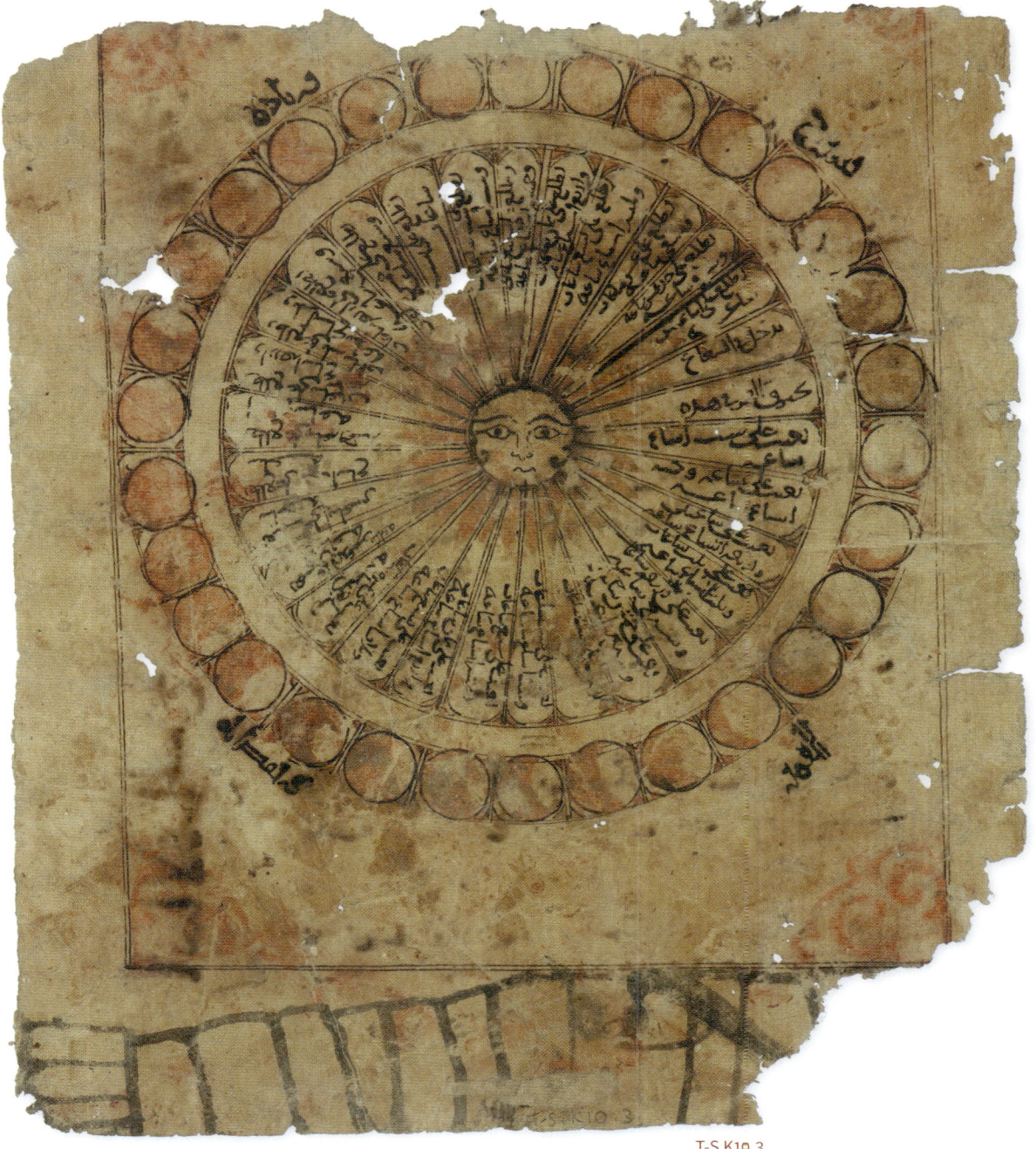

T-S K10.3

Kalila wa-Dimna

Kalila wa-Dimna is a book of Arabic fables with moral lessons that has roots in the Sanskrit and Persian literary traditions. It was very popular with people of all faiths in the medieval Middle East. The stories centre around a pair of jackals, named Kalila and Dimna, and their encounters with other anthropomorphised animals. Medieval manuscripts of *Kalila wa-Dimna* frequently included elaborate illustrations of the animals' adventures.

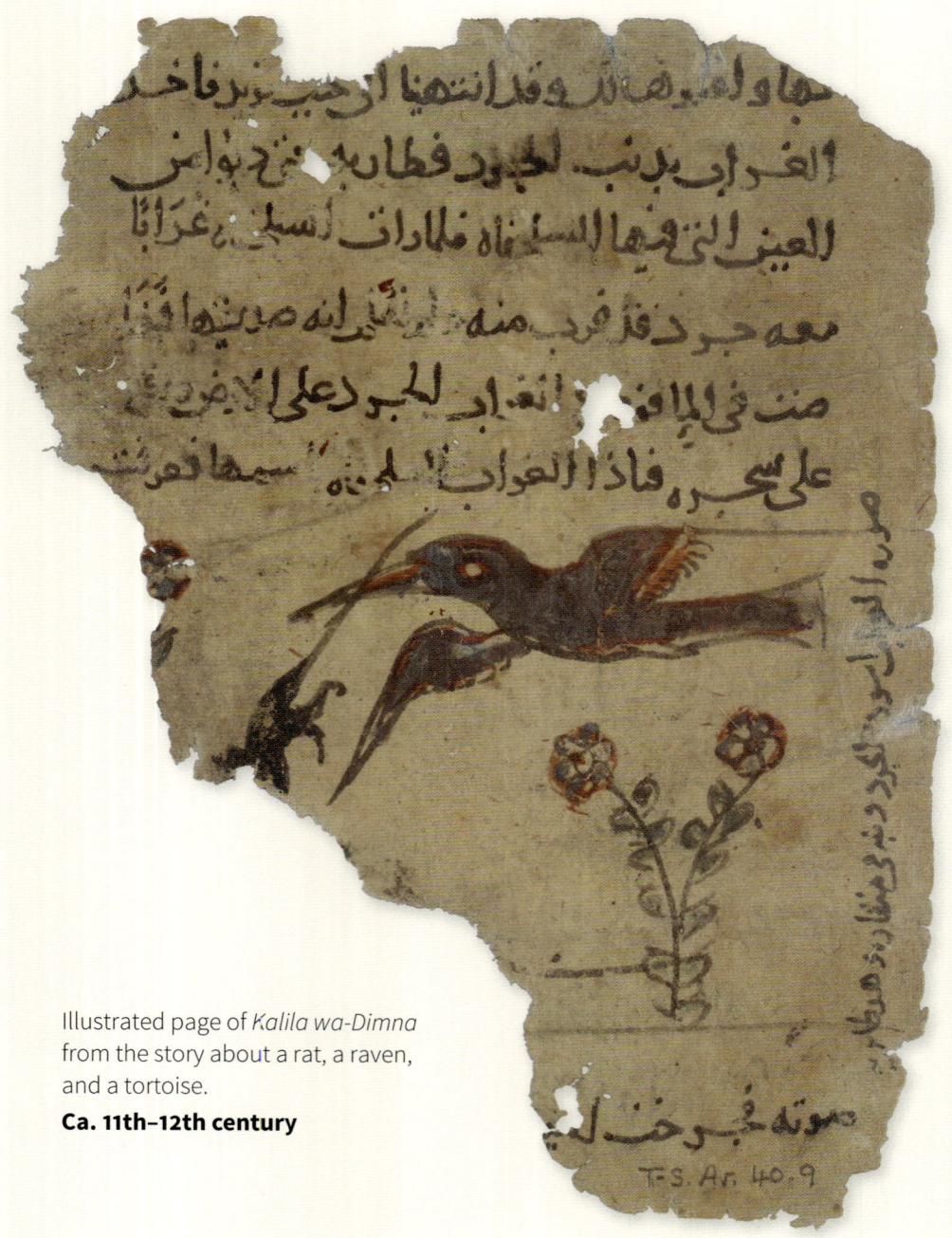

Illustrated page of *Kalila wa-Dimna* from the story about a rat, a raven, and a tortoise.
Ca. 11th–12th century

T-S Ar.40.9

T-S Ar.51.60

Illustrated page of *Kalila wa-Dimna* picturing a lion and his wise lioness mother. This copy has much finer Arabic calligraphy and more sophisticated artwork than the previous fragment. The paper is also larger and the margins are wider, both of which indicate that this book was more expensive (more blank space = more paper required). This manuscript would have been a valuable prestige item for whoever owned it, most likely a Jew in Fustat.

Ca. 13th–14th century

Sticking It to the Man

Sometimes we just come across a tiny ancient stick figure. This fragment is barely six centimetres wide and was probably produced by a young child, perhaps four or five years old – the age at which children begin to draw people with separate bodies and add details like fingers and belly buttons. There are a few hints of practice Hebrew writing, so it may be torn from the corner of a child's homework assignment (☞ Chapter IX).

Ca. 11th–13th century

T-S AS 221.204

T-S AS 183.272

Good Luck Charm

Arabic amulet featuring a drawing of a turbaned man, wishing great fortune for the bearer. Long, thin slips of paper like this were rolled and stored in cylindrical amulet cases that could be worn as pendants around the neck (☞ Chapter V).

Ca. 11th–13th century

One Fish, Two Fish

Another amulet, this one featuring decorative Arabic and pseudo-Arabic calligraphy around an illustrated medallion of a fish. The text above and on the reverse side is religious poetry in a mix of Arabic, Judaeo-Arabic, and Hebrew. The two fragments of the drawing were separated long ago. Solomon Schechter brought one half with him when he returned to Cambridge from Egypt in 1897, but Jacques Mosseri collected the other half in Cairo between 1909 and 1912. It was only a few years ago that Genizah researchers spotted that the two halves belong to the same manuscript.[2]

Ca. 11th–13th century

Mosseri IV.198.1

T-S Ar.51.115

Drawing of a Hunt

Drawing of an armed man on horseback pursuing two four-legged animals, one of which may be a hunting dog. Arabic pen tests and other sketches surround the picture. This scene appears on the back of a legal document written by one of the Genizah's most prolific scribes, the 12th-century Jewish court clerk, Halfon ben Manasseh.

Ca. 1100–1138 CE

T-S AS 154.491

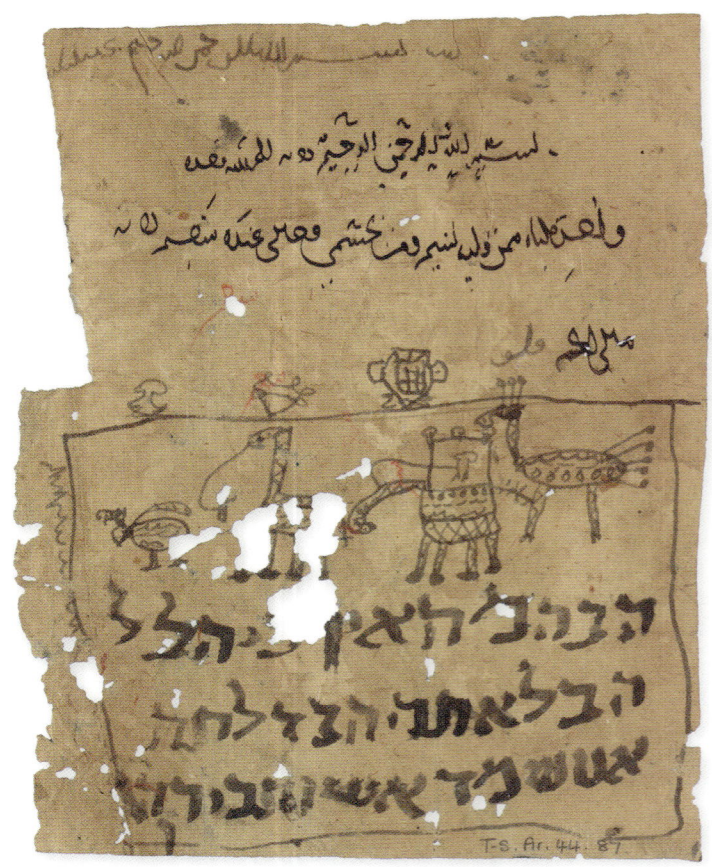

T-S Ar.44.87

Medieval Zoo Pals

Draft sentences in Arabic – written by a skilled hand – followed by several rough drawings and a child's Hebrew writing practice (from a prayer recited at the end of Yom Kippur). If you ask us, that's a chicken, two camels, and a peacock.[3]

Ca. 12th–13th century

Temple Schematic

A building plan of the Jewish Temple in Jerusalem, drawn more than 1000 years after its destruction. It is labelled in Hebrew, including the central altar and southern cistern for collecting rainwater. The image is similar to one found in Maimonides' commentary on the Mishnah. There was originally an adjoining page that depicted the public side of the temple.[4]

Ca. 12th–13th century

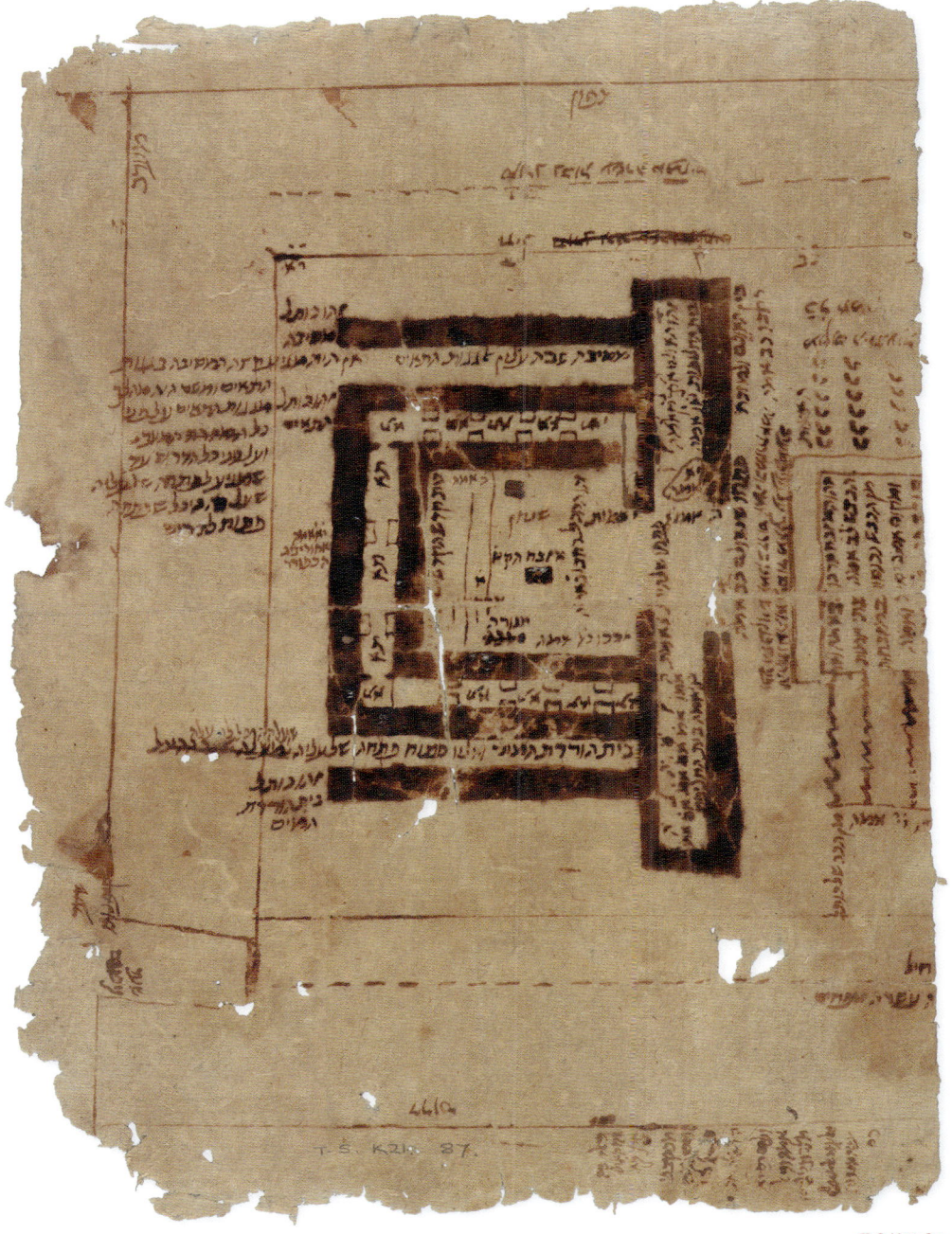

T-S K21.87

Amulet with Flute or Blunderbuss

Magical amulet designed to give charm and grace to a man named Berakhot ben Khulul ben Joseph Yefet (and also protect him from demons). It is written in a mix of Hebrew, Arabic, and Aramaic, with the 8 columns in the centre listing different Hebrew names for God each 13 times. The matrix in the lower left includes some magical symbols (☛ Chapter V). The drawing at the bottom is, as a previous cataloguer put it, an "image of a gun or a sword." To us, it also looks a bit like a mizmar, a type of reed instrument common in the Middle East and North Africa.

Ca. 12th–14th century

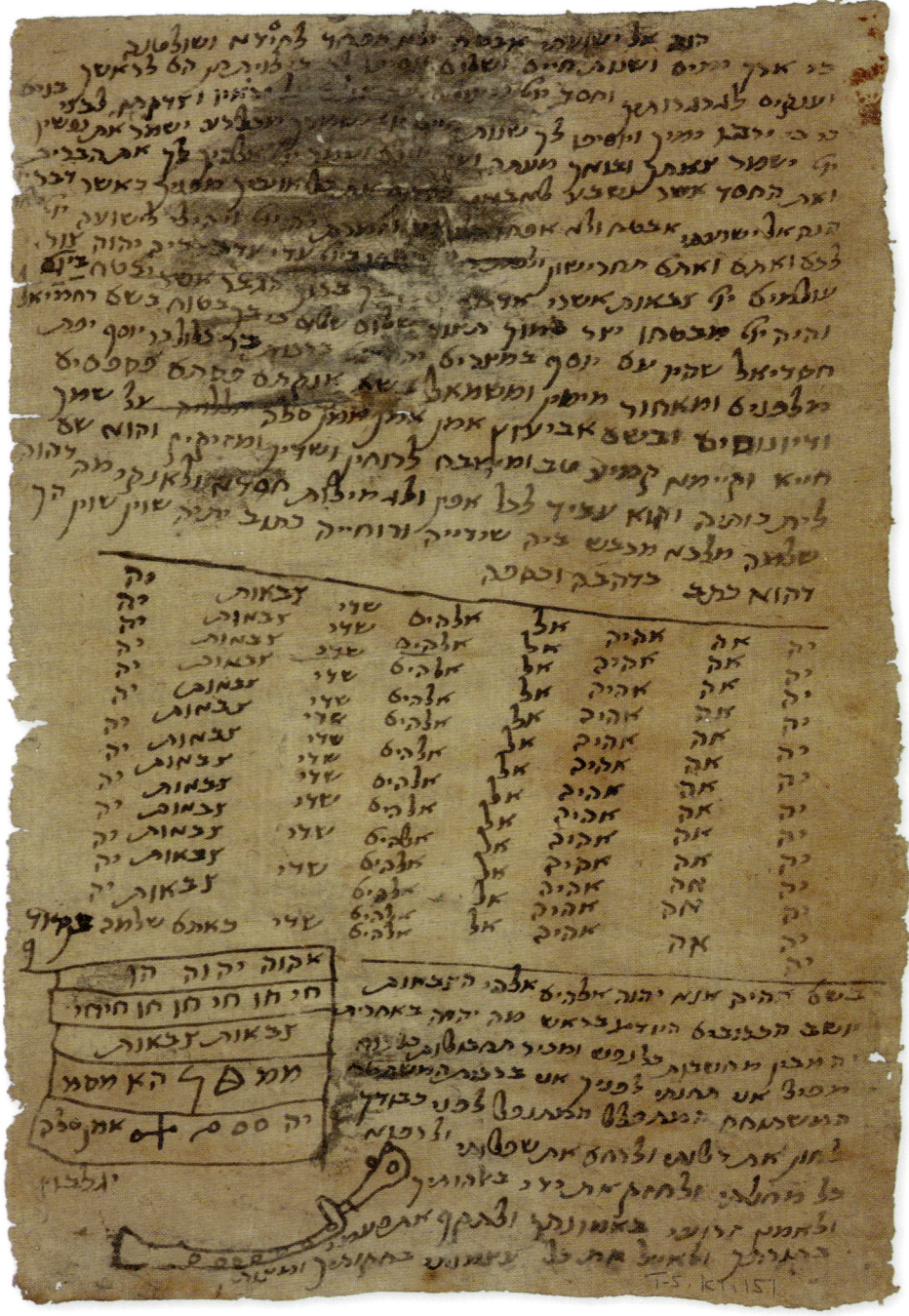

T-S K1.151

Magic Square with a Drawing of a Bug

Magic square arranged with letters from the Arabic, Coptic, and Hebrew alphabets, though the Hebrew seems to have been added by a later hand. Arabic phrases praising God appear in the bottom row next to a sketch of some kind of insect. Notice the creases that show how the whole page was once folded up to just a single square.

Ca. 12th–14th century

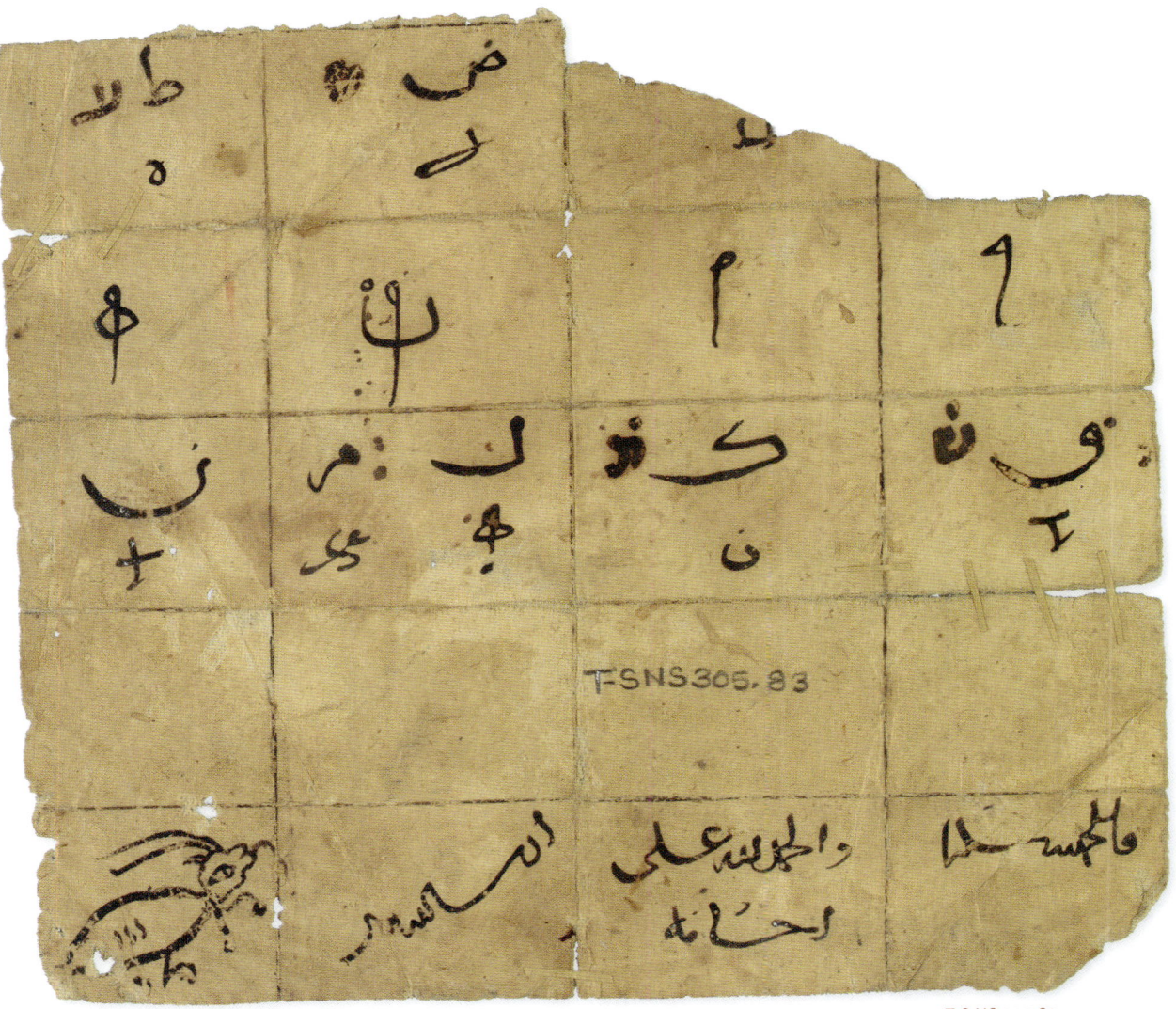

T-S NS 305.83

L-G Talmud 2.68

Menorah Diagram

A page from Maimonides' *Mishneh Torah* (*Repetition of the Torah*), the most influential book of Jewish law in the Middle Ages (☛ Chapter II). This copy was probably made within a century of his death in 1204 CE. The illustration is a labelled diagram of a menorah with straight branches.

Ca. 13th–14th century

Trimming the Sails

Drawing of an oared galley with three sailors on deck. Its triangular sail features a Star of David and a broken Judaeo-Arabic caption runs along the top and bottom. Several surviving illustrations of boats show the importance of the Mediterranean Sea and Indian Ocean trade routes for the people of medieval Egypt. This one has, unfortunately, been torn and we've yet to find the missing piece.[5]

Ca. 13th–15th century

Mosseri III.11.4

T-S K6.184

Scrap Paper with Doodles

Spare paper leaf with sketches and jottings, including the names Abraham Meron ha-Levi, Judah ha-Levi, and Jacob ben Moses. The text runs in several directions and some other phrases are repeated, so this is likely scrap paper for something else. It seems someone has drawn a rough self-portrait.

Ca. 14th–15th century

Marginal Cavalry Charge

This fragment comes from a Hebrew ethical work called *Sha'are Teshuvot* (*The Gates of Repentance*) by the 13th-century Catalonian Rabbi, Jonah Gerondi. The paper was made later though, so this copy was produced well after his death. The sketches in the margin depict a bearded horseman and archer locked in combat. They may be based on European or Mamluk warriors of the 14th and 15th centuries.[6]

Ca. 14th–15th century

T-S NS 324.3

Calendrical Hand Book

Diagram of a hand from a calendrical text on the divisions of the seasons (*tequfot*), with Hebrew instructions for doing calculations using the fingers. The script is an Ashkenazi style, which suggests that the scribe was most likely a Jew from Central or Eastern Europe.

Ca. 16th–17th century

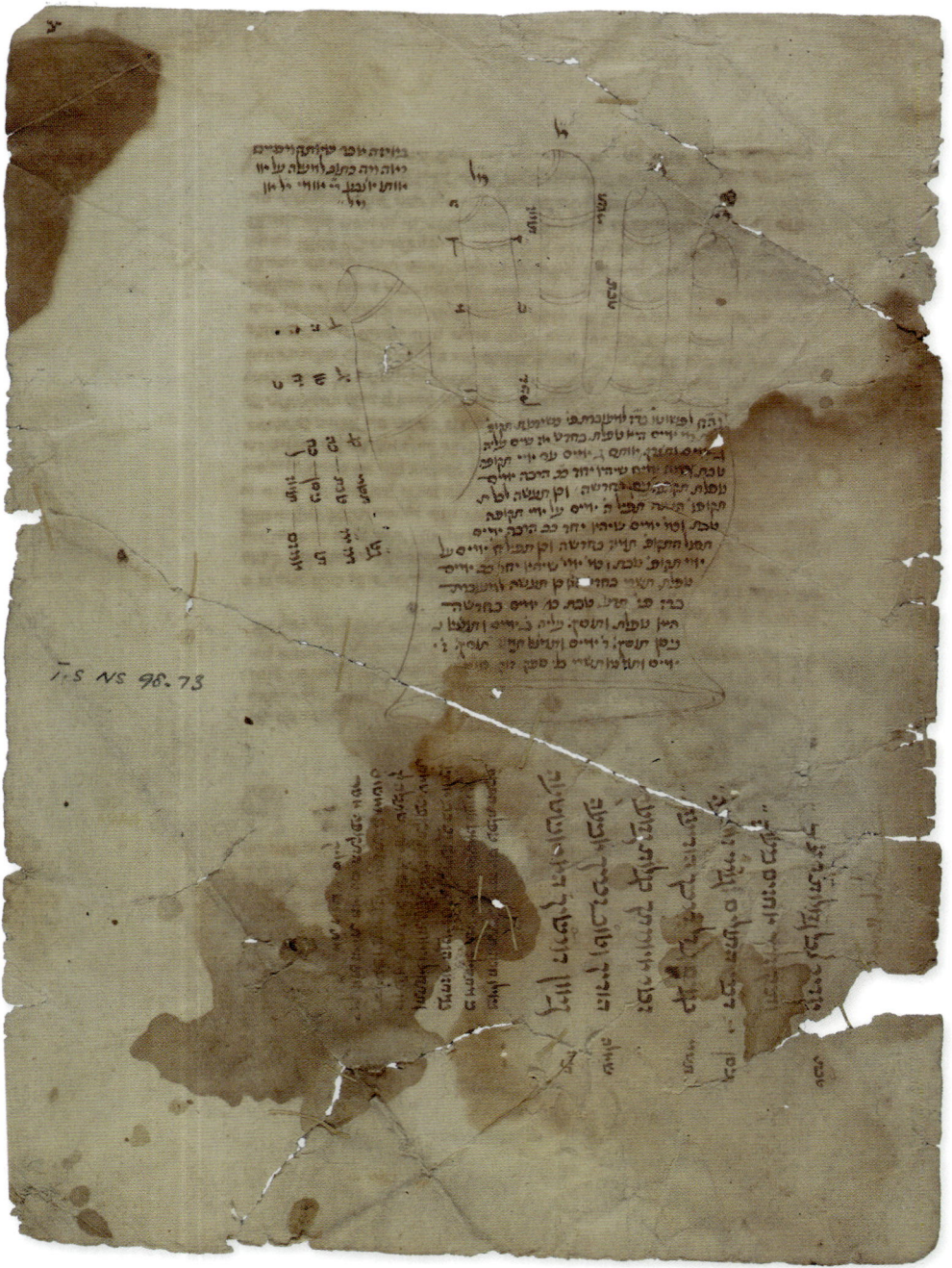

T-S NS 98.73

Flower Powder

Ottoman-era painting of a soldier standing on a wheeled cart while firing a cannon which appears to be exploding with flowers. While not the first Middle Eastern empire to adopt gunpowder weaponry, the Ottomans famously used cannons to crack the Byzantines' walls and conquer Constantinople in 1453 CE. You can see how the left side of the page is torn off, so there was once more to this scene.

Ca. 17th–19th century

Or.1081 J55

Late Communal Records

Hebrew ledger listing betrothal and marriage contracts in the Jewish community of Cairo near the end of the 18th century. It includes the names of married couples, their trousseau lists (☛ Chapter VIIIa), and the values of wedding presents. The script is a late Sefardi style, typified by long horizontal cursive strokes that sometimes resemble Arabic. The scribe also employed (Indo-)Arabic numerals, visible just above the three birds.[7]

1790–1792 CE

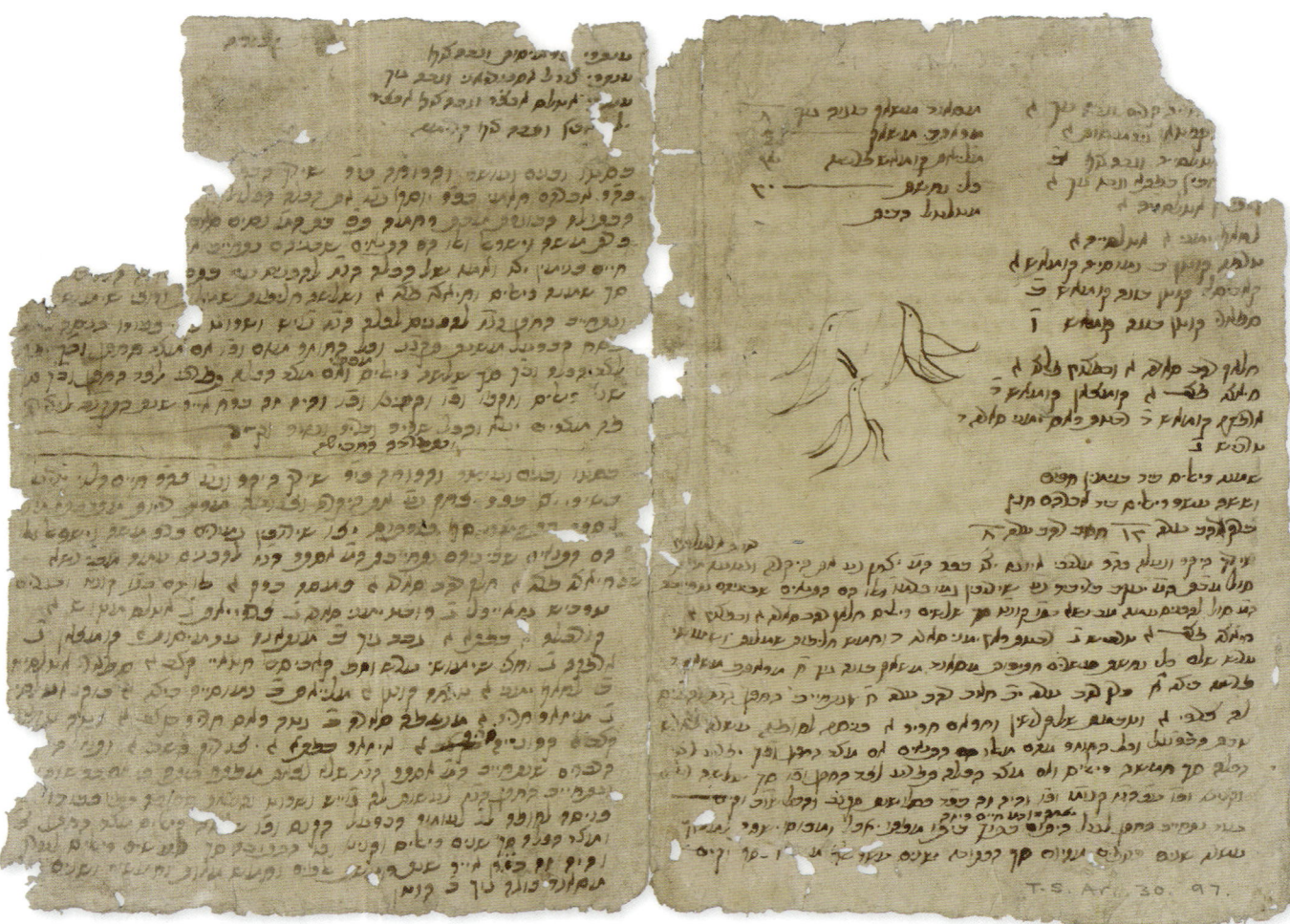

T-S Ar.30.97

Hebrew and Judaeo-Arabic Wall Calendar

Calendar of the 12 Jewish months and the holidays that take place in them. It was originally meant to be hung on a wall, so someone used the large blank space on the back to copy a writing exercise. The front includes the date "Muharram 1231" in the Islamic Hijri calendar (AH), equivalent to Heshvan 5576 in the Jewish calendar (AM) and December 1815 in the Gregorian Christian calendar (AD).

1815 CE

T-S K2.75

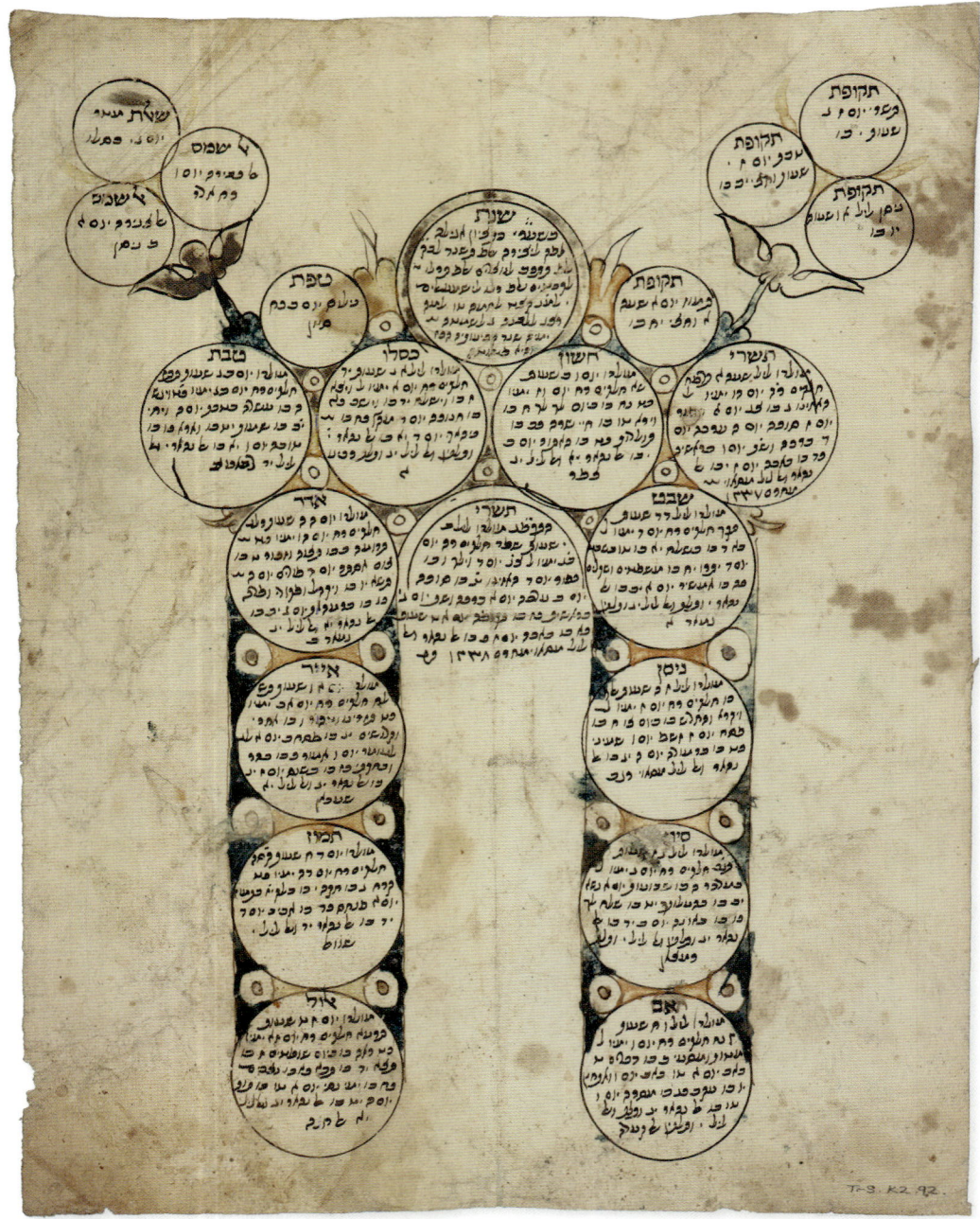

T-S K2.92

Illuminated Wall Calendar

Hebrew and Judaeo-Arabic wall calendar for the year 5582 of the Era of Creation (1821–22 CE), giving the date according to the Jewish, Gregorian, Coptic, and Hijri calendars. Each circle is a month containing dates for Jewish festivals with the corresponding Muslim month. It also provides dates for regular changes in the wind patterns on the Mediterranean coast and the date of the annual flood of the Nile.

1821 CE

Schematic Map of Gravesites

Painted diagram of important graves at sites in Palestine, listing biblical figures and influential rabbis supposedly buried in Shechem, Meron, and the ancient cemetery at Safed. The names include Joseph, Jethro, Zipporah, and Rabbi Akiva. The back is blank, suggesting that the picture was meant to be hung on a wall.[8]

Ca. 1880–1897

T-S K10.13

Notes to Chapter III

1 For more on the 'spontaneous gelatinisation' of manuscripts, see our *Genizah Fragments* interview with Cambridge University Library Senior Conservator, Deborah Farndell (https://www.lib.cam.ac.uk/genizah-fragments/posts/qa-wednesday-gelatinisation-early-parchment-fragments-t-s-new-series-deborah).

2 The join between these two fragments was discovered by Athina Pfeiffer and publicised on social media by Alan Elbaum of the Princeton Geniza Project.

3 Thank you to Amir Ashur for identifying the Hebrew text.

4 Thank you to Ben Outhwaite and Amir Ashur for helping to identify this fragment.

5 Not to worry, they are still sailing half a ship.

6 Thank you to Amir Ashur and Estara Arrant for identifying this text and extensive palaeographic analysis to estimate a date for the script style.

7 Information in part from Alan Elbaum of the Princeton Geniza Project (https://geniza.princeton.edu/en/documents/20485/). See Pierre Delbes, 'Les documents datés de la Geniza du Caire (Université de Cambridge) (Westminster College Cambridge): Liste chronologique des documents datés Répertoire' (École des hautes études du judaisme, 1992), 251.

8 Thank you to Amir Ashur for helping to date this fragment.

IV.
Letters

Thousands of letters were deposited into the Cairo Genizah, and through them the daily concerns of Egypt's communities come to life. We learn firsthand about family dramas and heartfelt greetings sent to absent friends, read commercial news on the prices of fine textiles or rare spices from abroad, and receive terrible reports of earthquakes, wars, pirate attacks, and devastating plagues. Through letters, the heads of the rabbinic academies in distant Babylonia (i.e. Iraq) and Palestine ministered to their respective flocks in Egypt, soliciting donations, providing political leadership, and dispensing legal rulings, ever watchful of the shifting allegiances of the diaspora communities. But merchants' letters, letters from travelling husbands to their wives back home, and letters of introduction or solicitation – how did they end up in the Genizah alongside sacred texts? Well, every letter, no matter how mundane, had an opening blessing, a rousing Bible verse, or a closing wish for God to protect the reader's family. Writers often invoked the Almighty in all sorts of turns-of-phrase, whether sharing good news, wishing long life to a friend, or cursing the name of a rival. It is easy to see why the Jews of Cairo treated their mail with a degree of sanctity.

Physically, the letters are remarkably varied. Some are small, rectangular pieces of paper with every margin filled to the brim with writing, while others are great lengths of parchment. Delivery was similar, though: letters were uniformly folded over and over until only a thin strip remained, upon which were written the sender's and recipient's names. These strips were tucked into the deep sleeve pockets or luggage of messengers, couriers, travelling merchants, or pilgrims – whoever was going in the right direction to carry it. Such correspondence arrived in Egypt from all around the Mediterranean Sea and even from beyond the Indian Ocean.

A Complaint from a Babylonian Gaon

In an attempt to halt the decline in his community's fortunes, Sherira ben Hananya, Head of the Gaonic Yeshivah ('Academy') at Pumbeditha (on the site of modern Fallujah, Iraq), reached out to his Jewish compatriots in Fustat. Reproaching them for their failure to send regular donations to the Academy, Sherira expresses his disappointment in elegant Hebrew. He stresses that without their financial support – which their forefathers always gave – the resident scholars will drift away, and there are no eager pupils to fill their places. Sherira was fighting a losing battle. The diaspora communities were gradually turning away from the old Jewish centres in Iraq, as the intellectual centre of gravity moved west to Spain and North Africa. With the death of Sherira's son Hai in 1038, the Pumbeditha Academy would stumble on for only a few years before disappearing from the record.[1]

Ca. 970 CE

T-S 13J25.5

…many of the children of the talmudic scholars are leaving for other occupations and taking their place among the wage-earners or emigrating away. From generation to generation we are becoming fewer…

…the worms crawl from our flesh while we are alive …

T-S 16.18

Funding the Lepers of Tiberias

People seeking treatments for skin ailments were drawn to the hot springs of Tiberias, and a leper colony formed there in the 11th century. To raise funds, community leaders sent out graphic letters describing their sufferings in gruesome detail, like this one addressed to Samuel ben Ezra in Jerusalem. Sometimes one of the sufferers might accompany the letters to collect the donations in person, as a vivid example of their plight.[2]

Ca. 1030 CE

Aftershocks in Ramla

In 1033 CE, a violent earthquake shook the whole of Palestine with destructive force. The writer of this account, Solomon ben Semah, describes people in the city of Ramla who abandoned their houses when they noticed the walls bulging. They left all their belongings behind, only to see their homes collapse into rubble, with some still trapped under the ruins. Nevertheless, there were things to be grateful for. The writer thanks God that the earthquake happened during the day, when most people were outside, and not at night "when everyone would have been asleep in their beds." The Fatimid governor of the city arranged for tents to be put up for those left homeless.[3]

1033 CE

…many died under the rubble because they had no means of escape. Everyone came out of their houses, each one leaving behind all that they had, and fled for their lives…

T-S 18J3.9

The 'Kyiv' Letter

This is the famous 'Kyiv' letter, a letter of introduction written for Jacob bar Hanukkah, who needed to raise money to repay his murdered brother's debts. Among the signatories – presumed to be members of the *Bet Din* (Rabbinical Court) in Kyiv – are some who have non-Hebrew names. Some cryptic letters towards the bottom of the document have been interpreted as Turkic Runes. Early scholarship suggested this manuscript was proof that Khazars, a Turkic tribe that converted to Judaism, had lived in Kyiv during the Middle Ages. Recent research, however, suggests that the names in the letter may have Slavic, rather than Turkic, origins, and the letter's connection to the Khazar kingdom is unproven. Thanks to water damage and fold lines, even the proper reading of the name 'Kyiv' is contested, although 'multi-spectral' imaging (seen here alongside the normal photograph) suggests it is the most likely interpretation.[4]

Ca. 10th-11th century

… We, the community of [Kyiv], are informing you of the affair of this Mar Jacob bar Hanukkah… we have sent him out among the holy communities so that they can show him mercy. And now, our lords, raise your eyes heavenwards and act in your usual good way…

T-S 12.122

Letter from an Elderly Hai Gaon

Letter by an elderly Hai Gaon, Head of the Yeshivah (Academy) at Pumbeditha in Iraq, writing to Nehemiah ben Abraham, a member of the Babylonian congregation in Fustat. Nehemiah had quarrelled with his fellows and swore not to lead services for them anymore, but the quarrel has now been resolved, and Hai writes to officially release Nehemiah from his vow. The letter is dated at the bottom to 1037 CE, which would mean Hai Gaon was 98 years old when he – or more likely, his scribe – wrote this letter. He died the following year at the age of 99. The top half of the manuscript is preserved in the Taylor-Schechter collection, while the lower half is in the Mosseri collection.[5]

1037 CE

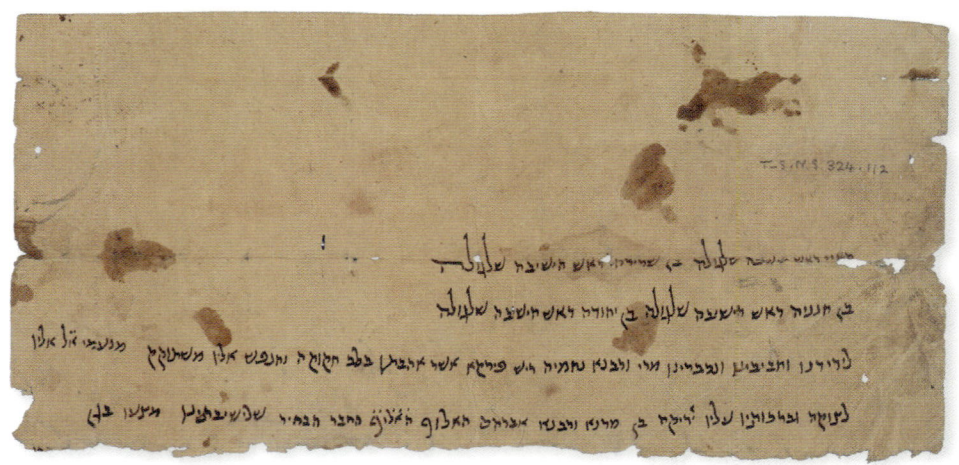

T-S NS 324.112

…Hai, Head of the Yeshivah of the Exile, son of Sherira, Head of the Yeshivah of the Exile, son of Hananya, Head of the Yeshivah of the Exile, son of Judah, Head of the Yeshivah of the Exile…

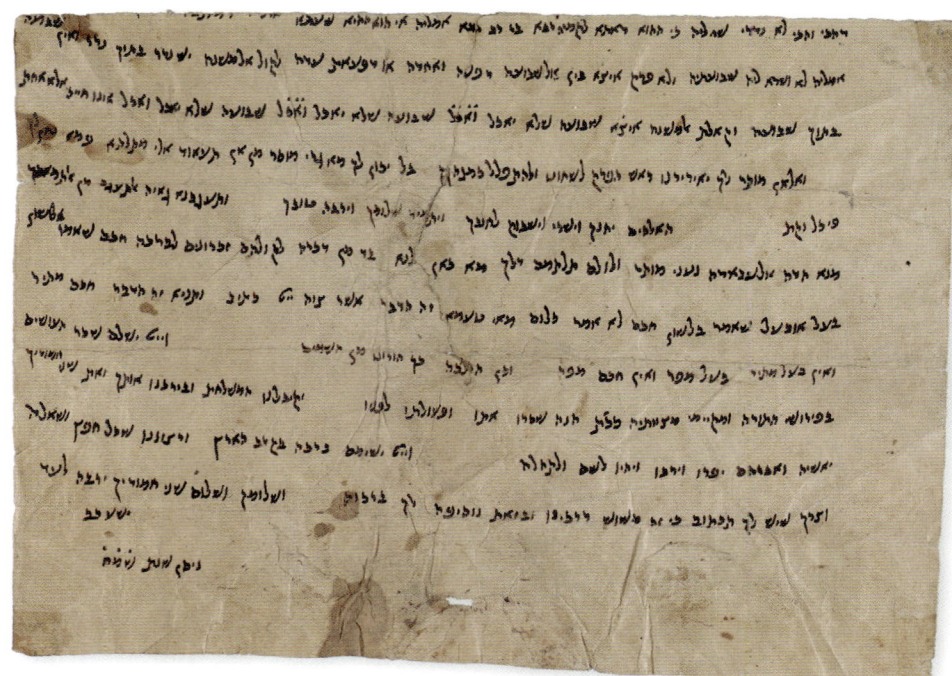

Mosseri VII.157

T-S 16.261

…be warned and warn others not to read his letters if they should come to you, because his letters are iniquitous scribings and mischievous missives…

Rivalry in the Palestinian Yeshivah

Life was difficult for Solomon ben Judah. He was unpopular, had rivals to his position as Gaon of the struggling Palestinian Yeshivah (Academy), and he was even forced to borrow from the poor fund to feed and clothe himself. His eyesight was failing and his knees often ached. In this letter to a Jewish leader in Tripoli (modern Lebanon), Solomon announces the excommunication of his challenger, Nathan ben Abraham, and urges the Tripoli community to follow suit. It was the ultimate sanction against Nathan, who had garnered sufficient support in Egypt, North Africa, and Palestine to attempt to usurp the Jerusalem gaonate. Solomon limped from one disaster to another, but eventually outlived all his enemies. Dozens of his letters have been recovered from the Genizah.[6]

1039 CE

Pirates of the Mediterranean

Human trafficking in the Mediterranean is no recent phenomenon. Christian and Muslim pirates carried out a lucrative trade in captives, seizing travellers from each other's ships and selling them in distant ports. Captive Jews were often brought to Alexandria, and Jewish communities throughout Egypt held charitable collections to free those captured in acts of war and piracy. There was even a standard rate of 33 and a third dinars for an adult male. In this letter from Alexandria, Yeshua ben Joseph writes to Nahray ben Nissim, a wealthy trader, legal scholar, and community leader in Fustat, to report the rescue of captives sold by merchants from Amalfi.[7]

Ca. 1050 CE

…these three people were taken from a ship and were robbed by Byzantine soldiers of everything. They stripped them bare of their merchandise… and they enslaved them…

T-S 12.338

...growing bold, the tyrants of the city, its notables, its elders and the qadi there, called the Nephew of Abu l-Sayyar — may the name of the wicked rot! — conspired to cut off our water supply. For they said "How can the Hebrews drink from our water?"

T-S 13J26.13

Trouble in Damascus

Life under the rule of the Fatimid dynasty could be difficult for Jews, particularly the burden of the *jizya* poll-tax. But on the whole, the Jewish community of Egypt, at the heart of the Fatimid Empire, enjoyed a peaceful existence and was free to practise their religion. It was a different matter in the far reaches of the empire, where pressure from rival factions or Bedouin tribes threatened Fatimid control. This letter describes the breakdown of Fatimid authority in Damascus when Bedouin forces joined local citizens to establish their own rule. They immediately imposed heavy new taxes on the local Jews, restricted their access to the water supply, and banned them from performing kosher slaughter in the city. The Fatimids sent a new governor to re-establish control, but – as this letter complains – he only lifted the restrictions after a massive bribe from the Jewish community.[8]

Ca. 1050 CE

Vouching for a Political Dissident

When Qayn ibn Abd al-Qadir, a Muslim, fell out of favour with the governor of Ramla because of his political activities, a warrant was issued for his arrest. Solomon ben Judah, the head of the Palestinian Yeshivah – and with it, all the Jews of the Fatimid Empire – used his own political network to try to save him. Solomon wrote this letter to call in a favour from Abraham ben Isaac ibn Furat, a physician at the Fatimid court in Cairo, in the hope that his influence could reconcile Qayn with his political enemies.[9]

11th century

*Whatever he does to this man,
Qayn, he also does to me…*

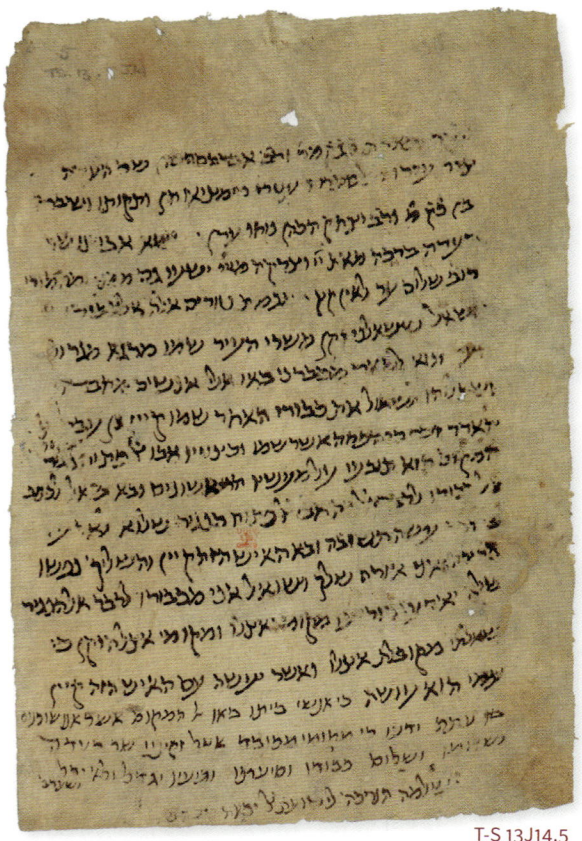

T-S 13J14.5

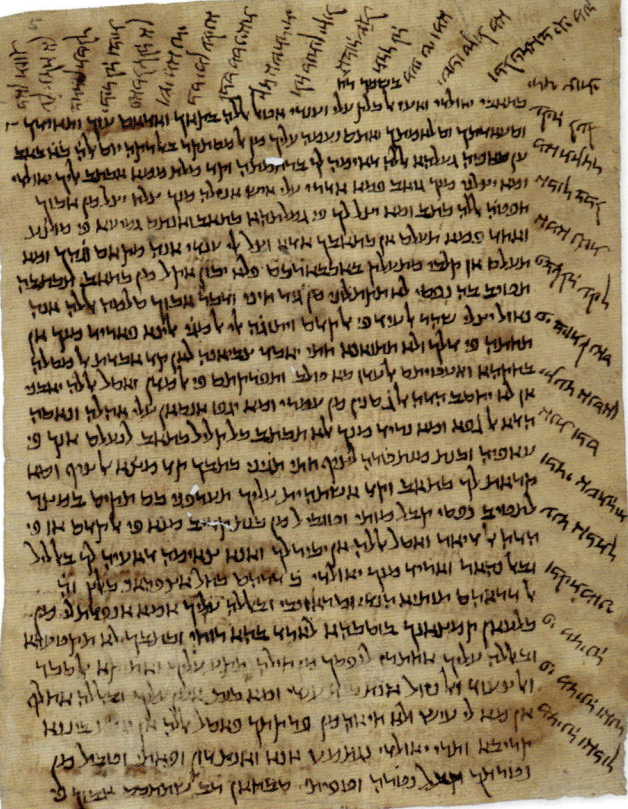

T-S 13J23.5

A Syrian Mother Misses Her Son

This elderly widow, the wealthy matriarch of the aristocratic Dosa family, was frustrated by her dependence on her sons – and perhaps by their independence from her. She sent this Judaeo-Arabic letter from Raqqa on the Euphrates to her son Abu Mansur Dosa ben Joshua in Fustat, complaining that they've abandoned her in her daughter's house and failed to keep in touch – even in summer, she points out, when letters are easier to deliver. A bundle of his dirty laundry would be a comfort to her now! She addressed the back of the letter in Arabic script, ensuring it would reach its destination across predominantly Arabic-speaking lands.[10]

Ca. 1067 CE

*By God, you must send me your
worn and dirty shirts to restore my
spirit. Do not withhold your letters…*

A Desperate Mother in Tripoli

A starving Jewish woman's account of her flight from the Seljuk Turks when they swept down into Palestine in the second half of the 11th century. After fleeing Jerusalem, which the Seljuks captured and held until 1098 CE, she escaped northwards with her children, taking shelter in Tripoli (Lebanon). She has so far avoided capture, but has come to believe it would be better if they were captured – even by the Byzantines – and fed than remain free and starving.[11]

1070s CE

L-G Misc. 35

I was with him on the day I saw them killed in terrible fashion… As far as I am concerned it is better to be captured by the Rum, for the prisoners find someone who gives them food and drink, but I am completely without clothing, and I and my children are starving…

T-S 13J13.16

As my sins and my transgressions increased, I developed a serious affliction upon my nose, and the infection spread, and it festered and my face was eaten away. This disease is worsening, and I cannot perform any work…

A Woman Facing Adversity

As her face rotted away from some sort of flesh-eating disease, this destitute woman threw herself upon the mercy of the "Great Prince," Exilarch David ben Daniel. A scribe composed her pleas into a Hebrew letter, requesting that David arrange a *pesiqa* ('charitable allowance') for her. She offers to relocate to another town if needed, as the cost of supporting the poor of Fustat was already a heavy burden on the Jewish community there.[12]

Ca. 1090 CE

The Jewish Elders of Ashqelon after Crusader Attacks

A year after the crusading 'Franks' captured Jerusalem, the Jews in the fortified city of Ashqelon were struggling to cope with the aftermath of refugees and epidemics. Notables of the city wrote this letter to update Egyptian Jews about their attempts to ransom back captives from the Crusaders. The Ashqelon community also bought back hundreds of books and Torah scrolls that had been pillaged from synagogues in Palestine. In an era before the printing press, manuscripts held considerable value, and invaders frequently took books when they sacked cities.[13]

1100 CE

… money that was borrowed and spent in order to buy back 230 codices, 100 booklets, and eight Torah scrolls. All these are communal property and are now in Ashqelon.

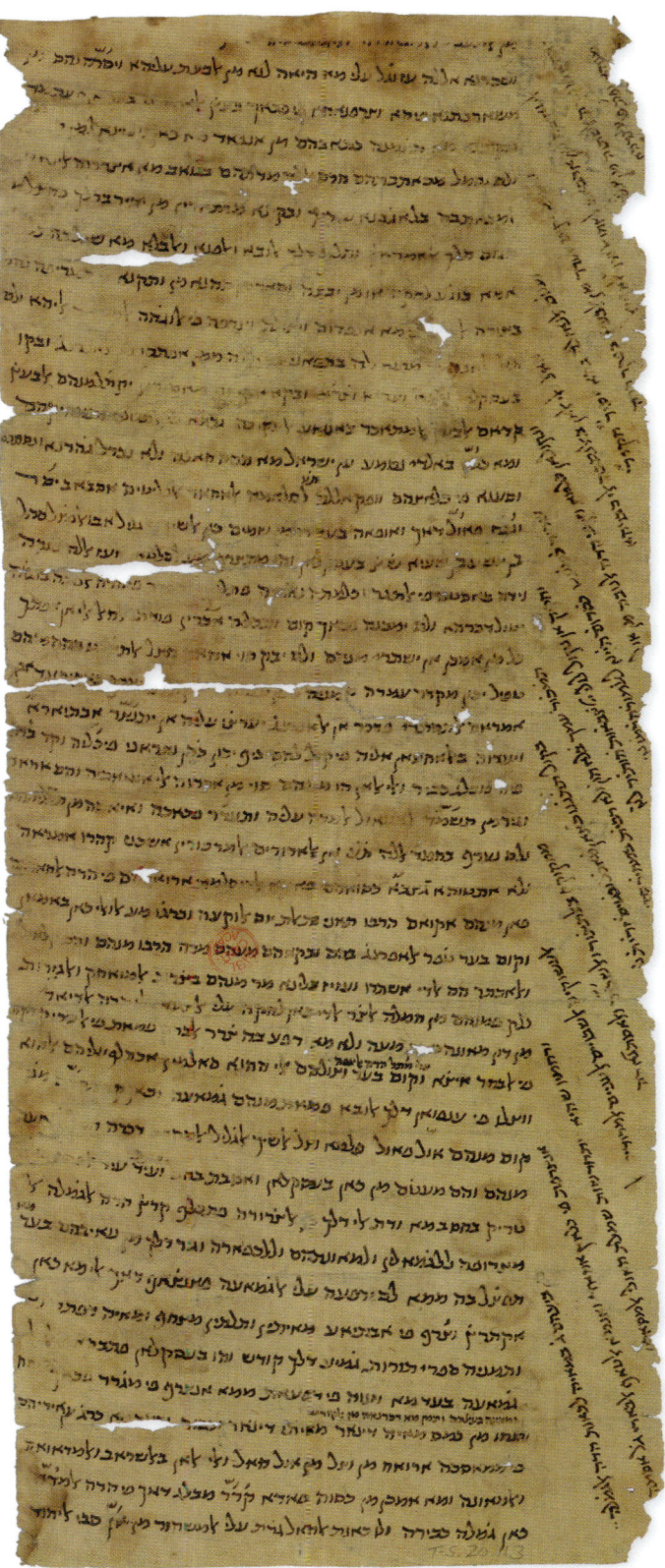

T-S 20.113

L-G Misc. 109

Good News from a Son

Sulayman sent this letter back home to his father, sharing the news of his wife's pregnancy and inviting him to visit for a holiday. The *basmala* ("in the name of God..."), which usually marks the beginning of Arabic letters, appears at the top in Arabic script, but the rest is in Hebrew characters. Poetry and other jottings in both scripts appear on the back.

Ca. 11th–13th century

God heaps goodness upon me, and as I congratulate you, I thank Him. The Torah is complete and indeed my wife is pregnant, for God is allowing me to achieve that blessing which you have always wanted for me…

Q: What's in a name?

A name can tell you a lot about someone. For Jews in Islamic lands, rather than a surname, the name of your father and grandfather would form part of your name: Abraham ben ('son of') Solomon ben Abraham. It was common for grandsons to share a name with their grandfather. Furthermore, you might be known by both Jewish and Arabic versions of your name: Abraham ben Solomon could also be called Ibrahim ibn Sulayman. Sittuna bat (Hebrew: 'daughter of') Moses could also be Sittuna bint (Arabic: 'daughter of') Musa. While Jewish women in Europe and Byzantium mainly went by biblical names like Sarah or Rebekkah, such names were not used publicly by Jewish women in Islamic lands. Instead, they used a wide variety of Arabic names. Some were originally titles but later came to be given as personal names, like Sitt al-Bayt ('Lady of the House') and Sitt al-Kuttab ('Lady of the Clerks'). Other names reflected personal qualities, like Karima ('noble'), Turfa ('cherished gift'), and Mu'ammala ('the one hoped for'). Some Jews also had Arabic nicknames that were plays on their Hebrew names. If your Hebrew name was Yefet ('beauty'), you might be called Abu al-Hasan ('father of beauty'). If you were Ephraim (from a root meaning 'to be fruitful'), you might be called Abu Kathir ('father of many').

In addition to a personal name, you might have a *kunya* name, a title of respect derived from the name of your eldest child: e.g. Abu al-Mansur, 'Father of Mansur', Umm Khalaf 'Mother of Khalaf'. You could also be known by your profession: e.g. al-'Attar, 'the perfumer', or by a *nisba* name referring to your family's place of origin: e.g. al-Siqilli, 'the Sicilian'. Some families even had a shared nickname: e.g. Ibn al-Qata if, 'son of the pastries'. If you were a Jewish male descendant of the biblical priestly tribe of Levi, you could add Levi, 'the Levite', or Kohen, 'the priest'. If you had any prestigious scholarly or communal titles, you could include those too, depending on the level of formality required: Haver, 'Fellow of the Academy', Shelishi, 'Third in the Academy', Av Bet Din, 'Father of the Court', Rosh Yeshivat Gaon Yacov, 'Head of the Academy of the Pride of Jacob', and Nasi or Nagid, 'Prince' (i.e. a descendant of the Davidic family).

Letter of Public Condemnation

A concealed entrance at the back of the Iraqi synagogue in Cairo allowed women convenient access to its upper gallery in privacy. This modest arrangement is now in jeopardy, as the congregation's charitable fund allowed a Muslim man named Ibn al-Masmudi to rent a house next to the women's entrance. An anonymous member of the community drafted this letter, in Arabic, protesting this failure of honour and assault on the women's modesty. The writer insists that they either evict Ibn al-Masmudi or permanently seal the secret doorway.[14]

Ca. 11th–13th century

O ye Jews! How can you face God?! …You are inflicting disgrace upon your women through Ibn al-Masmudi… Your sense of honour has obviously gone altogether. Peace!

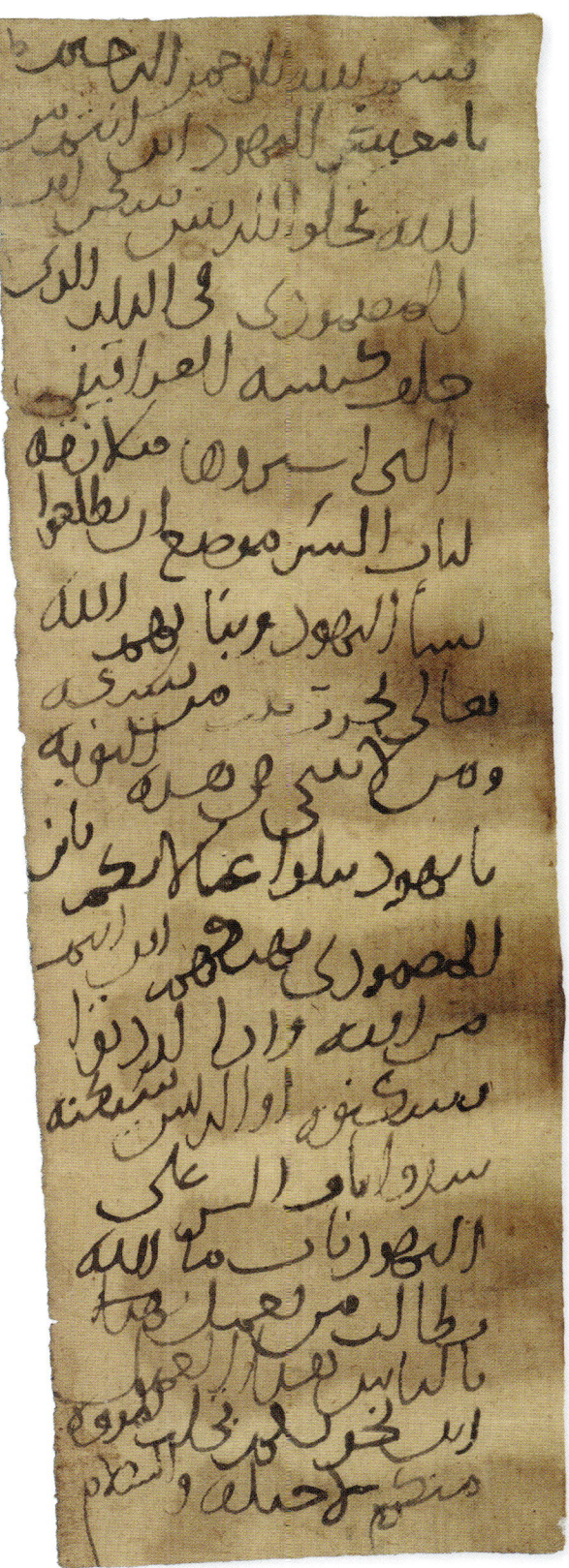

T-S 13J30.6

Judah Ha-Levi and the Case of the Captive Woman

Judah ha-Levi, the famous Spanish poet and philosopher (ca. 1075–1141), left us some of the most famous poems of the Jewish Middle Ages, as well as his monumental philosophical work, the *Kuzari*. He was also active in communal affairs. The Genizah preserves several letters that he sent to the Jews of Egypt, with whom he maintained close relations. In this one, Judah updates his wealthy friend, Halfon ben Nathaniel Dimyati, on progress towards paying the ransom of a Jewish woman from Toledo, for which Halfon had contributed money.[15]

1138–1139 CE

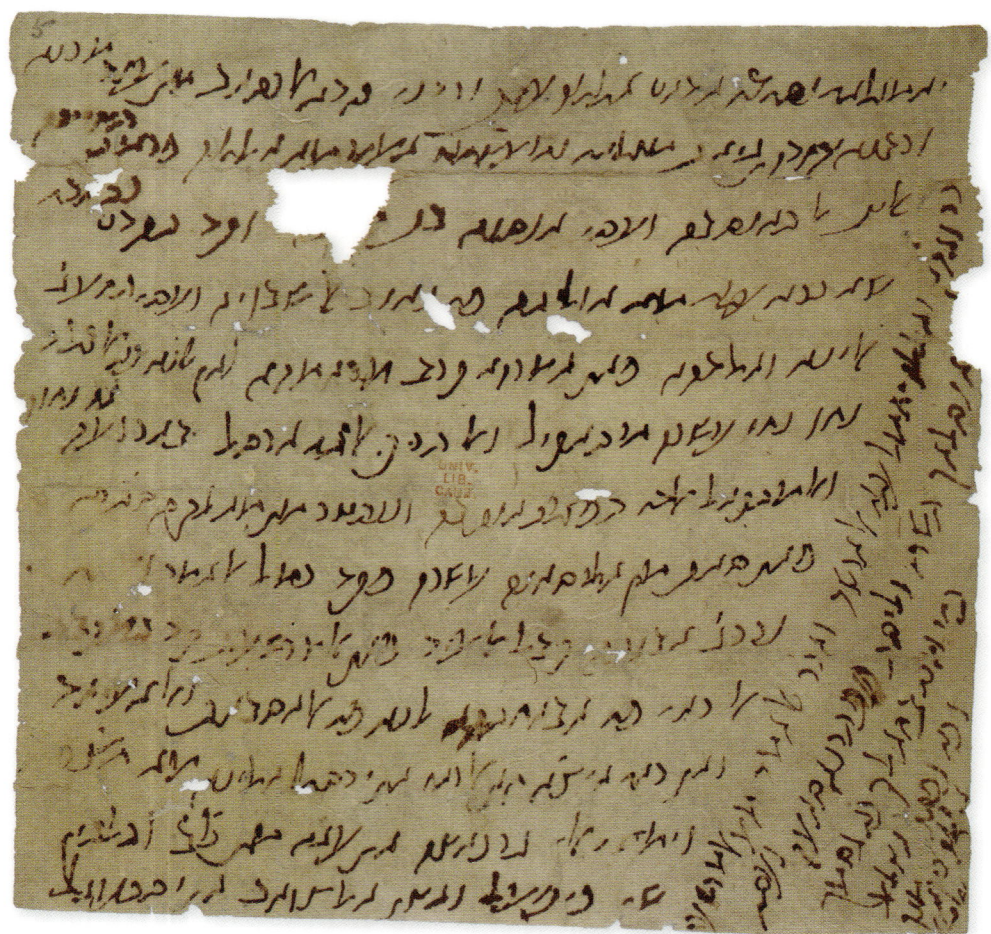

T-S 8J18.5

From Malaga we expect six [dinars], and when her father brings ten from Lucena, the matter will be settled and we may get his daughter out before the holidays. For that wicked woman has changed her mind and no longer permits us to take the girl out of the prison on Shabbats and holidays…

Appalled, of Byzantium

When Elijah ben Caleb ben Leon arrived in Egypt after a difficult journey from Byzantium, he was startled and disappointed at what he encountered. He had been expecting culture, erudition, and devout religious observance, but was disturbed by what he claims were the uneducated, smelly, and disrespectful hordes he found. He writes to Samuel ben Hananya, Head of the Jews in Egypt, in apparent distress, and hopes the community of Fustat will be of higher calibre.[16]

1140s CE

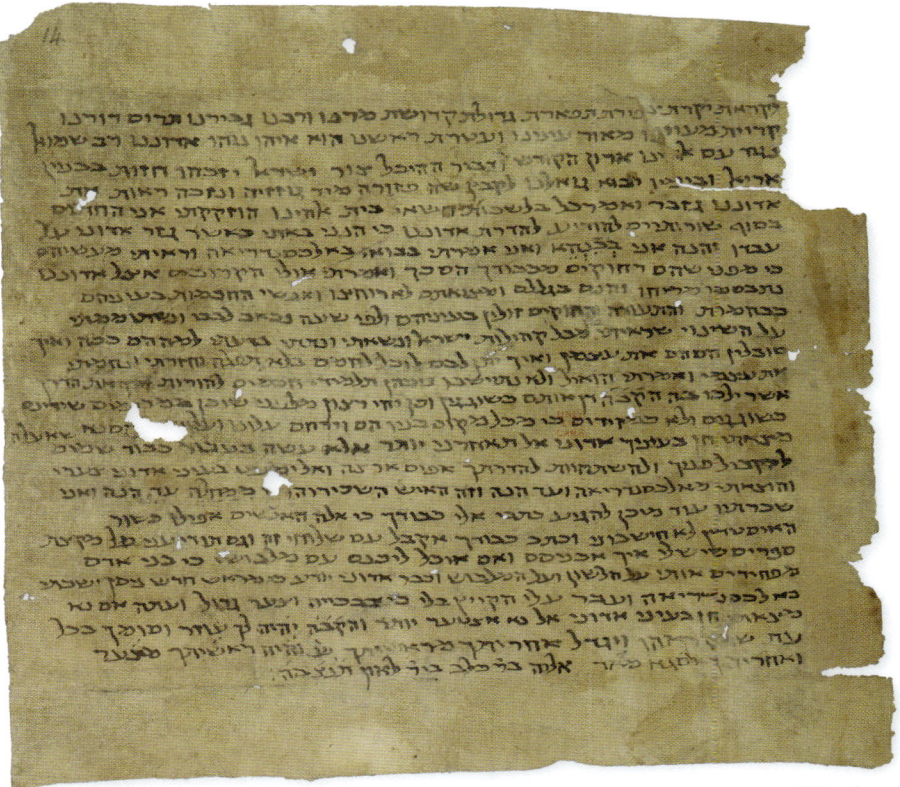

T-S 10J9.14

…When I arrived in Alexandria and saw how the people behaved, I thought that it was due to their distance from your honour that they behaved in such a way, and I said to myself that perhaps those nearer to our lord would be perfumed by his scent. But instead they wallow in their own dung and remain unwashed of their filth! Men of learning are as animals in their eyes; the Law and the statutes are worthless in their eyes. My heart was immediately pained and I was astounded…

Letters from Merchant Traders

Egypt sat at the centre of a vast international trading network that stretched from Spain in the west to India, and beyond, in the east. Jewish merchants made use of their familial and religious connections to trade over long distances, relying on bonds of trust to ensure a smooth flow of goods and the settlement of debts. Business letters with news of sales, receipts, losses, market prices, and orders – as well as greetings to family, friends, and business associates – travelled constantly back and forth. Hundreds of these commercial communications are preserved in the Cairo Genizah. They are our most important first-hand source for understanding mercantile practices, manufacturing, and international trade in the Middle Ages.

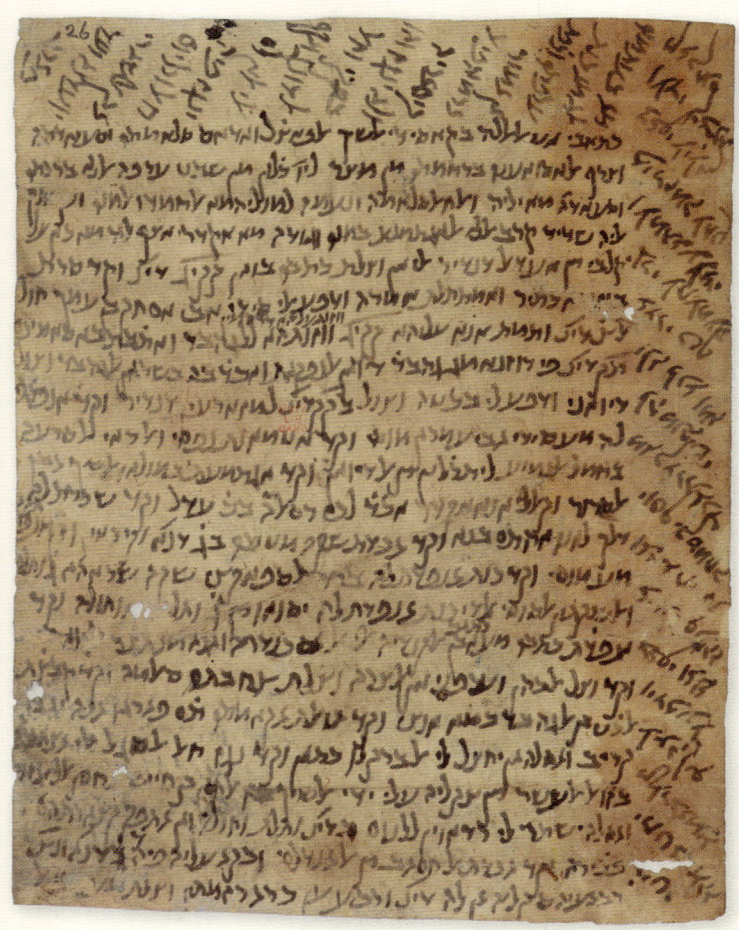

Flax, Tax, and Bureaucrats

A business letter from the prominent Maghrebi textile merchant, Nahray ben Nissim. He writes from Fustat to his associate, Barhun ben Musa al-Taherti, who was out in the Egyptian hinterland in the town of Busir. Nahray had paid 500 dinars – a huge sum – to a state bureau in Cairo to procure a shipment of flax. The payment was not for the flax directly, but rather a tax advance paid on behalf of peasants cultivating the crop. Flax (the fibre from which linen is spun) was one of the most important crops in Egypt in the 11th century, overtaking grain as the primary export. Merchants like Nahray cooperated with state institutions to secure access to this valuable commodity, and kept a watchful eye on the quality of the crops in the flax-growing towns of the Egyptian countryside.[17]

1053 CE

T-S 10J12.26

I paid the clerk here and he entered 500 dinars on our account in the account book of the clerk of the Office of Expenditure. Against this, Bushran, the clerk, took out official receipts and handed over to me receipts with his signature amounting to 200 dinars for the farmers of Dandir…

Unsteady News from Aden

As representative of the merchants and superintendent of the harbour in Aden, and eventual Nagid (head) of the Jews of Yemen, Madmun ben Hasan oversaw customs, fixed market prices, and even struck agreements with pirates and chieftains who controlled the sea lanes between Egypt and India. He sent this letter from Aden to his business partner, Abraham ben Yiju, in India. There is much to report: the ruler of Kis has led a failed naval campaign against Aden, pepper is not selling well, an elderly fellow merchant is showing signs of dementia, and Madmun lost his own investments when his ship sank on the way to Mangalore, India. He also shares the galling news that Ben Yiju's Hindu servant, Bama, has been living the high life in Aden on his employer's dime – repeatedly turning up at Madmun's office blind drunk.[18]

1135 CE

The news from Egypt was mediocre – goods sold poorly, and there was no demand for even a dirham's worth of pepper…

... do not worry. He who saved me from the desert ... will save me while on the sea.

Or.1081 J1

David Maimonides' Final Message

David Maimonides, the younger brother of Moses Maimonides, was a merchant specialising in gems and pearls who went south to trade at the Sudanese port of ʿAydhab in 1170 CE. After travelling down the Nile to Qus, he missed the caravan he planned to cross the desert with – a trip normally lasting seventeen days – so he had to make the dangerous trek with only a single companion. When they arrived in ʿAydhab, David discovered that the caravan had been waylaid by bandits, and he might have perished if he had been with them. But he had also been slow, and there were now no goods worth buying in ʿAydhab. Determined to make the trip profitable, David disregarded his older brother's warnings and resolved to set sail across the Indian Ocean. He drowned shortly after sending this letter. Moses was devastated and wept over his brother's letters for years to come.[19]

Ca. 1170 CE

Help for a Man from Morocco

When he served as Head of the Jews in Egypt, Moses Maimonides was often called upon to assist with acts of charity. He wrote this letter of introduction for an immigrant from North Africa, asking the local Jewish community to come together and pay his *jizya* – the poll-tax that Muslim rulers imposed on their *dhimmi* (Christian and Jewish) subjects. *Dhimmis* were free to practise their religion and were exempt from the *zakat* (almsgiving) tax paid by Muslims, but the *jizya* was still a considerable burden. The Jews of Egypt established many charitable institutions to assist the poorer members of their community. Maimonides signed his name in full at the bottom of the letter: "Moses, son of the scholar Maymun of blessed memory."

Ca. 1168–1204

…help the bearer (of this letter), Isaac al-Dari, because he is one of our acquaintances. May he tell the Haver – God preserve him – to entrust his problem to the community and see (the money for) his poll tax collected from among you, because two payments of tax are due from him and from his son. If his honour is able to take steps to have this paid from among you in Minyat Zifta, then may he do it, for he is a newcomer and he has not yet paid a thing…

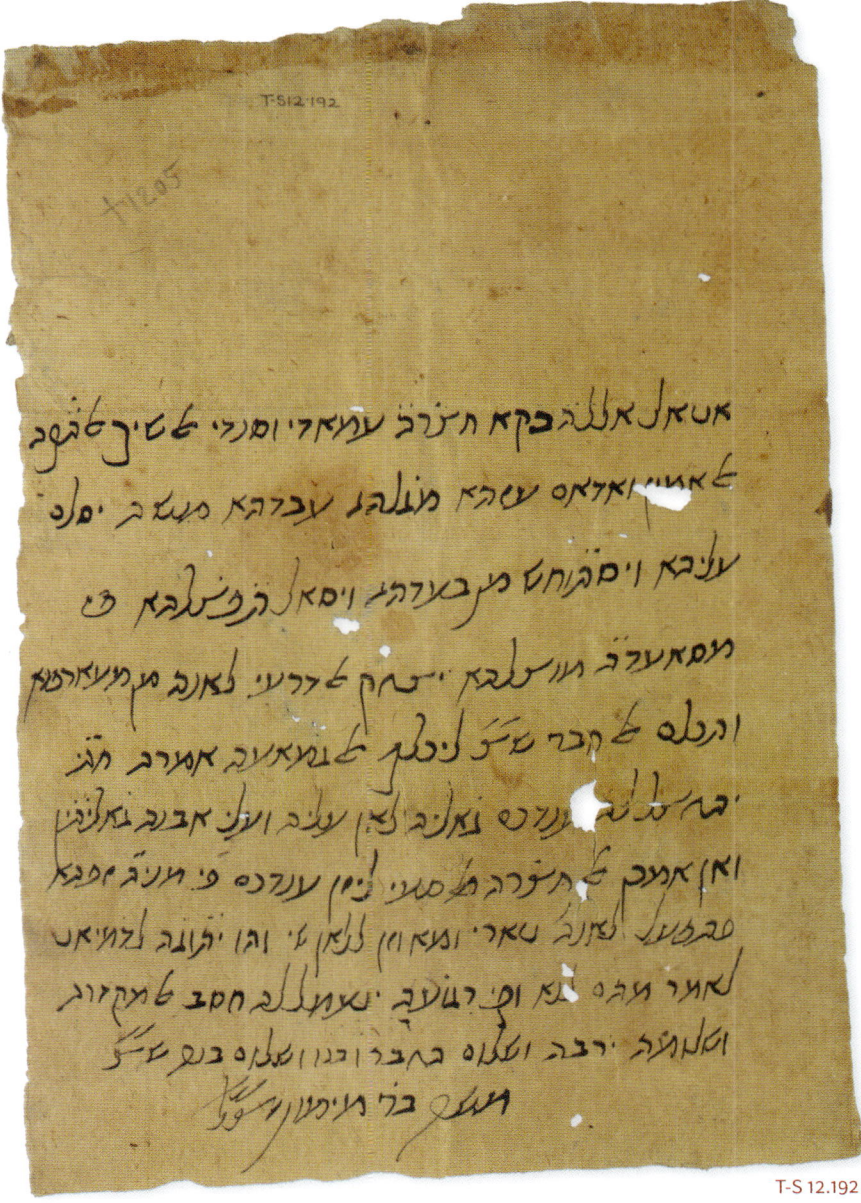

T-S 12.192

How much I miss you and pray to God that he reunites us for good…My people spoke of my brother-in-law's advice, "Release him from the obligation to pay the ketubbah money, and I will provide whatever you need." Now, were I to release you…

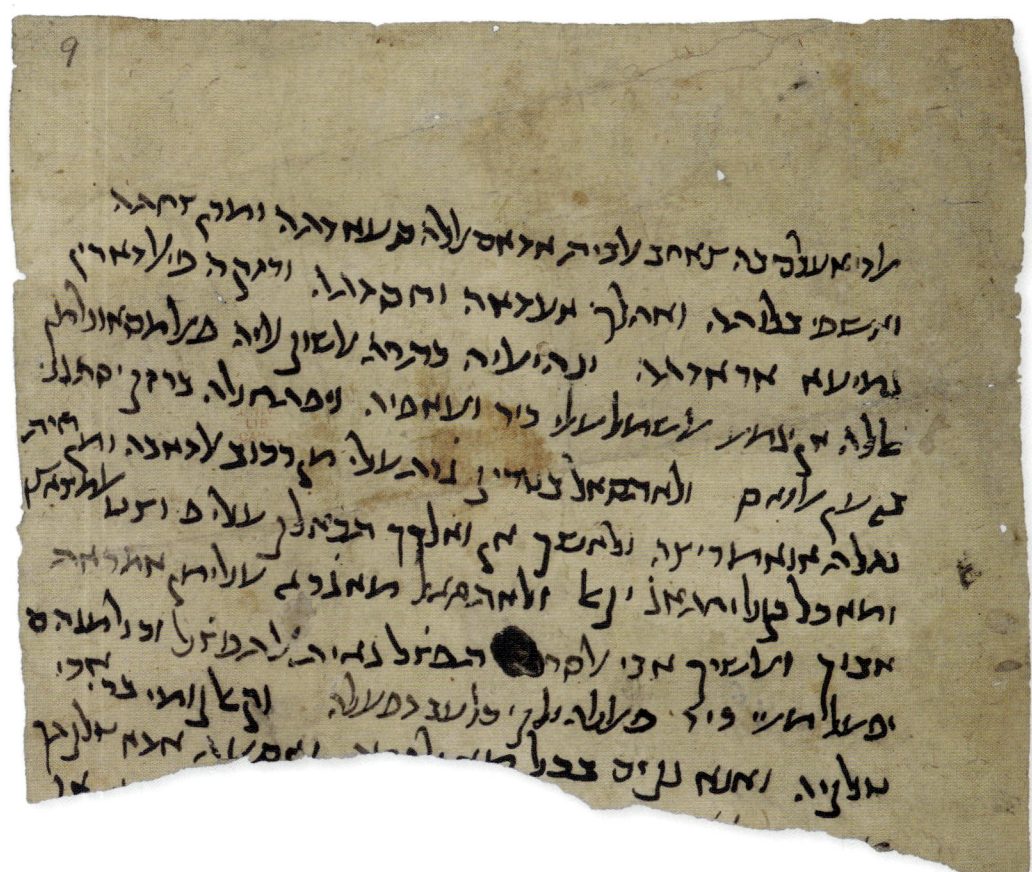

T-S 10J15.9

Letter from a Loyal Wife

Letters between close relatives who have not seen each other for many months are fairly common in the collection, as Egyptian merchants often travelled for months or years at a time to trade at ports in al-Andalus (modern Spain) and across the Indian Ocean. A Jewish woman dictated this letter to her husband who is away, and it was written down by the court clerk Solomon ben Elijah. She expresses her love for her husband but also mentions that his own brother has been offering her support if she will only give up her right to the ketubbah money her husband would have to pay in the event of a divorce. According to Jewish law, any romantic moves made by an ex-husband's brother would be regarded as incest.[20]

Ca. 13th century

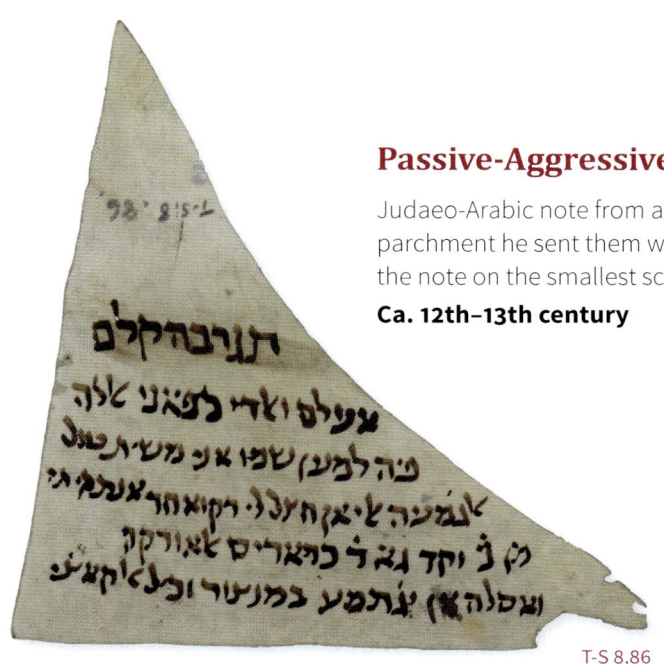

Passive-Aggressive Note

Judaeo-Arabic note from a scribe, informing their father that the parchment he sent them was a bit short. It seems the scribe wrote the note on the smallest scrap left to underscore the point.

Ca. 12th–13th century

Know, father... I spent the whole week before it occurred to me, when I finished the last piece of parchment from the 50(?), that four quires had come missing a leaf...

T-S 8.86

A City Under Siege

Judaeo-Arabic letter sent from Alexandria during the Fifth Crusade's invasion of Egypt. At the time, a Crusader army was besieging Damietta on the other side of the Nile delta. The Jewish writer explains that every man in Alexandria was drafted to dig a defensive ditch around the city. He also describes a Christian doctor who made a cast for a Jewish woman – free of charge – after a door fell and injured her leg.[21]

1219 CE

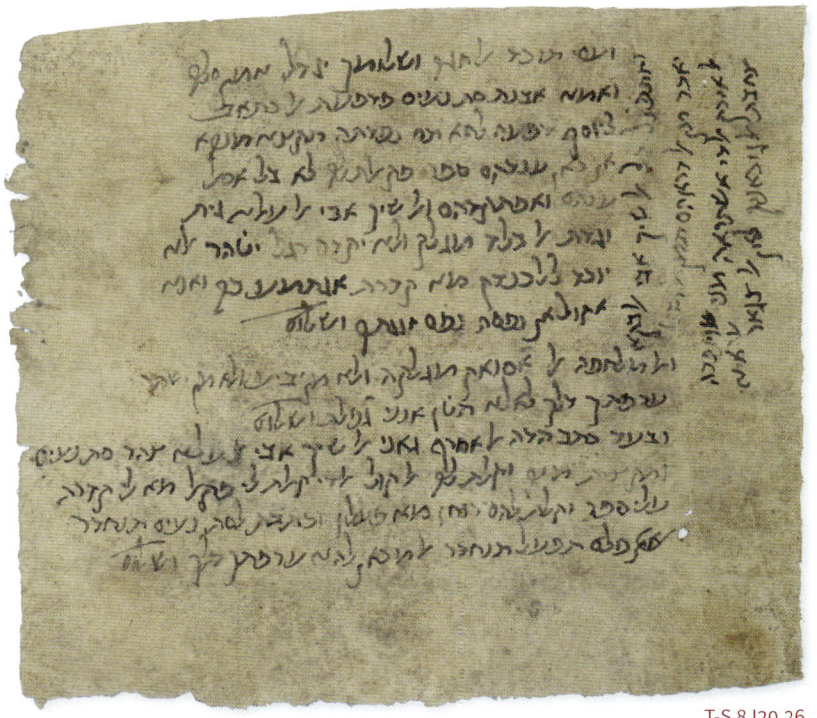

T-S 8J20.26

The city is in a dire state because of the digging of the ditch. The city is locked up, and forced labour is imposed upon the population.

A Warning for a Bad Husband

Solomon ben Elijah was a member of a prominent family and appears frequently in the Genizah (his Shavuot shopping list appears in Chapter I). When he decided to take a wife, his first-choice cousin rejected him, so he married a different one, Sitt Ghazal, instead (marriage between cousins was very common, even seen as ideal, at the time). Their union was not a happy one. Solomon complained that Sitt Ghazal failed to comb her hair, wear perfume, or apply kohl eye makeup. Her uncle, Abu l-Barakat, sent this letter from Alexandria when he heard that Solomon was mistreating her. He was afraid of gossip and wanted to make sure that Solomon knew the family had their eyes on him.[22]

13th century

As to what you say, that she's shameless and insolent – she's your own, and belongs to you – she's your maternal aunt's daughter! … How do you expect anything of the housework to be done perfectly if you use her as a maid? For you know she is alone…

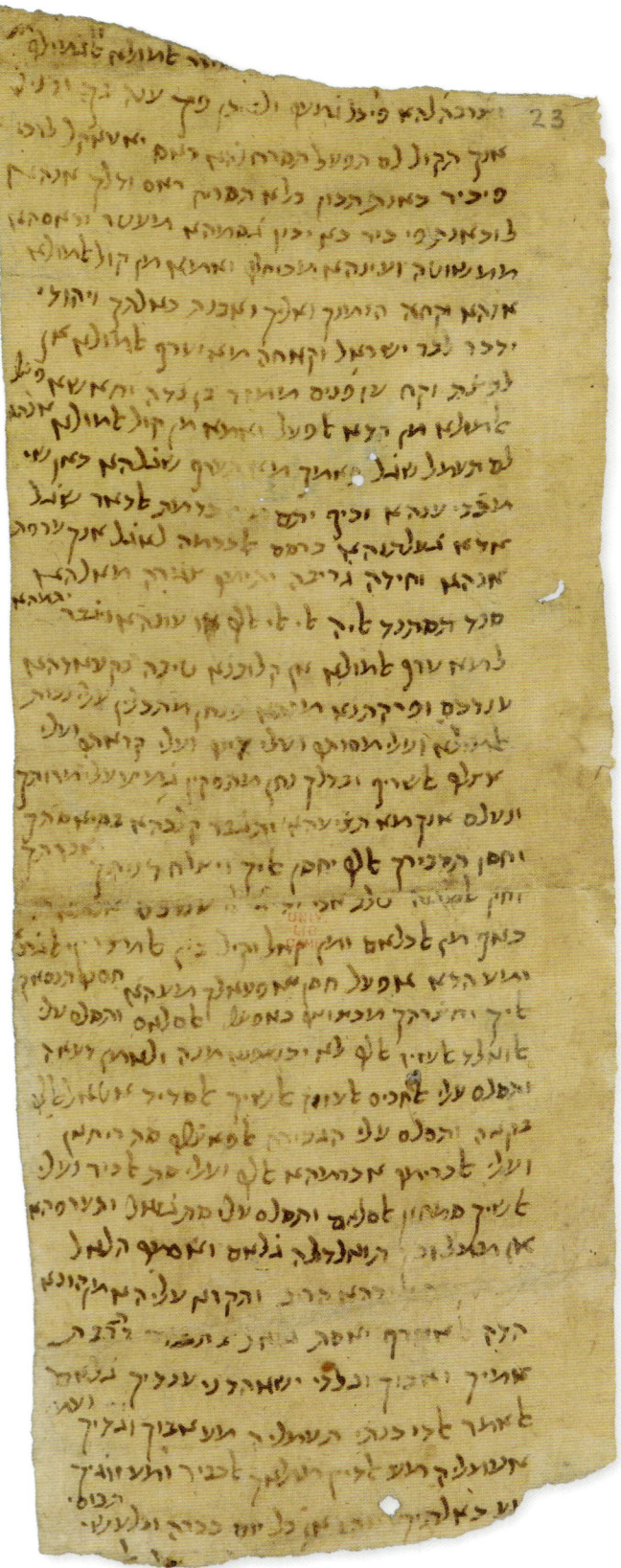

T-S 13J8.23

Family News for Alexandria

Two Judaeo-Arabic letters sent to Abu al-Fada'il "the Jew" in Alexandria, with the address line in Arabic script. Abu al-Fada'il's mother wrote the first letter, telling him of an illness she was suffering from, describing an arduous journey on the Nile, and offering advice. Another relative wrote on the back of her letter, though their penmanship is more rudimentary. The final line, written in an even rougher script, simply reads "and *shalom*." We like to think this was a young child adding to the message for Abu al-Fada'il.[23]

Ca. 13th–14th century

 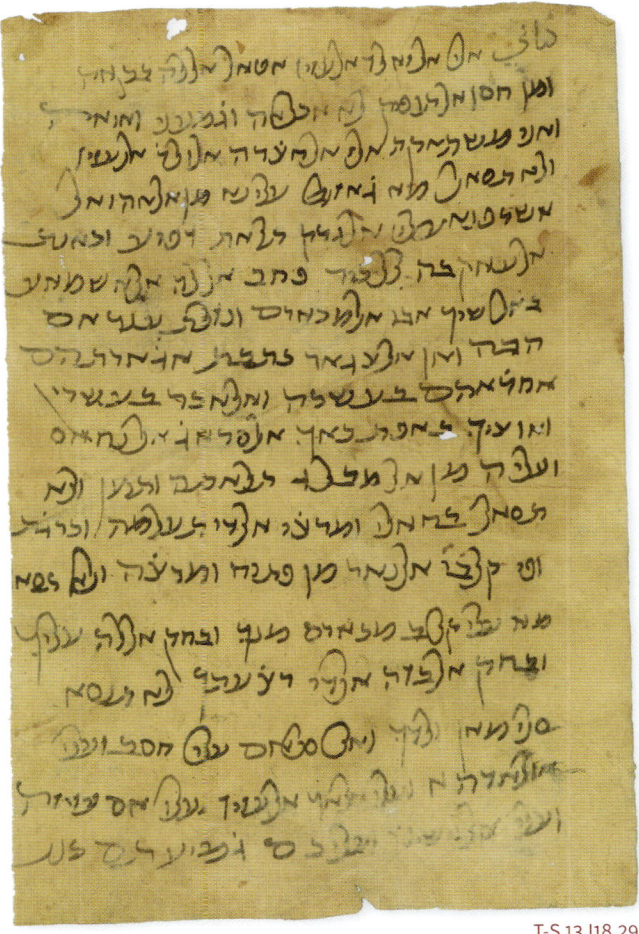

T-S 13J18.29

…we nearly drowned three times! But the end was good. God willed that we meet with the Shaykh Abu al-Makarim, and I stayed with Umm Hiba…

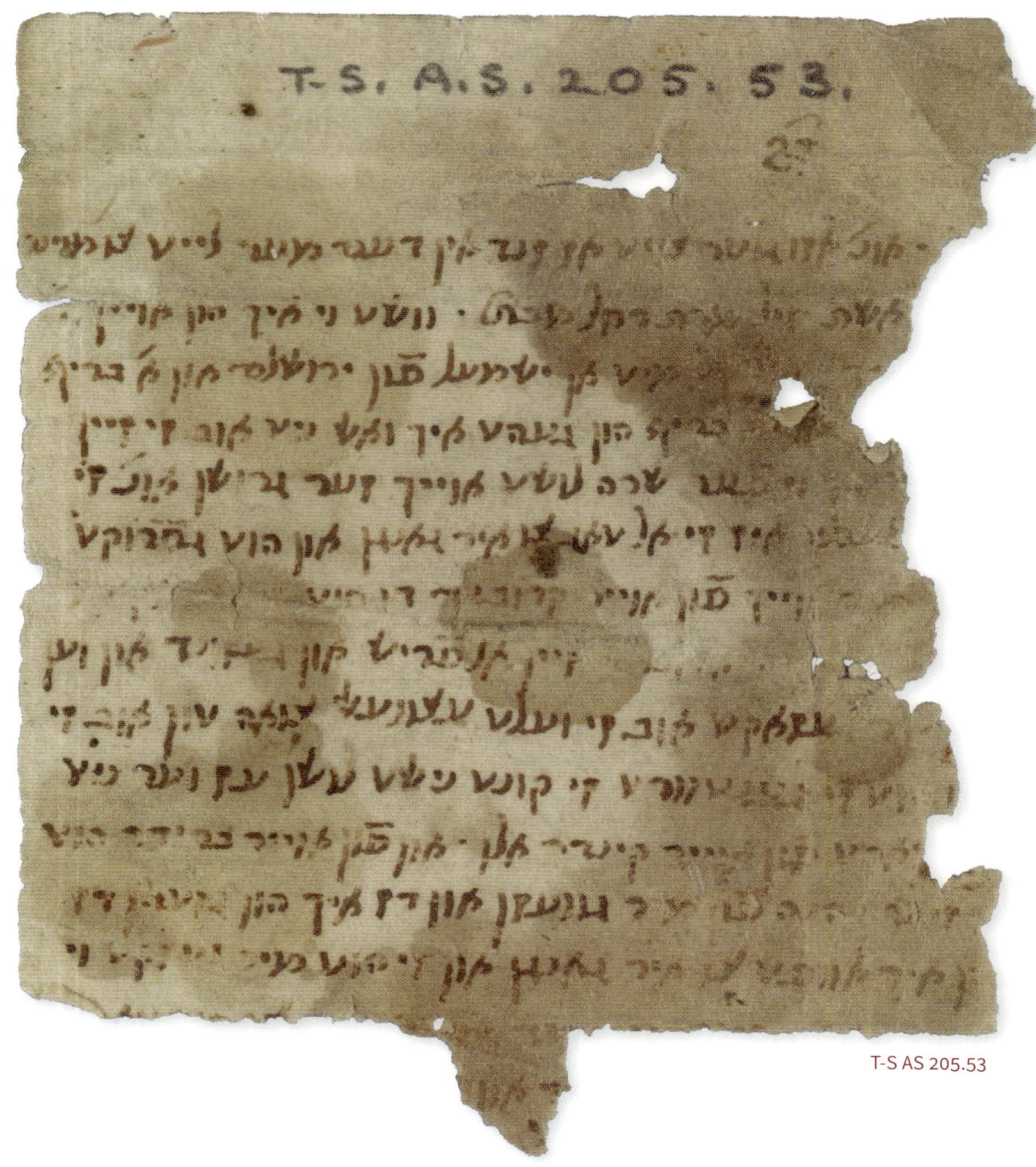

T-S AS 205.53

…may God forgive you that you made me so sad…

A Yiddish Mother in Jerusalem

The Genizah preserves five Yiddish letters from Rachel Zusman, a woman from Prague who lived in Jerusalem during the 16th century. She wrote all of them to her son Moses, in Cairo. Rachel is optimistic about life in Jerusalem, or is perhaps talking it up in the hope that Moses and his family will join her there. She suggests he might be able to study and there are opportunities for his wife's parents to open a shop. Sometimes Rachel strikes a more despondent note, admonishing her son for his numerous shortcomings.[24]

1560s CE

Warning about a Plague

Letter sent from Solomon Agostaro in Cairo to his son Nissim in Alexandria. He describes a plague and warns Nissim not to travel to Cairo until it has passed. The letter is undated but may refer to the bubonic plague outbreak that occurred there in 1513–14 CE. The paper was made in Italy and has a watermark (☛ Chapter X) known from Venice around 1600 CE.[25]

16th–17th century

Every day, one or two people die…

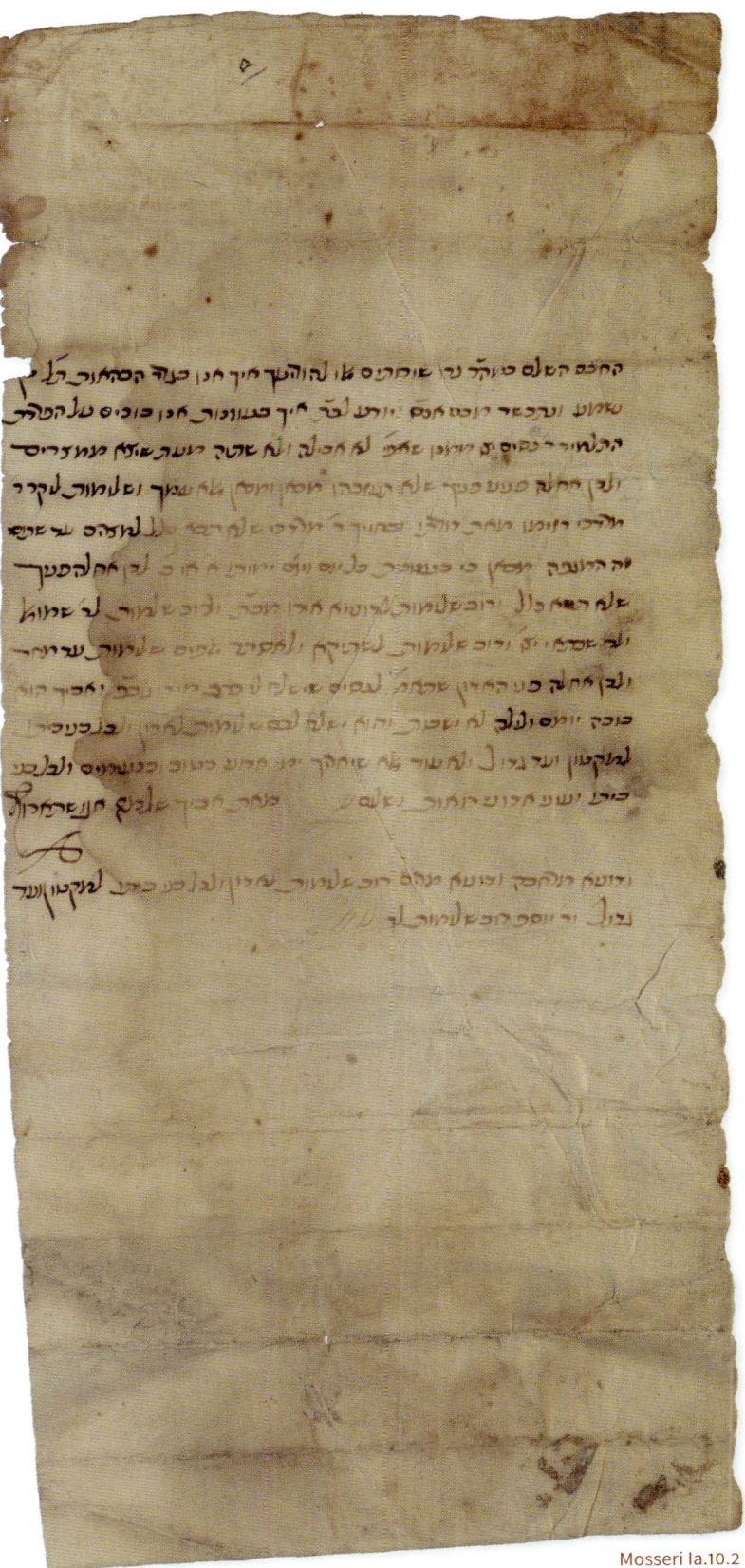

Mosseri Ia.10.2

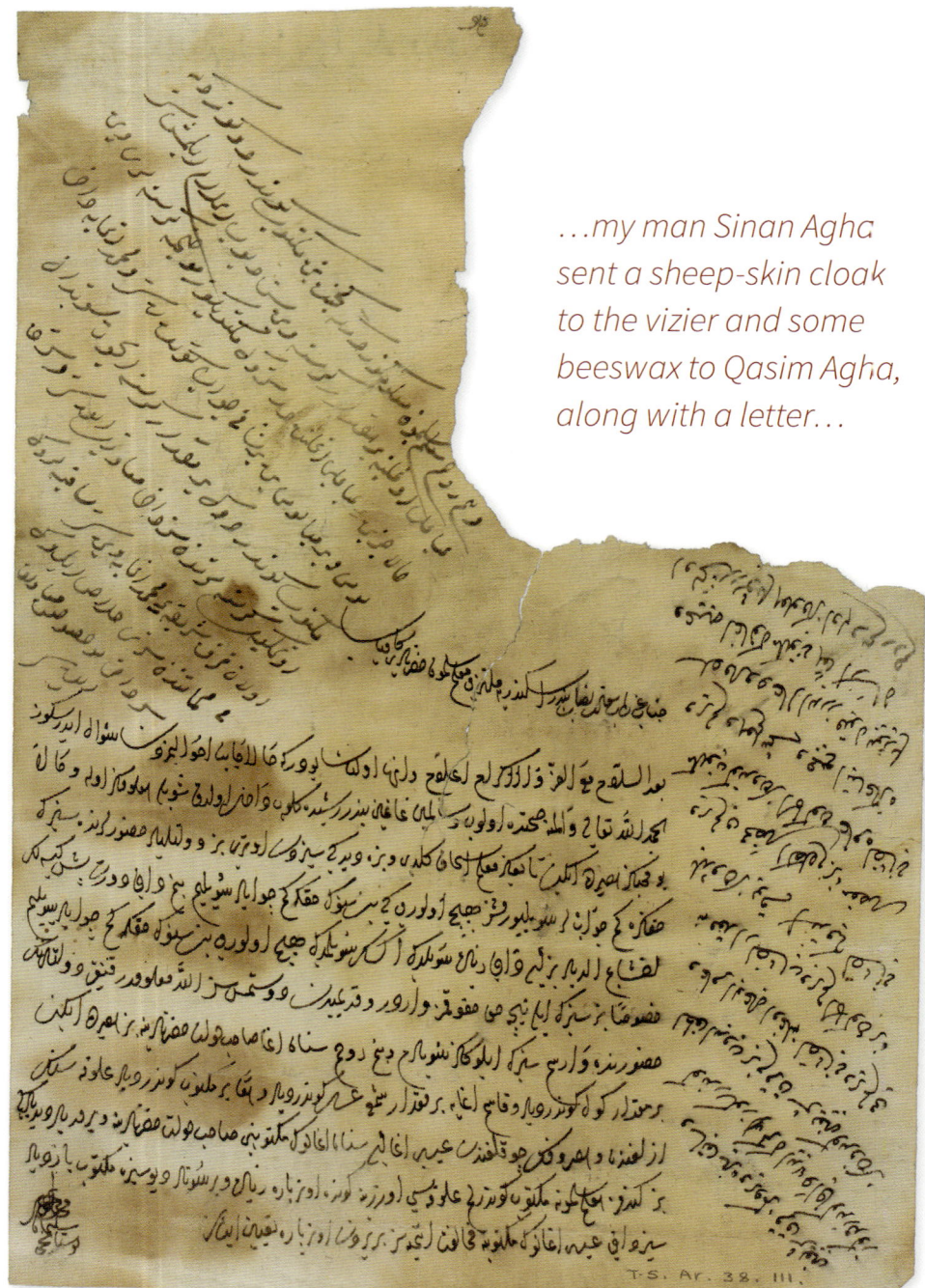

...my man Sinan Agha sent a sheep-skin cloak to the vizier and some beeswax to Qasim Agha, along with a letter...

T-S Ar.38.111

Imperial Military Communications

Bureaucratic letter in Ottoman Turkish, the administrative language of the Ottoman Empire, sent from Sulayman Bostanci in Istanbul to Maʿallim Salmun in Alexandria. Sulayman was likely a member of the Ottoman imperial guard, and his message discusses payments and other correspondence between several members of the Ottoman military. Two stamps on the back indicate that the letter was successfully sent and received.[26]

Ca. 16th–18th century

Financial Letter from Lebanon to Egypt

This letter, switching fluently between Hebrew, Aramaic, and Ladino, was sent from Joseph ben Joyya and Mas'ud Bunan in Sidon, Lebanon, to Abraham Monson and Judah Asec in Cairo. The writers discuss the community's finances, including difficulties faced by students at the academy in Rashid (Rosetta). The Hebrew script is a late Sefardi style and the elaborate, decorative signatures are typical of the Ottoman period. The paper is European, probably produced in Italy.[27]

1758 CE

…regarding the Yeshivah of Rashid, its time has passed, and its students – may God lengthen their lives – wander [looking for] bread, since it was a year of drought. For this reason we have written… for when there is trouble in the world, the Holy Congregation of Egypt – may the Lord bless and keep them – have always taken pity upon the poor of the land of Israel…

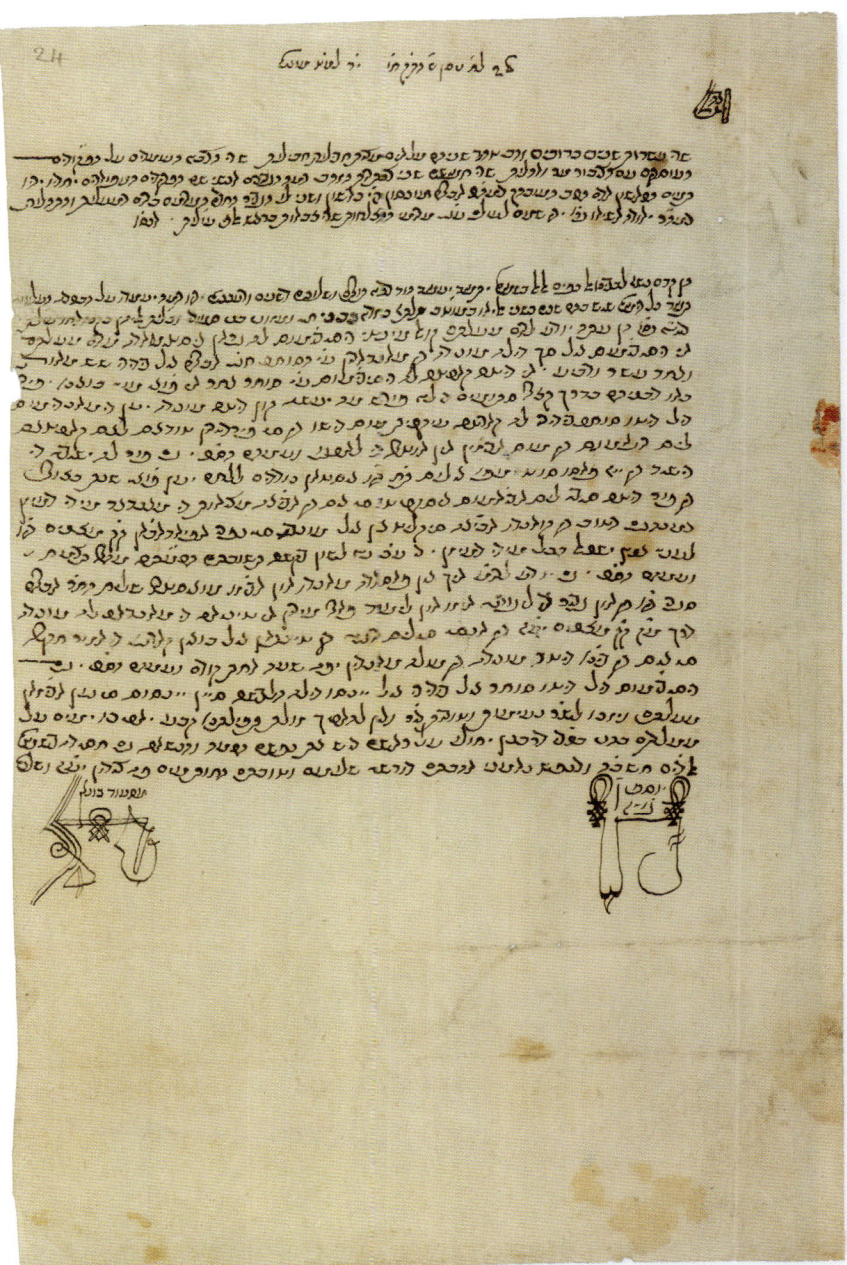

T-S 18J3.24

Letter of Recommendation

When Jewish travellers were planning to visit places far from their homelands, they sometimes procured letters of recommendation to introduce themselves and coax support from foreign communities. Samuel Jonas Bondi – a founding rabbi of the Orthodox community in Mainz, Germany – wrote this letter for Barukh Loeb in August of 1842. Barukh became a leader of the Jewish community in Livorno, Italy, and he acquired several more recommendation letters during his European travels over the next decade. He eventually ended up in Cairo, and his letters – including others from Zagreb, Livorno, and Turin – ended up in the Genizah.[28]

31 August 1842

…the unfortunate situation of the worthy rabbi Mr Barukh Loeb from Poland, who is highly recommended by his fellow believers, not only because of his renowned ancestors…

T-S Misc.34.26

Late Letter to Monsieur Aghion

A letter in Judaeo-Arabic, written at Alexandria and kindly addressed in French to one Brahim Aghion. The Aghions – along with the Mosseris and Cattauis – were among the wealthiest and most influential Jewish families in 19th-century Egypt. This letter is dated to a period when they were establishing new Jewish schools in Alexandria. Many of Egypt's educated elite (and members of the British colonial occupation) used French as a prestige language at this time.[29]

1885 CE

T-S AS 145.108

Monsieur Brahim Aghion, si vous plez,
deliver it immediately…

Q: Are all of the Cairo Genizah manuscripts from Egypt?

Some of the manuscripts in the Ben Ezra Synagogue's genizah chamber – records of the local *Bet Din* (Rabbinical Court), for example – were written just a few yards from where they were eventually discarded. But many of the manuscripts had already travelled long distances before they came to rest in the dusty piles of Cairo's genizot. A letter sent to an Egyptian family member or business colleague may have originated as far afield as Spain or India. Some manuscripts were owned and handled by many people over the centuries before eventually becoming too damaged for use, as numerous marks of ownership attest. Prayer books and Bibles were not only sacred, but also valuable property, and many books arrived in Egypt in the hands of refugees fleeing disasters and conflicts around the Mediterranean Sea. The most significant causes of Jewish refugees fleeing to Egypt were the Almohad takeover of Morocco and al-Andalus in the late 12th century, the Crusader invasions of Syria-Palestine between the 12th and 14th centuries, and the Christian expulsion of all Jews and Muslims from the Iberian Peninsula in the 1490s. Other manuscripts reached Cairo through more peaceful means. The Genizah preserves evidence of an extensive trade in books between Europe, North Africa, and the Middle East up through the 19th century.

Notes to Chapter IV

1 Translation by Ben Outhwaite.

2 Translation by Ben Outhwaite. See also M. Gil, *Palestine during the first Muslim period 634–1099*. Vol. 2. (1983), 467–69 (Heb.)

3 Ben Outhwaite, 'T-S 18J3.9 the Ramla Earthquake: for this relief much thanks' (*Fragment of the Month*, August 2017).

4 Translation by Ben Outhwaite.

5 Moshe Gil, *In the Kingdom of Ishmael*. Vol. 2 (1997), 121–123 (Heb.).

6 Translation by Ben Outhwaite. Some of Solomon's other letters are found at T-S 13J23.11, T-S 13J14.5, and T-S 18J4.15 (accessible in the CUDL database, see Introduction).

7 Translation by Ben Outhwaite.

8 Translation by Ben Outhwaite.

9 Translation by Ben Outhwaite.

10 J.L. Kraemer, 'Women Speak For Themselves,' in S.C. Reif, ed., *The Cambridge Genizah Collections: Their Contents and Significance* (2002), 206–207. This is a friendly reminder to call your parents.

11 See edition in Moshe Gil, *Palestine During the First Muslim Period (634–1099)* (Heb.) (Tel Aviv: Tel Aviv University, 1983), vol. 3 and translation in S. D. Goitein, 'Tyre-Tripoli-'Arqa: Geniza Documents from the Beginning of the Crusader Period,' *Jewish Quarterly Review* 66, no. 2 (1975): 69–88.

12 Translation by Ben Outhwaite.

13 S.D. Goitein, 'Contemporary letters on the capture of Jerusalem by the Crusaders,' *Journal of Jewish Studies*, 3 (1952), 171–175. Translation amended slightly.

14 Translation by Shelomo D. Goitein, *A Mediterranean Society* II, 293 note 12 and V, ch. X, B, 1, note 47. Translation amended slightly. Information in part from the Princeton Geniza Project (https://geniza.princeton.edu/en/documents/8056/).

15 For further details and Spanish translation, see José Martínez Delgado and Amir Ashur, *La Vida Cotidiana de Los Judíos de Alandalús (Siglos X-XII): Antología de Manuscritos de La Guenizá de El Cairo (University of Cambridge)* (Córdoba: UCO Press, 2021), 61–65.

16 Translation by Ben Outhwaite.

17 Excerpt translated by S.D. Goitein, *A Mediterranean Society*, vol. 1 (University of California Press, 1967), 249. Edition by M. Gil, *In the Kingdom of Ishmael* (Hebrew), vol. 2 (1997), 749–753. For a discussion of the fragment see also https://www.lib.cam.ac.uk/genizah-fragments/posts/qa-wednesday-flax-tax-and-trade-hacks-lorenzo-bondioli. For more on trader activities in Genizah manuscripts, see J. Goldberg, *Trade and Institutions in the Medieval Mediterranean: The Geniza Merchants and their Business World* (Cambridge University Press, 2012).

18 Edition and translation in M.A. Friedman and S.D. Goitein, *India Traders of the Middle Ages: Documents from Cairo Geniza ('India Book')* (Leiden: Brill, 2008), 337–351.

19 S.D.Goitein, *Letters of Medieval Jewish Traders* (Princeton University Press, 1973), 207–212.

20 Translation by M.A. Friedman, 'Divorce upon the Wife's Demand as Reflected in Manuscripts from the Cairo Geniza,' *The Jewish Law Annual*, vol. IV (1981), 121–122, and updated in M.A. Friedman, 'Crisis in Marriage as Reflected in Geniza Documents and a Legal Strategem in Maimonides' Responsum and their Study' [Hebrew], *Pe'amim*, 128 (2011), 69–103.

21 S.D. Goitein, *A Mediterranean Society*. Volume 5, 56. See also Alan Elbaum's description for the Princeton Geniza Project (https://geniza.princeton.edu/en/documents/2064/).

22 A. L. Motzkin, *The Arabic correspondence of judge Elijah and his family (papers from the Cairo Geniza); a chapter in the social history of thirteenth century Egypt.* Vol 1, 183–187. (PhD diss. University of Pennsylvania, 1965).

23 Translation and additional details from Alan Elbaum and the Princeton Geniza Project: (https://geniza.princeton.edu/en/documents/5281/); see Shelomo D. Goitein, *A Mediterranean Society: The Jewish Communties of the Arab World as Portrayed in the Documents of the Cairo Geniza*, (Berkeley; London: University of California Press, 1967), I:424; III:246, 480.

24 E.M. Wagner, 'Rachel's Missing Letters?' *Genizah Fragments* 58 (2009).

25 Nükhet Varlik, *Plague and Empire in the Early Modern Mediterranean World: The Ottoman Experience, 1347–1600* (Cambridge: Cambridge University Press, 2015), 151.

26 Information in part from the Princeton Geniza Project (https://geniza.princeton.edu/en/documents/20707/). Thank you to Murat Bozluolcay and Christopher Whitehead for assisting with the translation.

27 Many thanks to Dov Cohen, Merav Bellaiche, Dotan Arad, José Martínez Delgado, and Estara Arrant for assisting with the translation of this letter.

28 Many thanks to N cole Karafyllis for assisting with the translation of this letter. T-S Misc.34 26 P2 is another letter from 1845. MS AIU VII.E.243 is a letter from Zagreb (December 1847 or 1849). AIU VII.E.239 has two more letters from Livorno (October 1852) and Turin (December 1852). Information in part from the Princeton Geniza Project.

29 Nick Posegay, 'Searching for the Last Genizah Fragment in Late Ottoman Cairo: A Material Survey of Egyptian Jewish Literary Culture', *International Journal of Middle East Studies* 54, no. 3 (2022): 433.

V.
Magic

The Egyptian tradition of popular magic transcends time, language, and religion. Magical manuscripts date back to the pre-Islamic, pre-Christian, pre-Greek days of ancient Egypt, and in the Genizah period they freely mix elements from Greek, Coptic, Arabic, Hebrew, and Aramaic traditions. Genizah manuscripts show us that belief in the magical properties of objects, places, words, rituals, angels, and demons were fundamental to the ways that common people understood the natural world. The surviving magical texts reflect their daily concerns: amulets to protect travellers, curses to discourage thieves, and spells to make people fight, make up, or fall in love. Whether or not these spells were effective is not the point – they show us that people *believed* they would work, and since they contained sacred elements, they also found their way into genizot.

In many cases, the people who created these artefacts were not the well-trained, highly educated scribes who made elegant biblical manuscripts and Torah scrolls (☞ Chapter II). Some were local magicians trying to make a bit of money selling cheap amulets. Others were individuals – even prominent community leaders – who copied amulets or bits of spellbooks for personal use. Given the contents of the manuscripts in this chapter, it is also likely that many of them were women. The Genizah shows us that people from all different levels of society were making, buying, or using magical manuscripts.

Ancient Spellbook

These two pages come from a longer manuscript detailing magical recipes, and there's a lot going on here. The primary text includes spells to protect against demons, cure headaches, prevent miscarriage, and make a man fall in love. Magic words have dots over them – that's the right-hand page covered in Hebrew script. The left-hand page also has some Hebrew script at the top and bottom, but it's faded and hard to decipher.

The middle of the page isn't Hebrew though. It's two lines of Arabic script followed by two lines of magical symbols. The Arabic inscribes more nonsensical magical words, but it's the script style that is most interesting. It shares some features with the 8th- and 9th-century Arabic handwriting that appears in papyrus manuscripts. Such papyri could've been contemporaneous with this book, which would make it a very early Genizah fragment. On the other hand, the scribe might have been writing as late as the 10th or 11th century, using an 'archaic' script style that had already fallen out of fashion to evoke a certain magical or aesthetic effect.

Finally, the bottom left corner was torn and repaired with stitches, but that work wasn't done by Cambridge conservators. It's an original medieval repair sewn by a previous owner.[1]

Ca. 9th–11th century

T-S K1.143

T-S K1.50

Separated Spell Scroll

Collected Hebrew and Judaeo-Arabic magical recipes in a horizontal scroll format, including instructions for abjuring demons and producing an amulet, with invocations of angelic names such as Michael, Uziel, and Gabriel. Another scribe used the back to copy a Judaeo-Arabic translation of an older pseudepigraphic work known as the *Treatise of Shem*. The scroll was torn into two fragments, but their images appear together here.

Ca. 10th century

T-S K1.133

Home Security Measures

The Cairo Genizah contains numerous manuscripts that Jews produced to protect their homes. One type of manuscript with this purpose is known as a *mezuzah* (plural: *mezuzot*), which is affixed to the doorframe of a Jewish house, as prescribed in the Bible: "Write them [i.e. the commandments] on the doorframes of your houses and on your gates" (Deuteronomy 6:9). A typical *mezuzah* is written on parchment, like a Torah scroll, and consists of two passages from the book of Deuteronomy, including the *Shemaʿ Yisrael* ("Hear, O Israel…") from Deuteronomy 6:4. Some medieval Egyptian Jews tried to amplify the protective power of their *mezuzot* through magical means, invoking the names of angels or adding mystical symbols that typically appeared in amulets. Maimonides expressly forbade these superstitious practices in his *Mishneh Torah*, stating that such people would not have a place in the world to come.

A classic amplified medieval *mezuzah*, beginning with the *Shemaʿ* and ending with the addition of abbreviated versions of the name of God, alongside five Stars of David. In other ways, this *mezuzah* is fully kosher, including the use of embellishing strokes (called *tagin*, 'crowns') above certain letters.

Ca. 10th–11th century

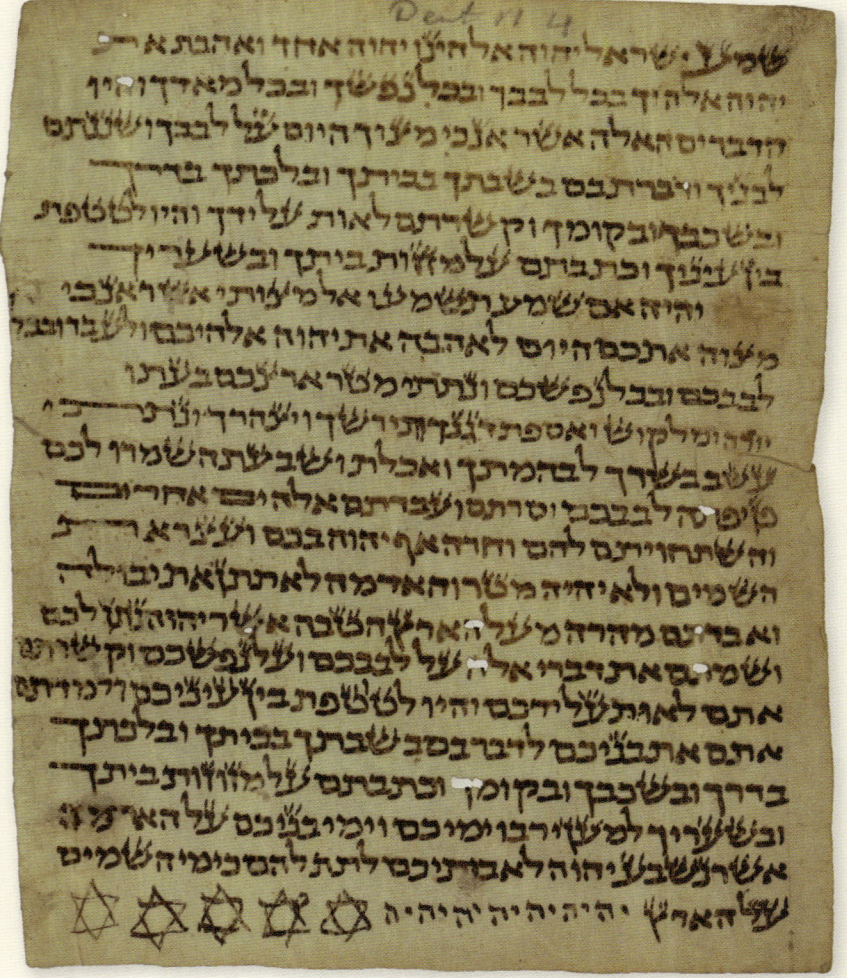

L-G Bible 3.47

T-S NS 290.58

While this *mezuzah* resembles the previous one, the scribe (or perhaps a later hand) added the Hebrew names of angels in boxes along the lefthand margin – the very practice that Maimonides would later condemn. They include Gabriel, Azriel, Zadkiel, Seraphiel, and Raphael.

Ca. 10th–11th century

T-S K1.62

This late amulet dates near the end of the Genizah period. The use of parchment in Egypt tapered off in the 12th and 13th centuries as paper fell in price and grew in popularity. Nevertheless, Jews continued to make certain types of manuscripts – like *mezuzot* and Torah scrolls – with parchment. The name of God repeats on all four edges, but the names of the archangels Michael, Gabriel, Uriel, and Raphael appear in the corners.

Ca. 17th–19th century

Greek and Coptic Hymn

Bilingual hymn in Greek and Coptic, likely used as a protective magical text. This is a rare example of a Genizah manuscript with writing in Coptic, the primary language of Egyptian Christians in Late Antiquity and the early Middle Ages. Arabic gradually replaced Coptic as the main spoken language in Egypt, but it still survives today as the liturgical language of Coptic churches.[2]

Ca. 10th–12th century

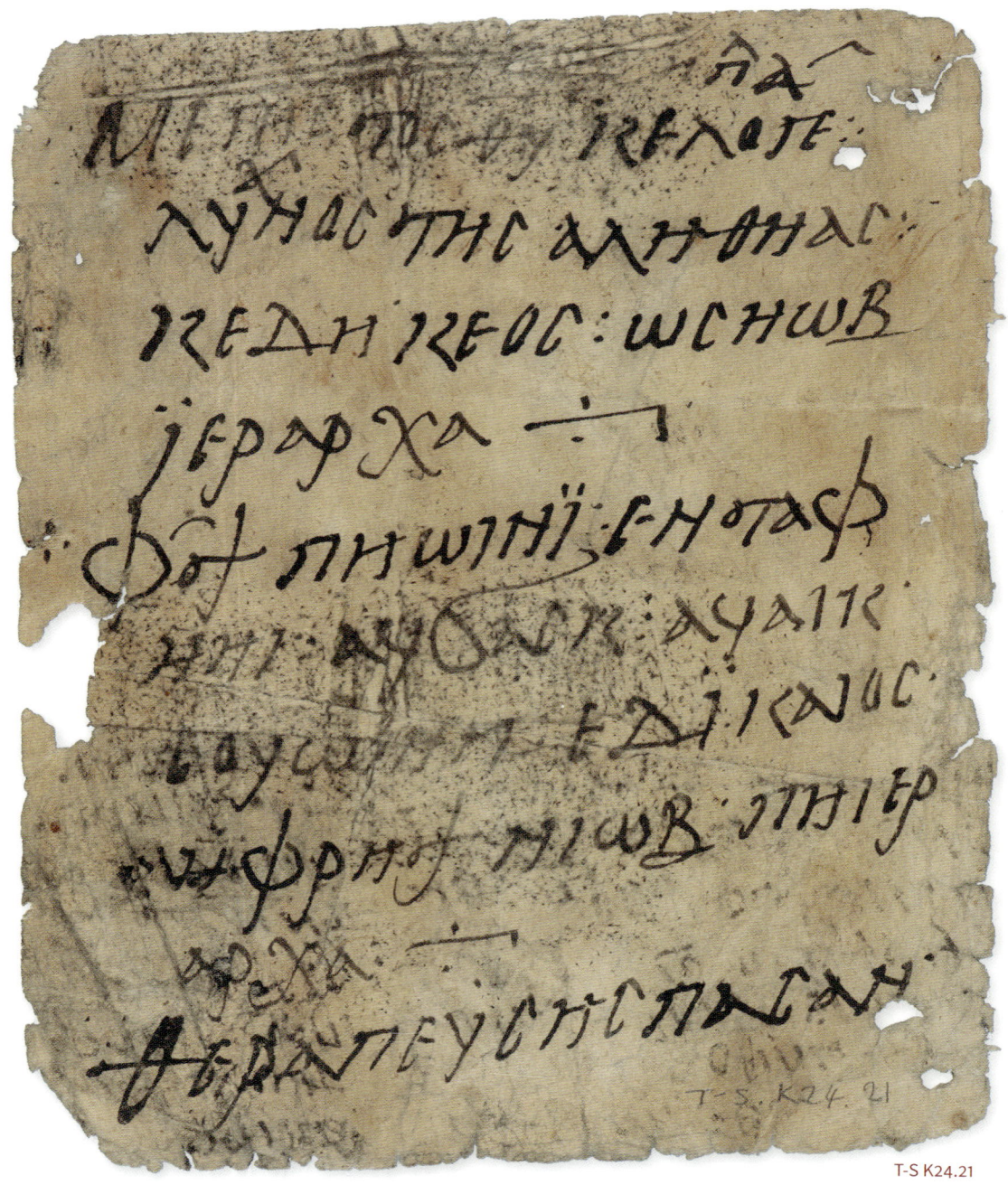

T-S K24.21

Seals for Demons

Hebrew and Judaeo-Arabic text with magical incantations and instructions for making seals, probably intended to protect the bearer against demons. The three human-like illustrations may be angels or the intended demonic targets.[3]

Ca. 11th–12th century

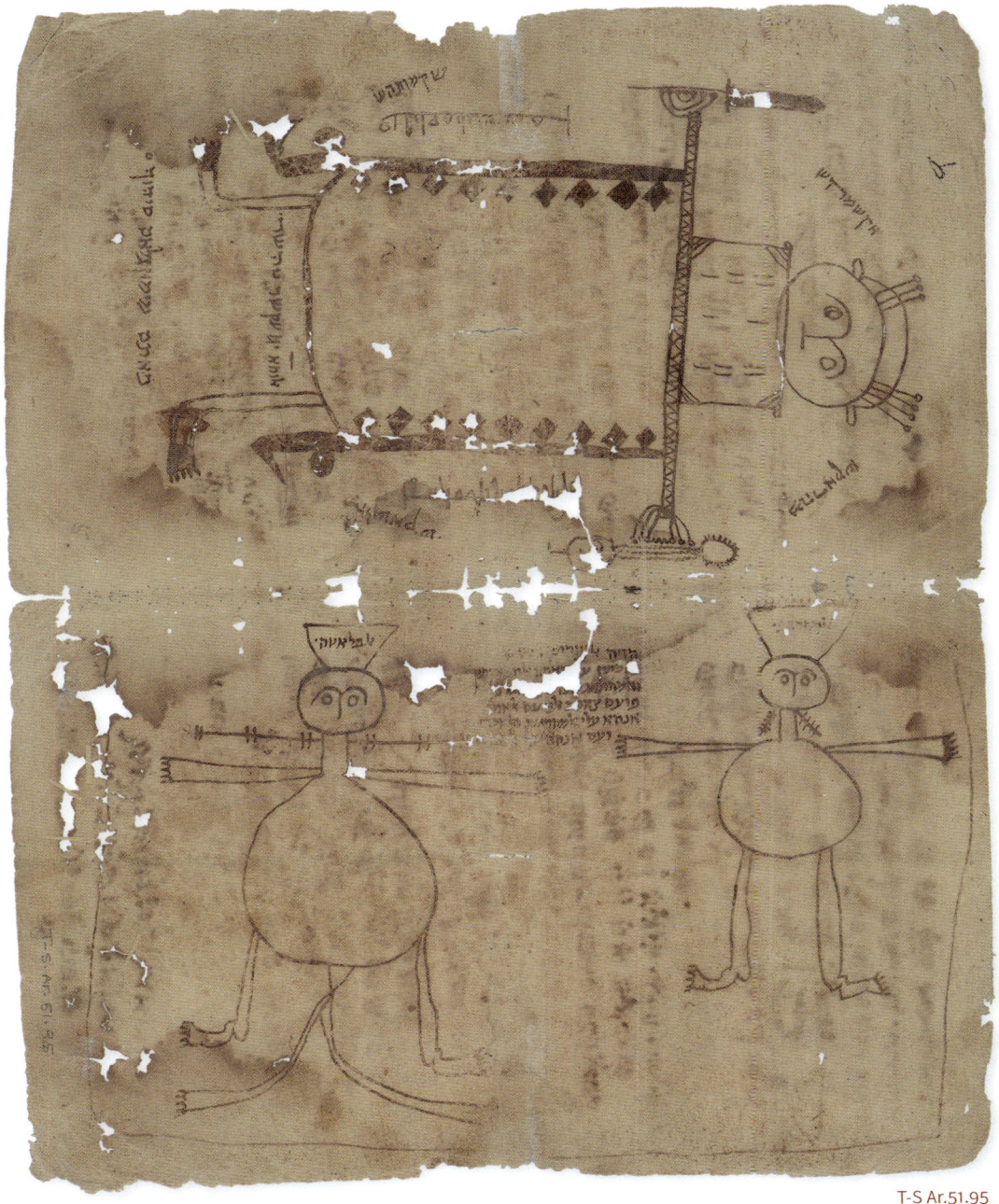

T-S Ar.51.95

Strange Figure on an Amulet

A damaged magical amulet featuring a human-like figure surrounded by Arabic incantations. The figure – which could be a human man, a jinn, or a demon – has a snake draped over its shoulders. The text is mostly nonsense sounds that were intended to invoke a magical effect when recited.

Ca. 11th–13th century

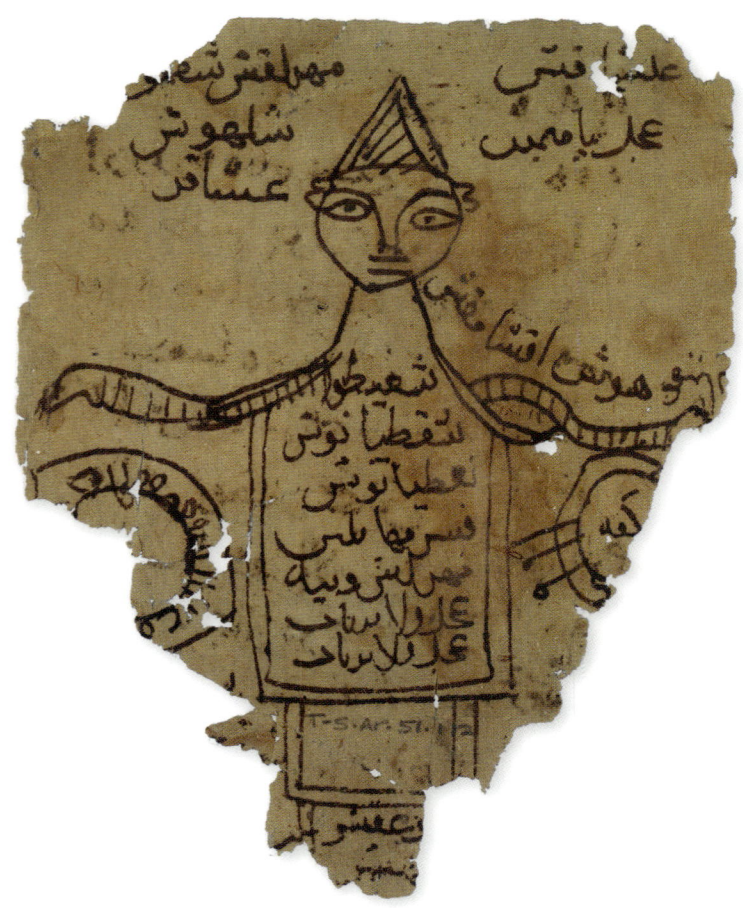

T-S Ar.51.112

Q: Did Jews in Egypt believe in magic?

For a religious archive, the Genizah contains a surprisingly large amount of superstitious and magical material, and we find significant numbers of formulae for both erotic and aggressive spells. The numerous magical fragments that survive provide clear evidence for the prominent position of magic in both Jewish and non-Jewish life, offering us a better understanding of popular beliefs. Amulets in particular are common, can be made of paper, parchment, or cloth, and are often intended for a specific individual and purpose. Even Masliah Gaon, the Head of the Jews in Egypt in the 12th century, used a magical amulet for personal purposes (to protect him, destroy his political enemies, and achieve success before the government). Unfortunately, it failed to save him when he supported the wrong side in a Fatimid court feud and was executed. The extant manuscripts show us that Egyptian Jews had magical recipes for a wide range of purposes: to remove a persistent headache, to find love, to detect an adulterous partner, to find treasure, to develop charm and grace, to protect travellers on dangerous voyages, to conceive a child, to avoid conception, to make a reluctant child take a bath, to protect against dog bites or scorpion stings, and to inspire fear in others – the whole gamut of human hopes and fears!

Pages from books concerned with the theoretical background of magical practice also survive in the Genizah. These works give detailed descriptions of the heavenly hosts, astrological observations, and instructions for divination techniques. Such magical beliefs and techniques even crossed religious boundaries. Many amulets and magical charms include verses from the Qur'an, and there was a popular belief among certain Jews that passages from Muslim scripture could give their magic extra potency.

Magic for Expectant Mothers

Two pages from a spellbook in Aramaic and Hebrew. It includes recipes to open locks, calm a storm at sea, protect against scorpions, alleviate fear, to help a woman who can't get pregnant, prevent miscarriage, and ease childbirth. The scribe added two rows of magical symbols and put dots over magical words. For this and many other magical texts, women were the likely target audience.[4]

Ca. 11th–13th century

T-S K1.19

T-S NS 297.84

Erotic Recipe on a Government Document

Judaeo-Arabic recipe for an erotic spell, featuring two drawings of snakes and several lines of 'linear Kufic' (also known as 'pseudo-Kufic') writing, a stylised, and usually nonsensical, type of Arabic script often used in magic. It refers to a woman called Sitt al-Ahl Wahshiyya and a man called Abu al-Khayr. The spell was written on the back of an official Arabic document. The Fatimid, Ayyubid, and Mamluk chanceries didn't maintain state archives. Instead, old documents were sold off or otherwise distributed as wastepaper, which Cairene communities recycled for new writing, like this recipe.[5]

Ca. 11th–13th century

Cure for Headaches

Part of a magical-medical manual containing recipes to treat headaches and toothaches. The text is mainly Arabic alongside magical symbols and linear Kufic in red ink. It was not uncommon for medieval physicians to combine aspects of medicine, magic, and alchemy to treat their patients.

Ca. 11th–13th century

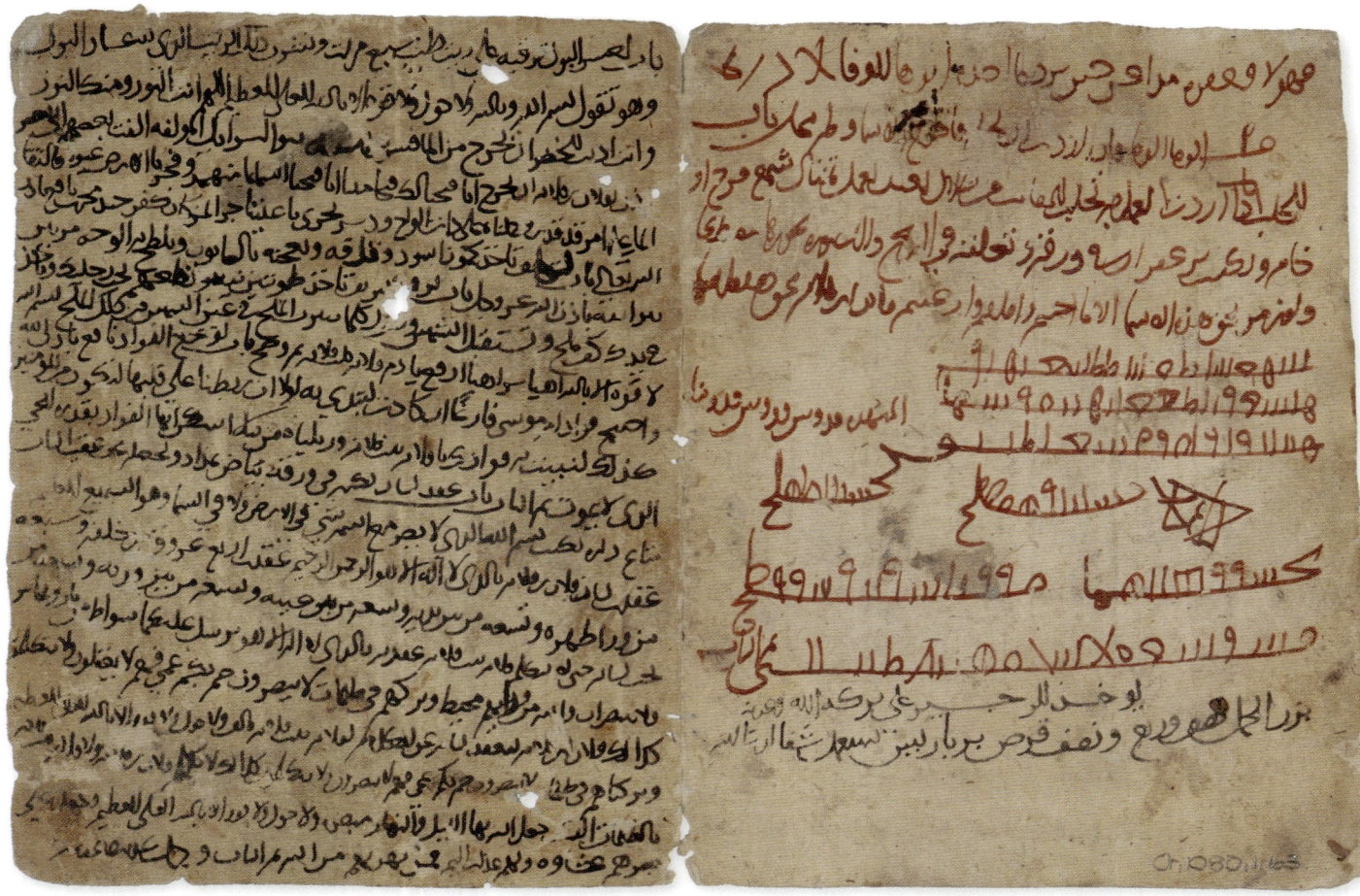

Or.1080 1.63

T-S K1.53

Jewish Amulet to Ease Childbirth

Parchment amulet to ease childbirth, invoking the Hebrew names of God in a magic square and quoting biblical verses (Exodus 11:3 and Psalms 142:8). There are traces of Arabic writing on the left side, probably transferred from another fragment that was stuck to it in the Genizah chamber.

Ca. 11th–13th century

Islamic Amulet to Ease Childbirth

This paper amulet is Arabic and references the Qur'an. Its purpose was to ease childbirth and aid those with problems passing urine. It is decorated mainly with pentagrams, but like some of the Jewish amulets in this chapter, it also invokes the name of God and has at least one six-pointed star (known as the 'Seal of Solomon' in Arabic). Elements of the long tradition of Egyptian magic often transcended religious boundaries.

Ca. 11th–13th century

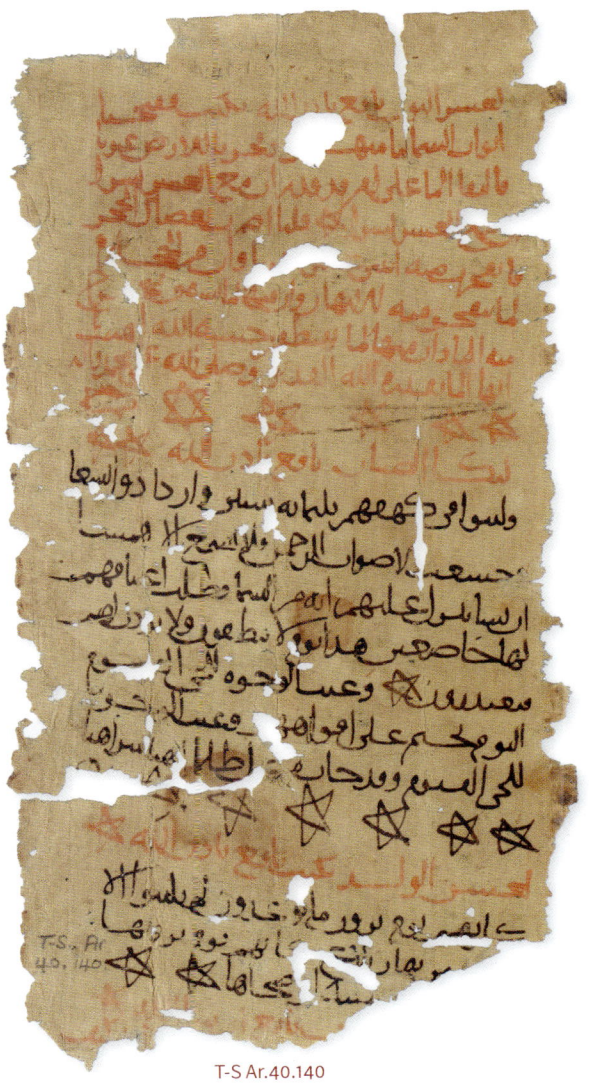

T-S Ar.40.140

Scorpion Amulets

Magical manuscripts reflect the everyday concerns of ordinary people. Spells to heal the sick, calm storms, ease childbirth, and protect travellers all survive in the Cairo Genizah. We find numerous amulets designed to ward off scorpions, suggesting that a fear of their deadly stings was a significant source of anxiety. We can also confirm that such amulets are effective: there have been zero scorpion-related incidents at Cambridge University Library since at least 2017.

Many of these amulets have illustrations of scorpions and, unexpectedly for Jewish manuscripts, invoke the name of the Greek goddess Aphrodite.

Ca. 11th–13th century

T-S AS 107.208

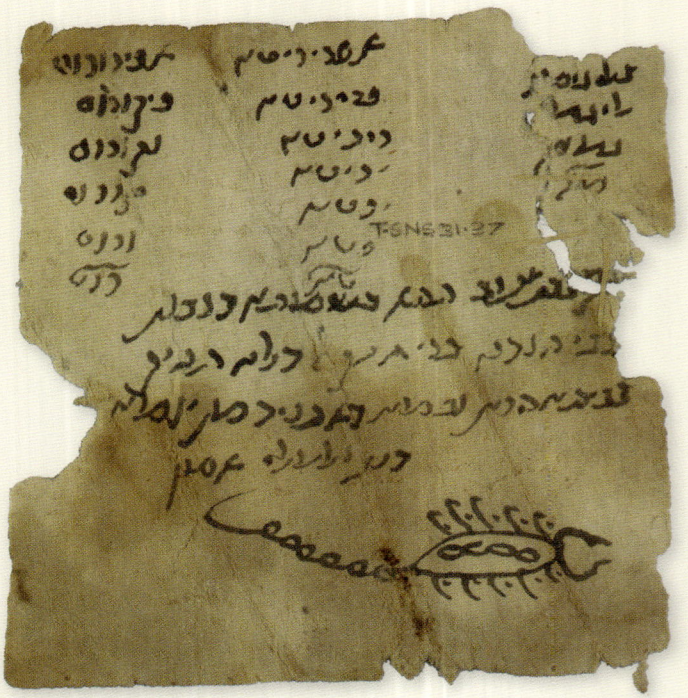

T-S NS 31.37

This amulet is in Arabic script, not Hebrew, but it was copied on the back of a Hebrew prayer text. The appearance of both languages attests to the multilingual culture of Fustat in the Middle Ages. People of all faiths spoke Arabic, but most Jews could also read and write in Hebrew.

Ca. 10th–11th century

Scorpion amulets were so popular, we even find that some magicians mass-produced them, repeatedly copying the same design across an entire sheet of paper. Several of these have been torn away and sold, although this magician may have overestimated the demand for their services.[6]

Ca. 11th–13th century

This mass-produced amulet is almost identical to another Genizah fragment held at the John Rylands Library in Manchester. It's likely they were both cut from a larger sheet by the same magician.[7]

Ca. 12th–13th century

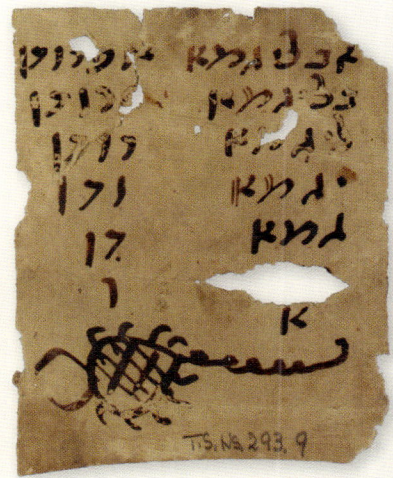

T-S NS 293.9

T-S AS 143.26

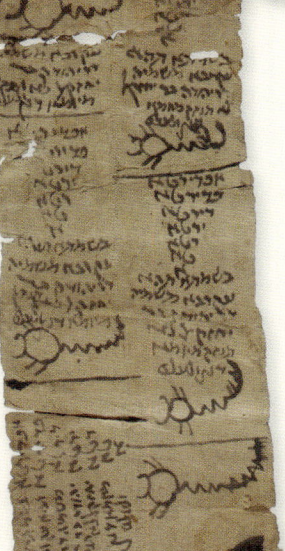

T-S AS 143.287

These two amulets have a different style. Rather than the name of the goddess Aphrodite, they invoke the cryptic letters 'ABLYGMA'. We still aren't sure who this refers to, or if it even is a name.

Ca. 11th–13th century

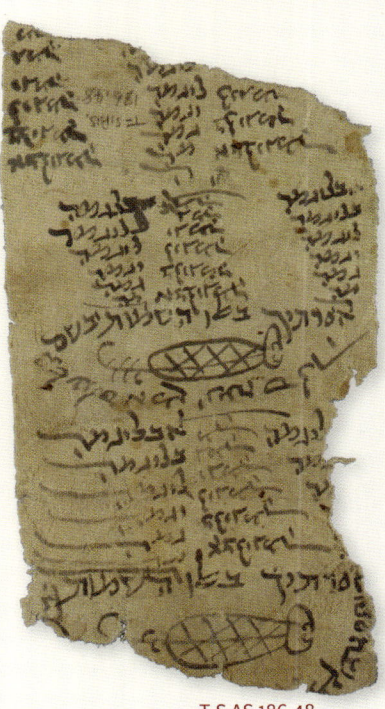

T-S AS 186.48

125

Love Spells by a Cautious Magician

This is one of the most intriguing spellbooks we've seen in the Genizah. It contains spells for invisibility, causing love and hate, knowing if a woman will become pregnant, protecting travellers, scrying in a mirror, and making people listen to what is being said. The last page has a magic square followed by a final spell for gathering demons, although it seems the magician had second thoughts and stopped writing after just four words.

Ca. 12th–13th century

T-S K1.132

Magical Maimonides

A leaf from Moses Maimonides' *Mishneh Torah* (*Repetition of the Torah*), copied 36 years after his death. This influential code of Jewish law was composed between 1170 and 1180 while Maimonides led the Jewish community in Cairo. A later scribe used this page to make a protective amulet, adding two ornamental knot designs and a blessing from Genesis 22.

1240 CE

Mosseri I.15

A Deadly Spell

Not all magic was for benign or protective purposes. This spell's user dabbled in dark magic with the aim of taking someone's life. The text – a combination of Judaeo-Arabic, Aramaic, and Hebrew – is a template in which a target's name could be inserted, entreating angels to invoke their destructive power. At the end, a satisfied customer left a positive review in Arabic: "Very effective for killing!"

Ca. 12th–13th century

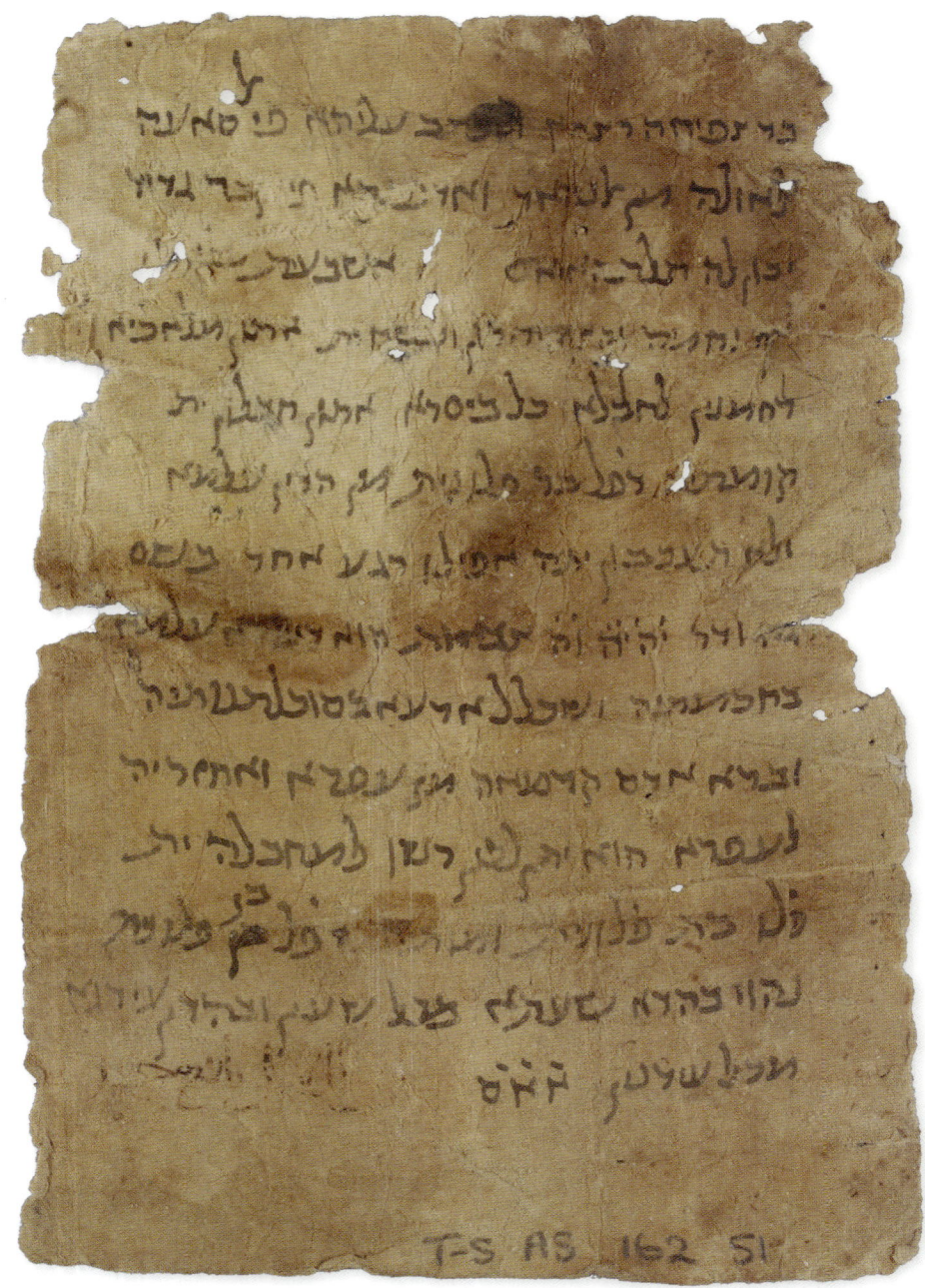

T-S AS 162.51

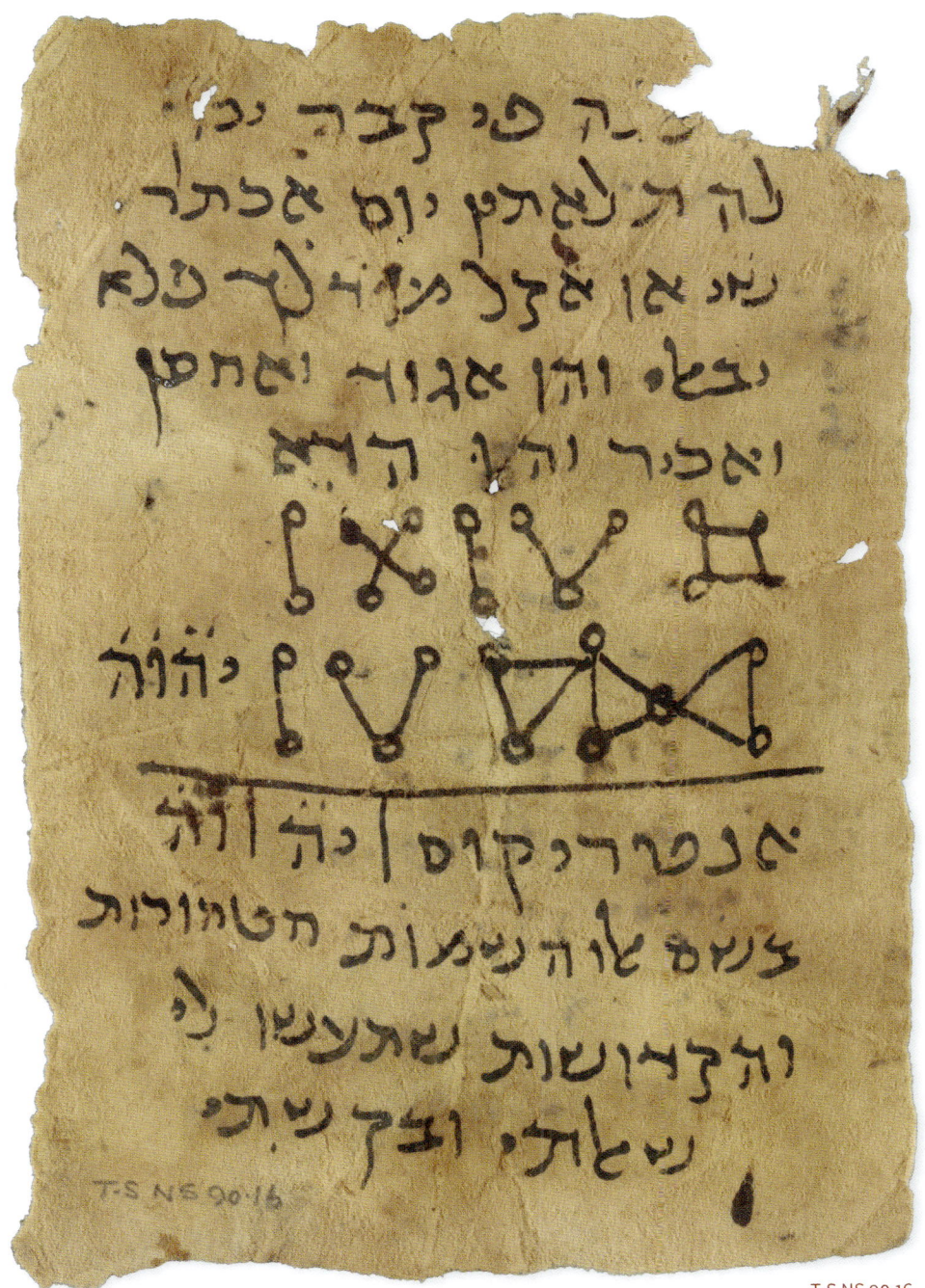

T-S NS 90.16

Magical-Medical Text

Magical characters within a Hebrew and Judaeo-Arabic text, invoking the names of God and angels to protect against severe disease. The back of the leaf includes a medicinal recipe requiring saffron and Socotran aloe.

Ca. 12th–13th century

T-S 12.41

A Dying Man's Curse

A curse upon anyone who steals a particular Torah scroll that was donated to the synagogue by a man on his deathbed. It contains the names of 10 angels marked by boxes or overlined, including Gabriel, Michael, Raphael, Uriel, and Zeganzel. The curses specify that the thief's wife will be widowed, his children will be orphaned, and he will be utterly destroyed.[8]

Ca. 12th–14th century

Book of Spells and Magic Symbols

Fragment from a Hebrew book of magic, including spells to cause fear, acquire treasure, find love, write quickly (we needed this one), gain charm and grace, preach well, and succeed in business without really trying. The type of symbol seen in the third line is common in magical texts of many different languages, including Greek, Arabic, and Hebrew.

Ca. 13th–14th century

T-S K1.96

Jewish Amulet to Ensure Victory

Another feature that connects Egyptian Jewish and Islamic amulets was their 'format' – that is, their layout in relation to the material they are written on. Regardless of the religion of the scribe, a popular format for amulets was a long, narrow, vertical strip, much taller than the page is wide. This practice dates back to the papyrus amulet tradition of ancient Egypt. The paper amulet here was written for a Jewish man named Fatum ben Sa'adyah, asking angels to assist him and ensure victory over his enemies.

Ca. 13th–14th century

Mosseri V.223

Menstruation and Mind-Reading

Magical spellbook with recipes for providing charm and grace, exorcising a chill-causing demon, stopping menstruation, and knowing what a woman thinks. The text mixes Hebrew, Aramaic, and Judaeo-Arabic elements with many of the geometric mystical symbols common to magical texts.

Ca. 13th–14th century

T-S K1.52

Applied Geomancy

Geomantic design consisting of dots and slashes arranged in groups of four rows. Geomancy, from a Greek word meaning 'foresight by earth', is a type of divination that uses patterns in sand and earth to predict the future. The Greek word comes from the Arabic name for the same practice, *'ilm al-raml* 'the science of the sand'. On the lower left of the fragment there are four lines in Ladino (also called 'Judaeo-Spanish'), which uses Hebrew characters to transcribe the Spanish language. Ladino appears in Genizah manuscripts from the 15th century onwards.

Ca. 16th–18th century

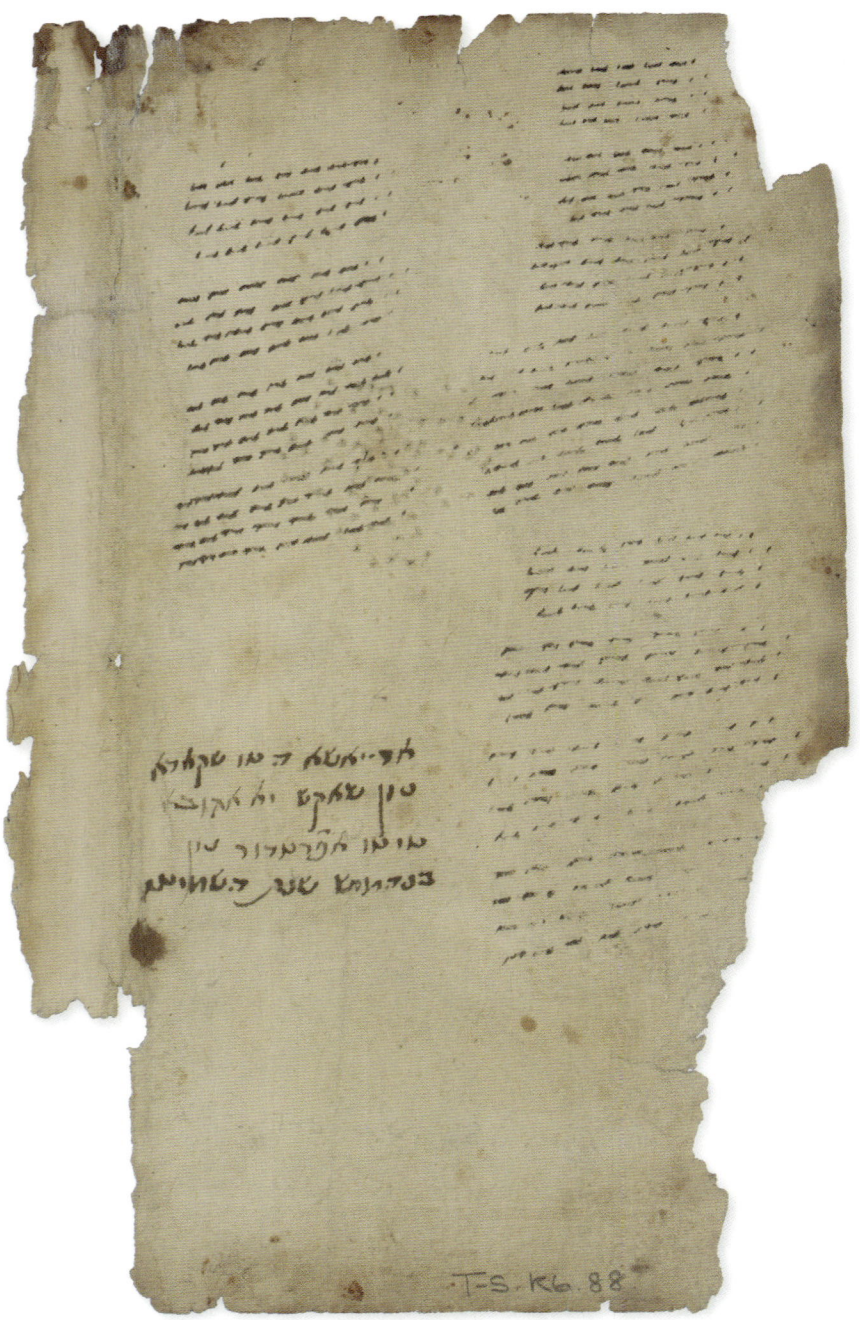

T-S K6.88

כשם הוה הוה ויהיה השבעתי
וגזרתי עליך אתה מזל אריה שתעמוד
כבל עץ ותגבורת ועוצם ותוקף ותעצם
נגד כל המזיקין והמכאוכים והמא חלי
איס את האשה חביבה בת זהרא ו
ותעמודו כשרה בתפילה ובארכה
לגני מלך מלכי המלאכים הרבה
נהבריית תיעלעה כל מיני שידין ועי
תין ולכן ולעלתין ותועין בישין ומזיקין
ומאזיקתין ורוחין בישין ובכורין וערכין
וכל מיני פחד ורעד ומורך ליבב ותלשת
הלב ותעויפת הלב וכל מיני מכאובשע
כאיבאריה או כגדיה כאומן שתהיה כה
ראה ושמועה מכל דבר רע מן כל היתים
די עאלין כת'יעתהון די כשייא ותעאכרן
זעיהו ולא תעיל את כרי כבועה על הבל
מכל הכתוב אתם עלוך שלא תביל לבר
שרי צבאות כאן לתעבדול עליה כשם
הקרוש הקה שהוא אדני וככות הציות
לנ וראא בכה ום ומה כשוא
ביל וכת צוא נת מן תוי מכ'
איום שלא תעבל אני רבת ורתכ
כבות התולאך השמוב על שבועתי דאת
קרביאל המוווע עליך שקא
התותנים על שבעת וככות שבעת התולאכים ילא
תוכאנל גבריאל סמ'ל רפאל
צדק יא"ל עניאל רפציאל ש
שתיתן כבור לין אתהי ישלאל

T-S K1.18

Amulet for Prenatal Health

Magical amulet copied for a pregnant Jewish woman – named Habiba bint Zuhra – to protect her from miscarriage and other complications. The text is a combination of Hebrew and Aramaic even though Habiba probably spoke Arabic in her day-to-day life. The handwriting is also fairly rough, which may suggest that she wrote it herself. The leaf was originally rolled up, likely to store in an amulet case that she wore as a necklace.

Ca. 16th–18th century

T-S NS 316.50

Printed Decalogue Amulet

While many magical texts invoke God or angels as part of a spell, others are more explicitly religious. This amulet features the first two Hebrew words of each line of the decalogue (also known as the 'Ten Commandments'). It was printed in the 18th or 19th century and has been folded in half, likely for someone to carry it in a pocket or amulet case.

Ca. 18th–19th century

Notes to Chapter V

1 Joseph Naveh and Shaul Shaked, *Magic spells and formulae: Aramaic Incantations of Late Antiquity*. Jerusalem: The Magnes Press, 1993, 189–209.

2 Korshi Dosoo, Edward O.D. Love, and Markéta Preininger (chief editors). 'KYP M736,' Kyprianos Database of Ancient Ritual Texts and Objects, www.coptic-magic.phil.uni-wuerzburg.de/index.php/manuscript/kyp-m736 (accessed 6 July 2023). Thank you to Hany N. Takla, Raquel Martín, Matt Boutilier, and Alan Elbaum for their assistance in identifying this manuscript.

3 See Colin F. Baker and Meira R.P. Polliack, *Arabic and Judeo-Arabic Manuscripts in the Cambridge Genizah Collections: Taylor-Schechter Arabic Old Series (T-S Ar.1a–54)*, Cambridge Genizah Series 12 (Cambridge: Cambridge University Press, 2001), plate 21.

4 Joseph Naveh and Shaul Shaked, *Magic spells and formulae: Aramaic Incantations of Late Antiquity*. Jerusalem: The Magnes Press, 1993, 158–164.

5 Gideon Bohak and Ortal-Paz Saar, 'Genizah Magical Texts Prepared for or Against Named Individuals', *Revue Des Études Juives* 174, no. 1–2 (2015): 77–110.

6 Gideon Bohak, 'Some "Mass-Produced" Scorpion-Amulets from the Cairo Genizah', in *A Wandering Galilean: Essays in Honour of Sean Freyne*, ed. Zuleika Rogers, Margaret Daly-Denton, and Anne Fitzpatrick McKinley (Leiden: Brill, 2009), 35–50.

7 MS Manchester, John Rylands Library, A 1252.

8 Shelomo D. Goitein, *A Mediterranean Society*, V, 337 and 599.

VI.

Science & Medicine

It makes sense that much of what we find in the Cairo Genizah is explicitly Jewish. Egypt's Jews needed a constant supply of items like Hebrew Bibles and Torah scrolls, and those are typical things to deposit in any genizah. But they also needed sources of information that were useful to people of any religion: books on medicine, astronomy, mathematics, cosmetics, alchemy, and other scientific topics. Most of these books were composed in Arabic, the scientific *lingua franca* of the time, used by Jews, Christians, and Muslims alike.

The manuscripts in this chapter show us how the people of pre-modern Egypt studied, created, circulated, and applied scientific knowledge to understand and interact with the world around them. Many of them are copies of works that were translated into Arabic during the so-called 'translation movement' of the 9th century. This movement saw the Abbasid Caliphate promoting the translation of as many ancient Greek texts as possible into Arabic, often with the help of bilingual Syriac Christian translators. The resulting Arabic adaptations of Greek and Syriac knowledge became widely popular in the Middle East, North Africa, and even Europe in the following centuries. The target audience for these manuscripts was often the wealthier, more educated classes of society, and many are calligraphically written or expensively decorated.

Alongside works of medical and pharmacological literature, the Genizah also preserves prescriptions, recipes, and other instructions from doctors – evidence for how medical theories were put into practice, as well as the kinds of ailments they aimed to treat.

Early Arabic Medical Treatise

Table of contents from a parchment Arabic medical treatise with chapters on the liver, stomach, teeth, and children's health. The script style is an early type of Arabic bookhand known from professional scribes of the 9th and 10th centuries. Given the high degree of scribal skill required, the original book was likely quite expensive.[1]

Ca. 9th–10th century

T-S Ar.11.36

T-S Ar.11.31

Galenic Perfumes and Ointments

Instructions for making perfumes and ointments, from an Arabic medical text on the preparation of drugs. The fragrance recipes are attributed to the ancient Greek physician Galen, and the preparations are based on Ibn Sina's medical encyclopaedia, *The Canon of Medicine*. The text is written in an early form of Judaeo-Arabic (Arabic in Hebrew script), but some headings are in a calligraphic Arabic script. Many medical texts show a similar level of scribal artistry as high-quality Bibles and Qur'ans, presumably because the target market was doctors who could afford to pay a bit extra.[2]

Ca. 10th century

Hebrew Transcription of an Arabic Translation of Greek Logic by a Syriac Bishop

This is the title page of a book copied in the 10th century, called *The Definitions of Logic According to Aristotle the Philosopher*. The text was compiled from Greek sources and translated into Arabic by ʿAbdishuʿ ibn Bahriz, a 9th-century Syriac Christian bishop who lived in Mosul, Iraq during the Arabic 'translation movement'. While this page is in Arabic script, the rest of the book is Hebrew characters, and thus intended for a Jewish reader. The penultimate line states that this copy belonged to someone named Sadaqa ibn Ishaq.

Ca. 10th century

T-S K6.181

Cosmetic Hair Dyes

This Arabic cosmetic text contains recipes for dark hair dyes. Its ingredients include henna, fig leaves, beet leaves, barley water, sesame, and natron. Based on the script style and parchment, we can estimate it was written no later than the 10th century.[3]

Ca. 10th century

Medieval Pediatrics

Two pages from a Judaeo-Arabic medical text describing ailments common to "children big and small," including fevers, coughs, rashes, stomach aches, and hiccups. It recommends remedies using common ingredients like salt, pepper, sesame, honey, and egg (though also some less-common ones, too, like ammonia and storax). One skin condition – circled on the top left – is alarmingly known as "the Persian Fire."

Ca. 10th–11th century

T-S Ar.45.20

Rose-Tinted Glassblowing

Instructions in Judaeo-Arabic for burning, washing, drying, and grinding metallic compounds, including copper, sulphur, and a reddish substance called *qulqutar* (probably iron sulphate). A crucible and a glass kiln are also required. It's likely that these are notes for a glassmaker on how to add colourful tints to their products.

Ca. 11th–12th century

Tabulated Medical Manuals

Around the 11th century, Arabic physicians began composing medical works with extensive tables of diseases, drugs, and treatments. This allowed for greater scribal creativity and made the books more enjoyable for readers to consult. Fragments from at least 5 different 'tabular' medical books survive in the collection, including the three shown here.

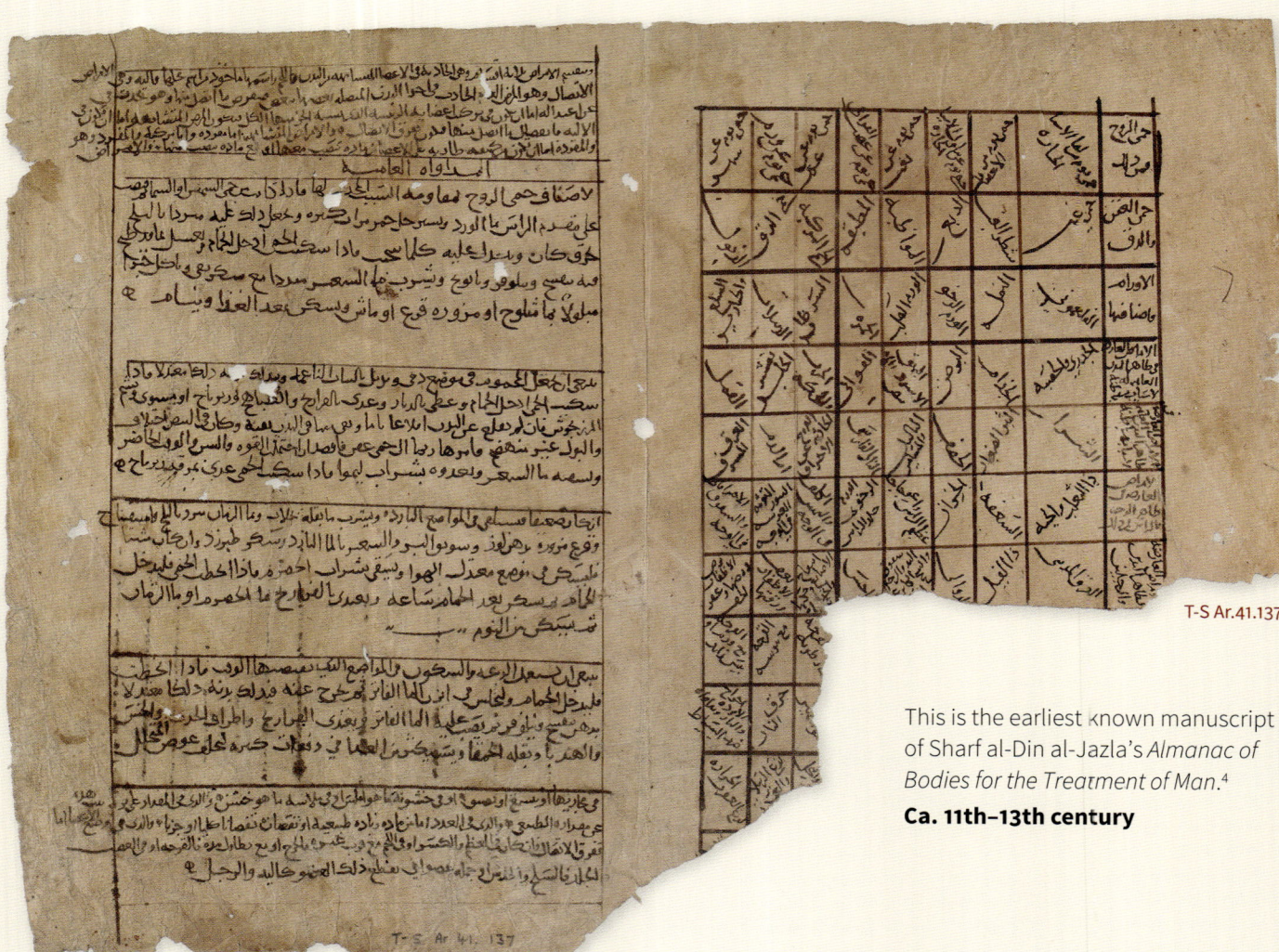

T-S Ar.41.137

This is the earliest known manuscript of Sharf al-Din al-Jazla's *Almanac of Bodies for the Treatment of Man*.[4]

Ca. 11th–13th century

Table of contents from a parchment medical textbook in a curiously long vertical format.[5]
Ca. 11th–13th century

T-S Ar.38.5

Book on ingredients with medicinal qualities, this time listing plants and their uses in a circular table (though there's another square table on the reverse side).
Ca. 12th–14th century

T-S Ar.44.12

Annotated *Canon of Medicine*

One of the most important books in the history of medicine was *The Canon of Medicine*, by Abu
'Ali al-Husayn ibn Sina (known as 'Avicenna' in Europe). Ibn Sina was a Persian polymath who
composed works of philosophy, theology, physics, grammar, medicine, poetry, logic, and alchemy.
European scholars translated many of these works into Latin, and *The Canon of Medicine* remained
part of European medical curricula into the 18th century. Whoever owned this Arabic copy heavily
annotated it, making corrections or clarifications in red ink and adding their own commentary in
the margins. Many medical books had wide margins specifically so readers could add notes like
this. This section deals with the anatomy of muscles in the arm and shoulder.

Ca. 11th–13th century

T-S Ar.40.114

Cosmetic Cream for Hairy Women

Instructions for making a hair-removal cream specifically for "hairy women." The recipe calls for ashes, yellow arsenic, and bird poo to be blended together and cooked. The resulting mixture was then applied in the bath. We have no idea if this worked and it's one recipe we aren't eager to test.

Ca. 11th–13th century

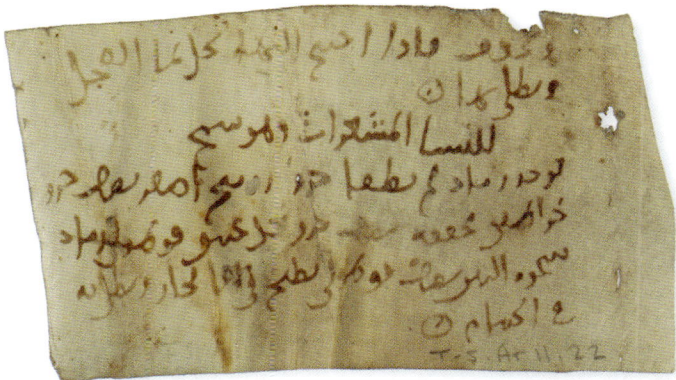

T-S Ar.11.22

Euclid's *Elements*

This is the ancient Greek mathematician Euclid's famous book *Elements*, translated into Arabic by the Sabian scholar Thabit ibn Qurra. Thabit participated in the 9th-century Abbasid Caliphate's 'translation movement' to translate Greek knowledge into Arabic. The large copy here was made a few centuries later and has been transcribed into Hebrew characters for use by Jewish readers. The messiest bits are Arabic notes and geometric diagrams of triangles, probably drawn by a student studying the book. The thinner fragment may come from a separate copy that was cut up to serve as binding material in another book (☛ Chapter X).

Ca. 11th–13th century

T-S AS 144.97

T-S NS 324.120

The Memorandum for Opticians

Numerous Genizah fragments of a book called *The Memorandum for Opticians* make it clear that eye health was important for the people of Cairo. A Christian physician, ʿAli ibn ʿIsa al-Kahhal, wrote this book in the 11th century, and his combination of ancient Greek and Arabic medicine proved widely popular in Europe and the Middle East. The text contains chapters on eye anatomy with treatments for various conditions, including basic surgical operations, and may be the first work in history to recommend the use of a surgical anaesthetic.

T-S Ar.40.41

There is a note attached to this Arabic copy of *The Memorandum* with instructions from a Fatimid government official. He orders a man named al-Hafiz, the owner of a book warehouse, to send this book to the amir Fakhr al-Din abu Mansur ʿIzz al-ʿArab. If you look very closely, you may be able to see a fingerprint in the left margin next to the last line.

September 1142 CE

T-S Ar.11.21

This is also *The Memorandum for Opticians*. The language is still Arabic, but this time it's copied in Hebrew characters for the benefit of Cairo's Jewish doctors. Moses Maimonides, who was a physician to the court of the Ayyubid Sultan Salah al-Din, likely had a copy that looked like this. Notice how the Hebrew scribe used red ink to mark section headings just like the Arabic scribe in the previous fragment.

Ca. 12th–13th century

Maimonides' Autograph Treatise on Sexual Dysfunction

Moses Maimonides, the head of the Egyptian Jewish community, personally wrote this draft
of an Arabic treatise on sexual dysfunction. An ageing Ayyubid prince, Taqi al-Din 'Umar, had
sought him out to solve the problem of his waning 'manly vigour'. Maimonides offers the prince
various aphrodisiac concoctions and recommends a diet that avoids 'cooling' foods like lettuce
and spinach. With the top doctor in Egypt telling his patients to stop eating salad, it's maybe no
surprise that people died younger back then.

Ca. 1179–1191 CE

T-S Ar.44.79

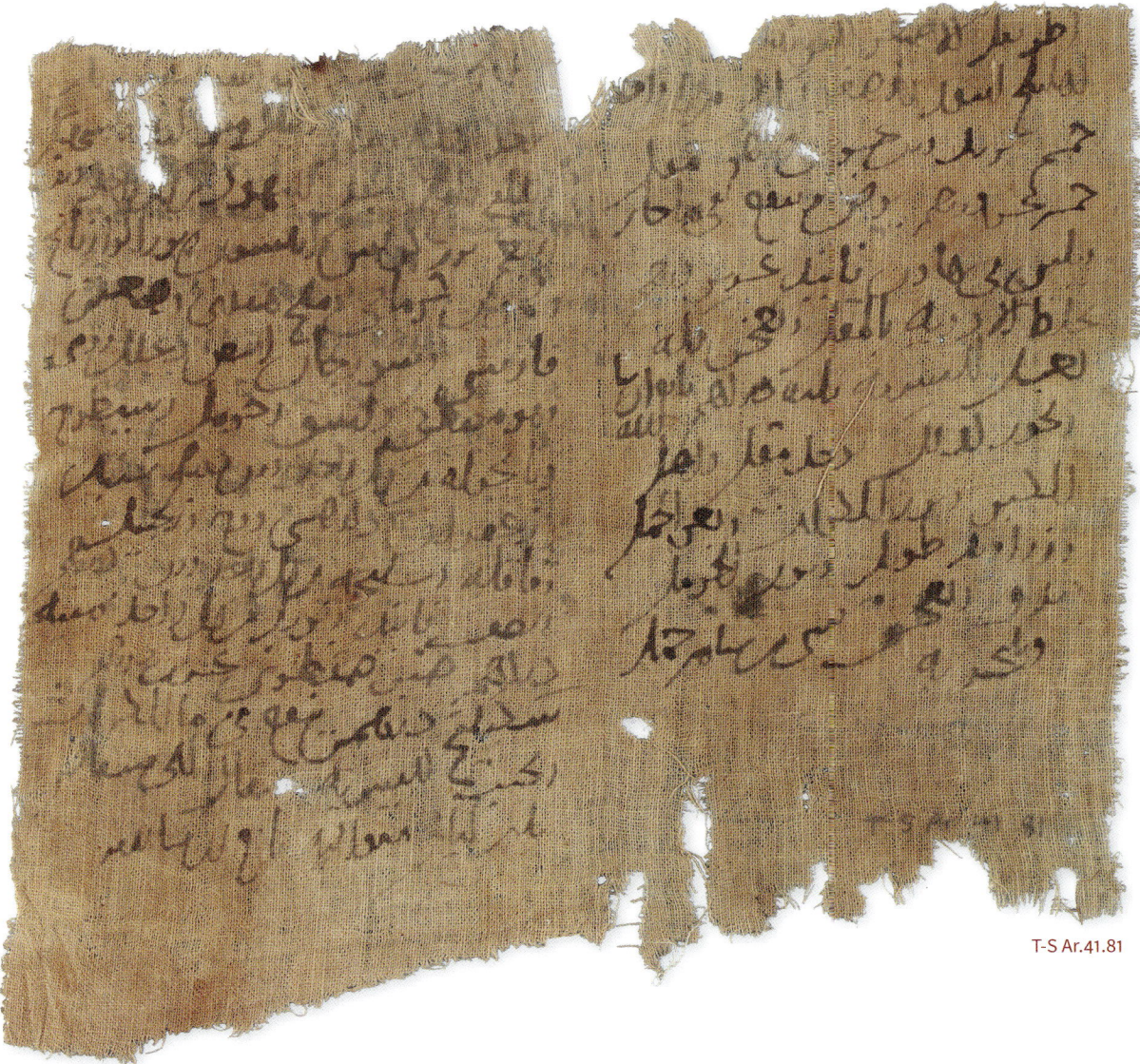

T-S Ar.41.81

Prescriptions for Haemorrhoids

Paper was cheap and plentiful in Egypt, but for Jewish merchants living and working in India, it was often in short supply. Abraham ibn Yiju, a trader based in Mangalore, used pieces of cloth for his correspondence and note-taking. Here, on the back of a court record from the Indian port of Baruch, Ibn Yiju copied two medicinal recipes. "Lesser tripha a for haemorrhoids: black, yellow, and chebulic myrobalan berries, each 5 dirhams; turpeth herb and […], 20 dirhams; bdellium resin, 15 dirhams. Crush and soak in hot water, and soften sugar candy in a mortar, 20 dirhams. Combine the bdellium with the drugs and knead all of it with honey. The dose is 3 dirhams. Beneficial, if God wills. And likewise possible: take bdellium, caper-root, leek seed, camel dung, long birthwort, and harmal seed. Grind and knead […] and sniff it up." Abraham spent almost two decades in India, raising a family with an enslaved local woman whom he freed and subsequently married. He eventually returned with his family to Egypt. Around 70 manuscripts detailing his life and business affairs survive in the Genizah.[6]

Ca. 1130–1150 CE

Autographed Introduction to Geometry

This is the opening page of the Arabic title page from Qusta ibn Luqa's *Introduction to the Art of Geometry*. Ibn Luqa was a 9th-century Melkite Christian translator who acquired ancient Greek manuscripts in the Byzantine Empire for the Abbasid Caliphate. This copy is written in a beautiful *maghrebi* ('western') script style typical of Arabic manuscripts from al-Andalus (modern Andalusia, southern Spain). On the back of this page there is a title page and a note in a different hand: "belonging to 'Ali ibn Muhammad al-Ansari, known as al-Qushubri." This al-Qushubri is a known scholar of geometry who was born in al-Andalus and died in Samarqand sometime before 1224. He likely took this book with him when he left Spain.[7]

Ca. 1175–1224 CE

T-S Ar.53.39

Ophthalmological Certification

Eye diseases are the most common medical problem that we see in Genizah manuscripts. This scrap paper contains an Arabic draft of a question intended for an Islamic judge, asking whether a Jewish eye doctor (specifically described as "beardless") can treat a Muslim family. It seems that this doctor had previously taken Muslim patients and already secured their testimony that he was trustworthy. We have little reason to think the doctor's request would have been denied, since the skill of Jewish physicians – such as Moses Maimonides – was widely recognised in Egypt at the time.[8]

Ca. 12th–13th century

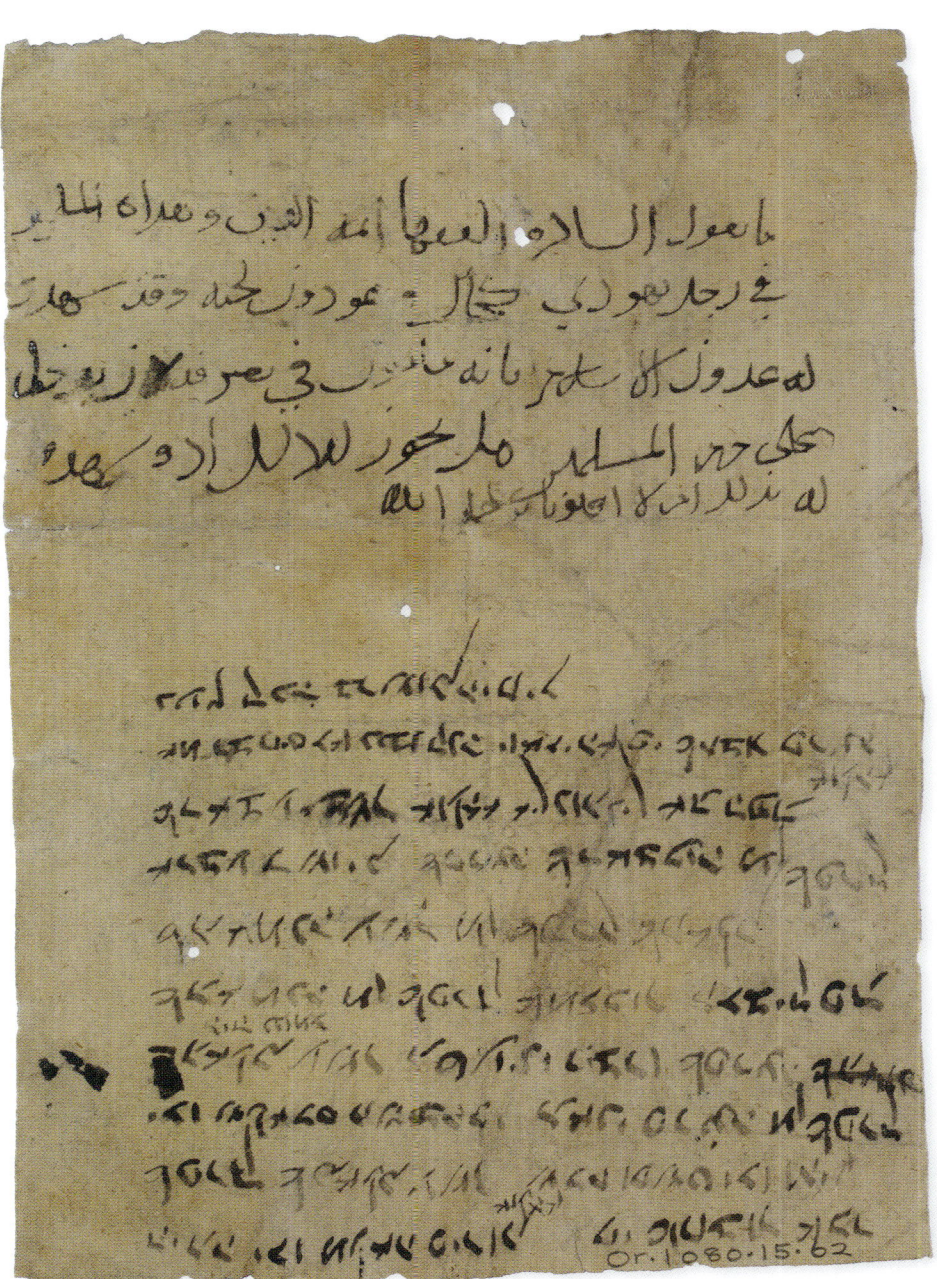

Or.1080 15.62

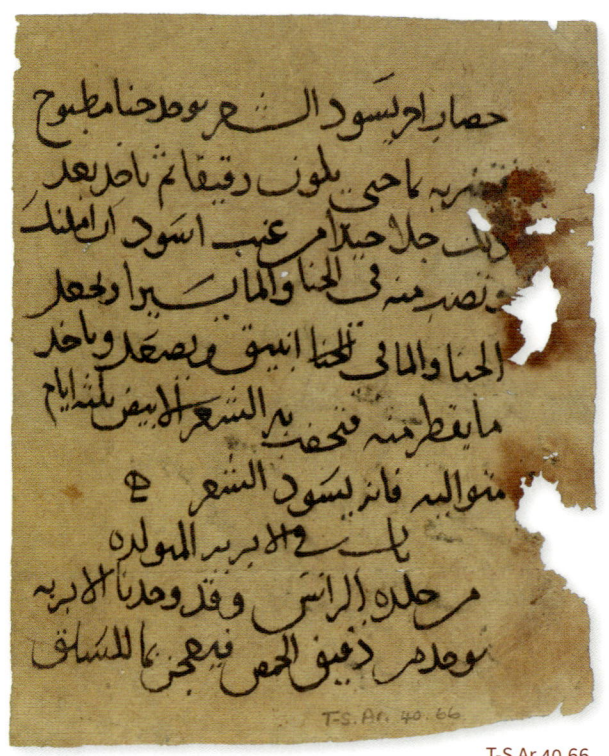

T-S Ar.40.66

Instructions for Hair Care

An Arabic guide for hair care. It contains a recipe for treating brittle hair and split ends using a mixture of tamarind, violet blossom, and plums. A second recipe recommends pine nuts to darken whitening hair. This leaf has been torn from a relatively small booklet, each page only about 4 x 6 inches, and may be a personal copy that an individual used at home.[9]

Ca. 12th–13th century

Q: How do scholars date the manuscripts?

Some documents include a date, so we know exactly when they were written. Court scribes, for example, would note the day, month, and year in which they were writing, and there were several different dating systems to choose from. Medieval Jews commonly calculated the date from the biblical Creation of the world (*Anno Mundi*, often abbreviated AM), the date since the destruction of the Jerusalem temple in 70 CE, or the date since the start of the Seleucid Greek calendar in 312 BCE (*Anno Graecorum*, AG). This Greek reckoning was also popular with Middle Eastern Christians, and Jews in the Genizah often refer to it as 'the Era of Documents'. Later fragments, particularly printed books (☛ Chapter XI), refer to the Gregorian Christian calendar (*Anno Domini*, AD), calculated since the approximate year of the birth of Jesus. Muslim documents in the collection are dated according to the Muslim Hijri calendar, counting years from the Hijra – Muhammad's migration from Mecca to Medina – in 622 CE (*Anno Hegirae*, AH). Some scribes even listed the date in multiple calendars, and conversion mistakes were common. The Leningrad Codex (B19a) – the oldest complete copy of the Hebrew Bible – gives the year according to five different systems, but each is a different date! The book you're reading now was first published in 2024 CE and AD, equivalent to 5784 AM, 1446 in the Hijri era, 1954 since the destruction of the temple, and 2336 in the reckoning of the Greeks.[10]

When a manuscript does not contain a date – and this is the case for most fragments from the Genizah – we estimate its age by palaeographic analysis (examining handwriting), linguistic analysis (examining language), codicological analysis (examining physical features of books), and other contextual clues. Handwriting style, language, and bookmaking practices change over time, so certain features can be associated with a particular area or time period. Perhaps the scribe's handwriting is also found in another document with a date? Or perhaps a type of currency is mentioned that narrows the possible range? The paper may even bear a watermark that pinpoints its time and place of production (☛ Chapter X). In extreme cases, carbon-14 dating can also be used to estimate when a piece of paper or parchment was made, but this process is expensive and requires the destruction of a small portion of the manuscript.

Astronomical Chart

An astronomical table in Arabic listing information about the days of the week, the phases of the moon, the sun, and the classical planets (Mercury, Venus, Mars, Jupiter, and Saturn). Muslim and Jewish scholars carefully tracked astronomical phenomena to measure their calendars, determine religious festivals, manage agriculture, and even – for some – to make astrological predictions or know the best times to perform magic and alchemy.

Ca. 12th–14th century

Treatise on Veins

Two pages from an Arabic medical text. It discusses the anatomy of the veins, including a process for drawing blood, and states that the knowledge was transmitted from Greek writings. Scholars of the Abbasid Caliphate translated and adapted numerous texts from Greek into Arabic during the 9th- and 10th-centuries, but the script style here suggests this book was copied several centuries later.

Ca. 13th–14th century

T-S Ar.40.70

Arabic Orbital Mechanics

Astronomical work discussing the cyclical movement of heavenly bodies (including such thrilling topics as the ecliptic orb, the epicyclic orb, the celestial equator, and the meridian cycle). The text is Arabic transcribed in Hebrew characters, but it appears to have been copied from a Classical Arabic original. The spherical diagrams are also labelled with Hebrew letters. The paper is European and the script style is Sefardi, perhaps written in Spain or by a scribe who immigrated to Egypt from the Iberian Peninsula.

Ca. 15th century

T-S AS 144.180

Galen in Hebrew

Hebrew translation of Galen's commentary on the medical works of Hippocrates. It is written in a calligraphic Sefardi script style on European paper that is datable to the second half of the 15th century. It may have reached Cairo with refugees fleeing the 1492 expulsion of Jews and Muslims from Spain. The surrounding marginal text – interestingly, resembling the layout of contemporary Talmuds – is a separate work on fevers and their remedies.[11]

Ca. 1450–1500 CE

T-S K14.45

T-S NS 192.72

Spanish Renaissance Pharmaceuticals

Fragment of Discorides' *Materia Medica*, an encyclopaedia of ingredients useful in medicine. Originally written in Ancient Greek, the humanist Andrés de Laguna translated it into Castillian Spanish during the 16th century for publication at the press of Jean de Laet in Antwerp. This fragment includes an article on myrrh (*la myrra*), a valuable ingredient for incense produced in East Africa and the Arabian Peninsula.[12]

1555 CE

Alchemical Compendium

Alchemy is an ancient branch of scholarship that combined elements of philosophy, theology, astrology, medicine, and metallurgy to examine the natural world. It comes from the Arabic word *al-kimiya*, ultimately from Greek *khumeia* (from which we also get 'chemistry'). Scholars in the Middle East and North Africa practised alchemy throughout the Genizah period, developing new knowledge and techniques that were precursors to modern chemistry. This Judaeo-Arabic collection of alchemical notes discusses tools used for measuring weights, the planets that correspond with different metals, and chemical ingredients like potassium sulphate and ammonium chloride. The language and distinctive script style suggest it was copied in the northern Ottoman Empire in the 17th or 18th century.[13]

Ca. 17th–18th century

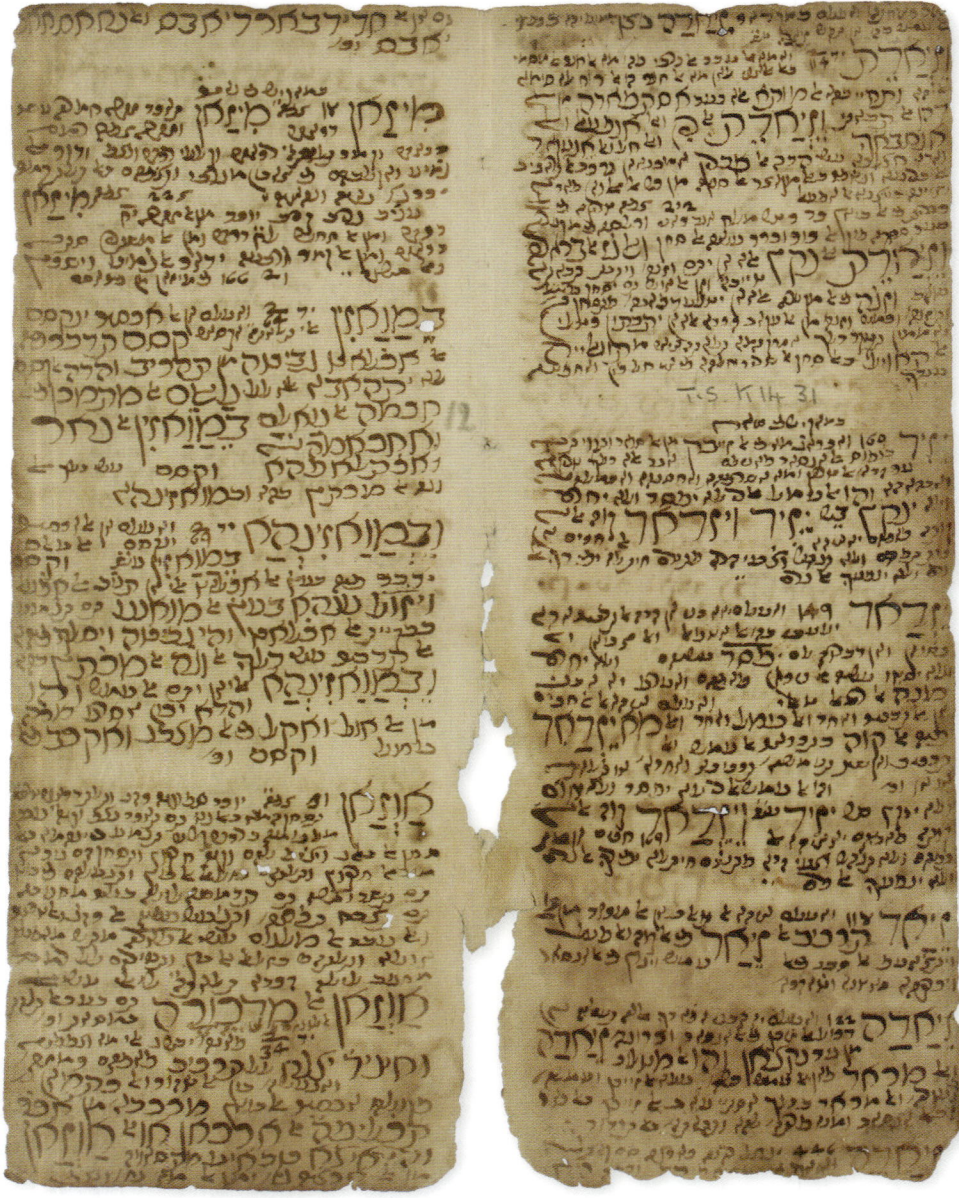

T-S K14.31

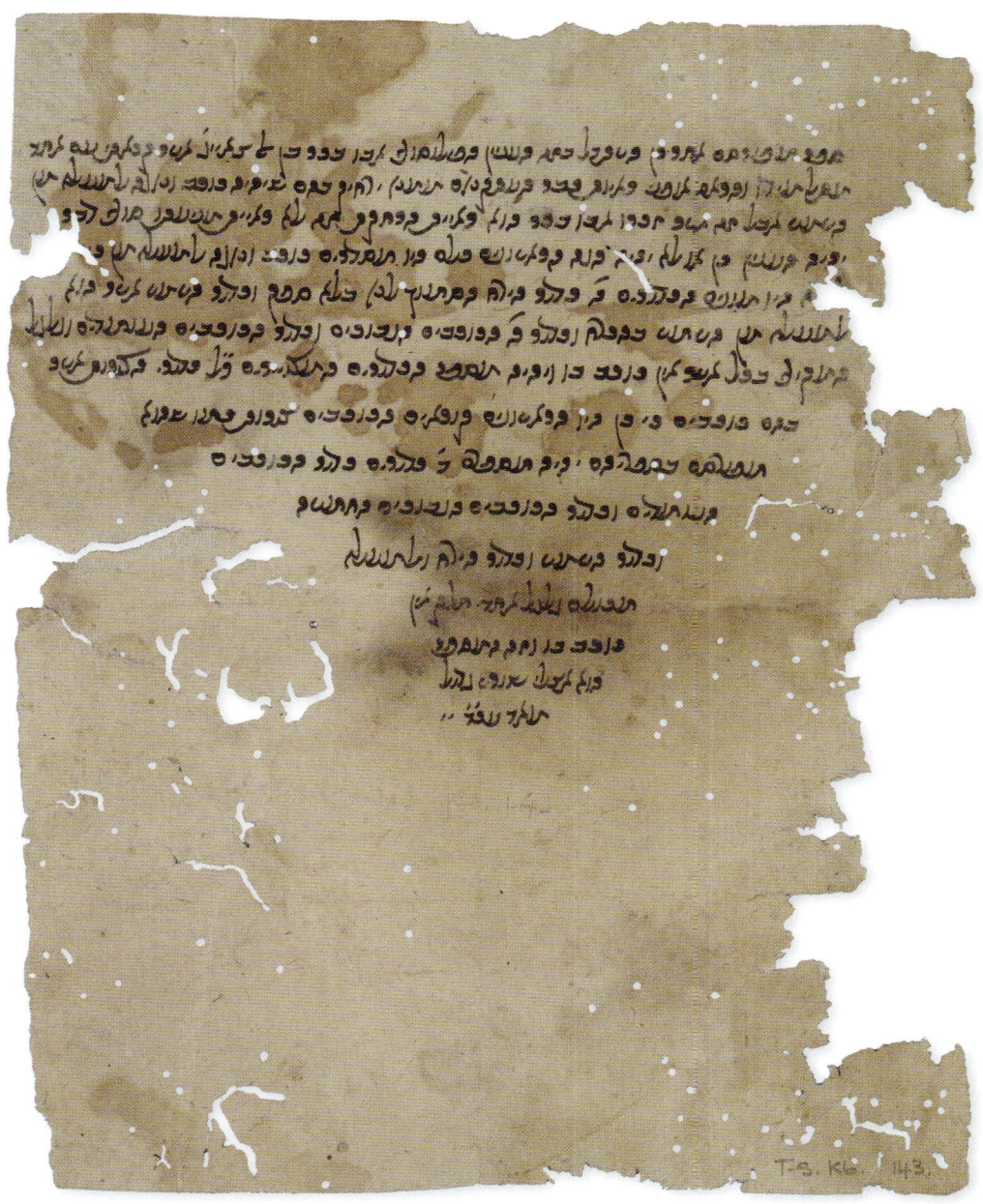

T-S K6.143

Celestial Bookworms

Astronomical treatise in Hebrew discussing the planets and the model of the universe. It mentions, among other famous astronomers, Ptolemy and Copernicus. The style of Hebrew script (with its long swooping leftward strokes) indicates it was copied late in the Genizah period, perhaps even in the 19th century. The holes across the page are spots where insects chewed through the paper while it was still inside a book.

Ca. 18th–19th century

161

Notes to Chapter VI

1   Haskell D. Isaacs, *Medical and Para-Medical Manuscripts in the Cambridge Genizah Collections*, Cambridge University Library Genizah Series 2 (Cambridge: Cambridge University Press, 1995), 9.

2   Information in part from Haskell D. Isaacs, *Medical and Para-Medical Manuscripts in the Cambridge Genizah Collections*, Cambridge University Library Genizah Series 2 (Cambridge: Cambridge University Press, 1995), 8.

3   Information in part from Haskell D. Isaacs, *Medical and Para-Medical Manuscripts in the Cambridge Genizah Collections*, Cambridge University Library Genizah Series 2 (Cambridge: Cambridge University Press, 1995), 67.

4   Efraim Lev, 'An Early Fragment of Ibn Jazlah's Tabulated Manual "Taqwīm al-Abdān" from the Cairo Genizah (T-S Ar.41.137)', *Journal of the Royal Asiatic Society* 24, no. 2 (2014): 200–201.

5   Thank you to Haim Gottschalk for helping to date this fragment.

6   Translation lightly edited from Efraim Lev and Leigh Chipman, *Medical Prescriptions in the Cambridge Genizah Collections: Practical Medicine and Pharmacology in Medieval Egypt* (Leiden: Brill, 2012), pp. 108–110. For more on the life and times of Ibn Yiju, see S.D. Goitein and M.A. Friedman, *India Traders of the Middle Ages: Documents from the Cairo Geniza: "India Book"* (Leiden: Brill, 2008); E.A. Lambourn, *Abraham's Luggage: A Social Life of Things in the Medieval Indian Ocean World* (Cambridge: Cambridge University Press, 2018); and Amitav Ghosh, *In an Antique Land* (London: Granta Books, 1992).

7   Thank you to Gowaart van den Bossche, Josef Zenka, and Muhammad Ali Abu Hamza for helping to decipher the ownership note. See Nick Posegay, 'The Long Road to Samarqand: Reverse-Engineering the Travels of a 12th-Century Andalusi Muslim (T-S Ar.53.39)', *Fragment of the Month (October)*, Cambridge University Library: Genizah Research Unit, 2023.

8   Geoffrey Khan, *Arabic Legal and Administrative Documents in the Cambridge Genizah Collections*, ed. Stefan C. Reif, vol. 10, Genizah Series (Cambridge: Cambridge University Press, 2006), 296.

9   Haskell D. Isaacs, *Medical and Para-Medical Manuscripts in the Cambridge Genizah Collections*, Cambridge University Library Genizah Series 2 (Cambridge: Cambridge University Press, 1995), 22.

10 And 47 ABY.

11 Information in part from Haskell D. Isaacs, *Medical and Para-Medical Manuscripts in the Cambridge Genizah Collections*, Cambridge University Library Genizah Series 2 (Cambridge: Cambridge University Press, 1995), 4.

12 Thank you to Daniel Newman and José Martínez Delgado for identifying this fragment.

13 Thank you to Amir Ashur and Estara Arrant for assisting with dating and suggesting locations for the copying of this fragment.

Arabic & Islam

When people think of the Cairo Genizah, they probably think of it as a Jewish collection, created by the Jews of Cairo, filled with Jewish manuscripts. To a great extent, this is accurate. The last 125 years of Cairo Genizah study has profoundly rewritten the history of Jewish culture in the Middle Ages and greatly enriched our knowledge of pre-modern Judaism in all its intellectual and social forms. But for most of the Genizah period, the Jews of Cairo spoke Arabic natively. Many of them read and wrote it fluently, and all were citizens of Muslim empires. For reasons that we are still only really beginning to understand, those same citizens deposited thousands of Arabic fragments into their genizot – at least 7,000 that are now in Cambridge alone. Many of these manuscripts are explicitly Islamic, including pages from the Qur'an, religious amulets, and prayer books. Others are the work of Muslim theologians and philosophers. They often display the elegant Arabic calligraphy expected of highly trained professional scribes. Some have been recycled or overwritten to create new Jewish manuscripts (☞ Chapter X), but others have not, suggesting that Jews were reading them and thought they were worth depositing in genizot.

We have selected the fragments in this chapter to demonstrate how the Cairo Genizah is not just a Jewish collection. It contains beautiful samples of medieval Arabic calligraphy and some of the oldest surviving copies of texts by famous Muslim scholars. These manuscripts crossed the boundaries between Egypt's different religious communities, revealing cultural connections and interfaith exchange in places that many people do not expect. We hope that readers with an interest in Arabic or Islamic history will enjoy them, but we especially encourage anyone whose primary interest is the Jewish side of the Cairo Genizah to spend some time here. You may even experience one of the few consistent truths of Genizah research: you never know what you'll find next.

Early Personal Qur'an

Possibly used as an amulet or good luck charm, this small parchment page contains Sura 11 (*Hud*) of the Qur'an, with a passage relating the story of Noah's Ark. The calligraphy is a style known as 'Abbasid bookhand', typical of Arabic scribes of the 9th and 10th centuries. This style has features of earlier 'Kufic' calligraphy as well as the later *naskhi* scripts that later came to dominate Arabic writing. The small red dots throughout represent vowel sounds in the Arabic text. Although the page originally came from a book, if you look closely, you can also see that it was once folded up into a thin strip, suggesting that it was stored in an amulet case (☛ Chapter V).[1]

Ca. 9th–10th century

T-S Ar.38.8

Book of Hadith

One of two surviving fragments (the other is T-S Ar.38.69) from a single book of hadith, the sayings of the prophet Muhammad as preserved by chains of transmitters across the centuries. This page is the beginning of a section of reports transmitted by ʿAdi ibn Hatim, a 7th-century Muslim convert. A later hand added comments in the margins.

Ca. 9th–10th century

Q: Why are Christian and Muslim writings found in the Cairo Genizah?

Some Arabic texts were preserved in the Genizah because the paper or parchment on which they were written was cut up and reused by writers in the Jewish community. Some of the earliest manuscripts in the Genizah are leaves from Christian translations of the Bible, originating from Palestinian monasteries, that were, centuries later, overwritten with Jewish liturgical texts (☛ Chapter I). Other manuscripts – particularly large Islamic legal documents – were recycled as scrap paper. As a result, we find many Genizah manuscripts with Islamic documents on one side and Jewish writings on the back (☛Chapter VIII).

The Genizah has also preserved considerable evidence of close relations between members of the different faiths of Egypt. We know that Jews, Christians, and Muslims tended to live together in the same neighbourhoods of medieval Fustat and Cairo, and

Jewish thinkers participated in the intellectual discourse of the Islamic world. Abraham Maimonides, the son of the great Jewish philosopher Moses Maimonides, for instance, was heavily influenced by Sufism, an Islamic mystical tradition. Scholars often refer to the shared culture of all people living under Muslim governments as 'Islamicate'. In contrast to 'Islamic', this term encompasses the diverse peoples and ideas that made up the societies where Muslims ruled, but is not necessarily related to the religion of Islam. Moses and Abraham Maimonides were 'Islamicate' thinkers, in addition to their roles as Jewish thinkers. Within this Islamicate cultural and intellectual world, works of science, philosophy, theology, and literature circulated between the different religious communities in Arabic, the common *lingua franca* of the day. Some Jews in Fustat treated these texts with reverence and deposited them into their genizot.

T-S NS 305.198

T-S NS 305.210

Christian Arabic Bible Translation

Arabic-speaking Christians used their own translations of the Old Testament. These two fragments are from Exodus 15. The red 'rubricated' heading indicates that it is the Song of the Sea, here labelled as "the first song by Miriam, sister of Aaron, and Moses." The script style resembles some of the earliest known Arabic Bible translations found at St. Catherine's Monastery in the Sinai Peninsula.

Ca. 9th–10th century

T-S Ar.38.75

Essay by al-Jahiz

Page from the literary essay *On Squaring and Circling* by the renowned Muslim author, al-Jahiz (d. 868/869 CE). Al-Jahiz was a rationalist scholar famous for employing irony and comedy to discuss serious topics. In this essay, he challenges widespread beliefs and superstitions related to the natural world. This page is from a chapter about animal life. It is one of the oldest surviving copies of al-Jahiz's work.[2]

Ca. 10th century

T-S Ar.51.73

Palimpsested Prayer Text

Parchment page from a Muslim prayer book. It preserves the text of a *du'a*, an Islamic prayer of supplication, known from 13th-century Shi'i sources. Written in an Early Abbasid script style, typical of Qur'anic scribes in the 9th and 10th centuries, this manuscript is likely the earliest extant version of this prayer. The back of the page was palimpsested (☞ Chapter I) and used as recycled writing material for notes in Hebrew.[3]

Ca. 10th–11th century

Two Books by a Prolific Scribe

Medical texts often resemble fine Qur'ans and Bibles in their elegant calligraphy and decoration, with the same professional scribes producing both types of manuscripts. The fragment below is a miniature Qur'an (just 2 inches wide) with two pages from Sura 2 (*The Cow*), copied in a distinctive 'New Style' Abbasid script and embellished with gold verse dividers. If you look very closely, you can also see a fingerprint in the left margin. The fragment to the right is a section of a medical text on the digestive system copied by the same distinctive hand as the Qur'an.[4]

Ca. 10th–11th century

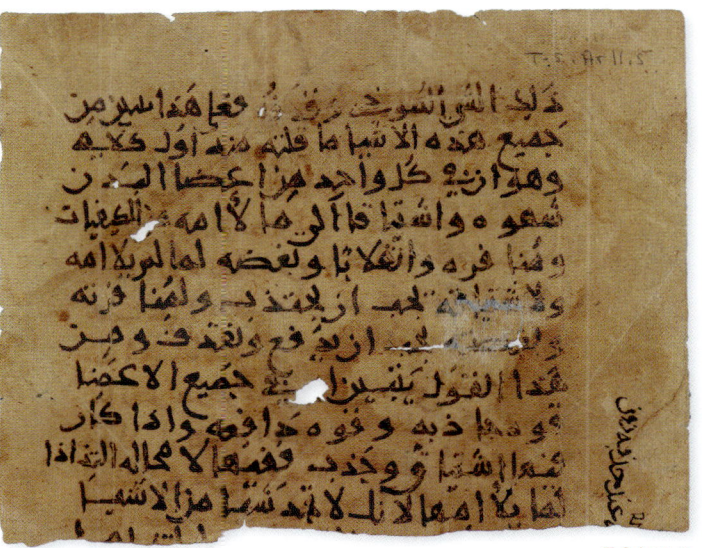

T-S Ar.11.5

T-S Ar.40.177

Muslim Prayer Book

Two pages from a pocket-sized book of *duʿa* prayers for requesting assistance from God. The original book was only about 3 inches wide, likely written by a professional scribe in Fatimid Egypt.[5]

Ca. 10th–11th century

T-S Ar.39.84

T-S Ar.38.70

A Unique Anthology

The Unique Necklace was an anthology claiming to contain all the knowledge that ought to be learned by a well-informed person. The author was Ibn ʿAbd Rabbihi, a 10th-century Arabic writer and poet born in the Umayyad Caliphate of what is now Spain. The script style of this parchment leaf suggests it was copied close to his homeland, either in al-Andalus or northwestern Africa. A later writer reused the back of the page to practise large Hebrew and Arabic writing.[6]

Ca. 10th–12th century

Instructions for Prayer

Instructions in Arabic for performing Muslim prayers. It is copied in a competent, if perhaps not professional, *maghrebi* style, most likely by a writer from northwestern Africa or al-Andalus. The light vertical lines along the full length of the page are impressions from the mould used to make the paper.[7]

Ca. 11th–12th century

T-S. Ar. 29.138

T-S Ar.29.138

T-S 16.353

Letter to the Jews of Khaybar

This Judaeo-Arabic text purportedly contains a copy of a letter that the prophet Muhammad sent to the Jews of Khaybar (in modern Saudi Arabia) in the year 630 CE. Conveniently, the letter exempts this Jewish community from the *jizya* tax that Muslim governments levied against non-Muslim citizens in their domains. While it is not impossible, many scholars doubt that Muhammad actually composed such a letter in the 7th century. This particular copy – one of two that survive in the Genizah – cannot be much older than the 11th century.[8]

Ca. 11th–12th century

Q: Did Egyptian Jews speak Arabic?

Arabic was the mother tongue for most Jews in the Middle East and North Africa for the majority of the Genizah period. It was the first language Egyptian Jews learned at home and the common language they would have spoken to conduct business with other Arabic speakers – including other Jews, Christians, and Muslims. Most Egyptian Jews also learned to read Biblical Hebrew, and would sometimes write letters in Hebrew, especially to communicate with foreign Jews who did not know Arabic. Interestingly, Jews in Arab lands typically wrote in a special writing system called 'Judaeo-Arabic', which uses the characters of the Hebrew alphabet that they learned in school to transcribe the Arabic language.

In later periods – especially after 1492 when Christian authorities expelled them from Spain – many European Jews settled in Egypt and the Ottoman Empire. They maintained distinct communities that continued to use languages like Ladino and Judaeo-Italian for generations afterwards, even into the 19th and 20th centuries. Depending on where they lived, many of these Jews learned Arabic or Turkish too. French also became an important language for Cairo's educated elite when European colonial powers took control of Egypt in the 19th century.

Maghrebi Qur'an

Qur'an fragment of Sura 26 (*The Poets*) and Sura 27 (*The Ant*), copied with the distinct looping tails of a *maghrebi* script style. This style is typical of Arabic manuscripts from North Africa and al-Andalus. At least two fragments of this Qur'an have survived in the collection. Like many *maghrebi* manuscripts, the scribe preserved an old Arabic custom of marking the letter *q* with a single dot above and *f* with a single dot below.

Ca. 11th–13th century

T-S AS 176.491

T-S NS 297.141

Prophetic Exegesis

This is one of a dozen fragments in the collection of *The Circumstances of Revelation* by the 11th-century Muslim scholar Abu al-Hasan al-Wahidi (d. 1075). It is an exegetical work describing the circumstances in which the prophet Muhammad received the words of the Qur'an. This book is the earliest and most influential representative of a subgenre of Qur'anic interpretation focused on the circumstances of prophecy.

Ca. 11th–13th century

Praises for the Prophet

A single page from a beautiful *maghrebi*-style Arabic text by a man named Zakariya ibn Ibrahim ibn Muhammad. He entreats God to bless the prophet Muhammad, quoting verse 33:56 of the Qur'an ("Indeed, God and His angels send blessings upon the prophet…"). The following lines are prayers for Muhammad, each beginning with "peace be upon you."

Ca. 12th–13th century

T-S Ar.19.24

T-S Ar.40.199

Ayyubid Chronicle

This is a history of the Ayyubids, the ruling dynasty of Egypt established by the Kurdish general Salah al-Din (better known as Saladin), presented year by year. Saladin subdued the Fatimid Caliphate and became the first Sultan of Egypt in 1171 CE. His successors ruled in Cairo until the rise of the Mamluk Sultanate in 1250 CE. The relatively brief period of Ayyubid rule produced one of the highest concentrations of manuscripts of any era represented in the Cairo Genizah.

Ca. 13th–14th century

Sayings of the Prophet

The Book of the Shooting Star by the 11th-century writer Abu ʿAbd Allah Muhammad al-Qudaʿi. This text collects sayings attributed to the prophet Muhammad. It is a literary work, but oddly, the Arabic script style resembles the messier cursive scripts common in documentary texts (☛ Chapter VIII).[9]

Ca. 13th–15th century

T-S Ar.19.6

Mamluk-Era Qur'an

Page from Sura 17 (*The Night Journey*) of a Qur'an produced in the late Mamluk or €arly Ottoman period. The calligraphy is a fine example of a *muhaqqaq* script style copied by a professional Arabic scribe.

Ca. 14th–16th century

T-S Ar.41.119

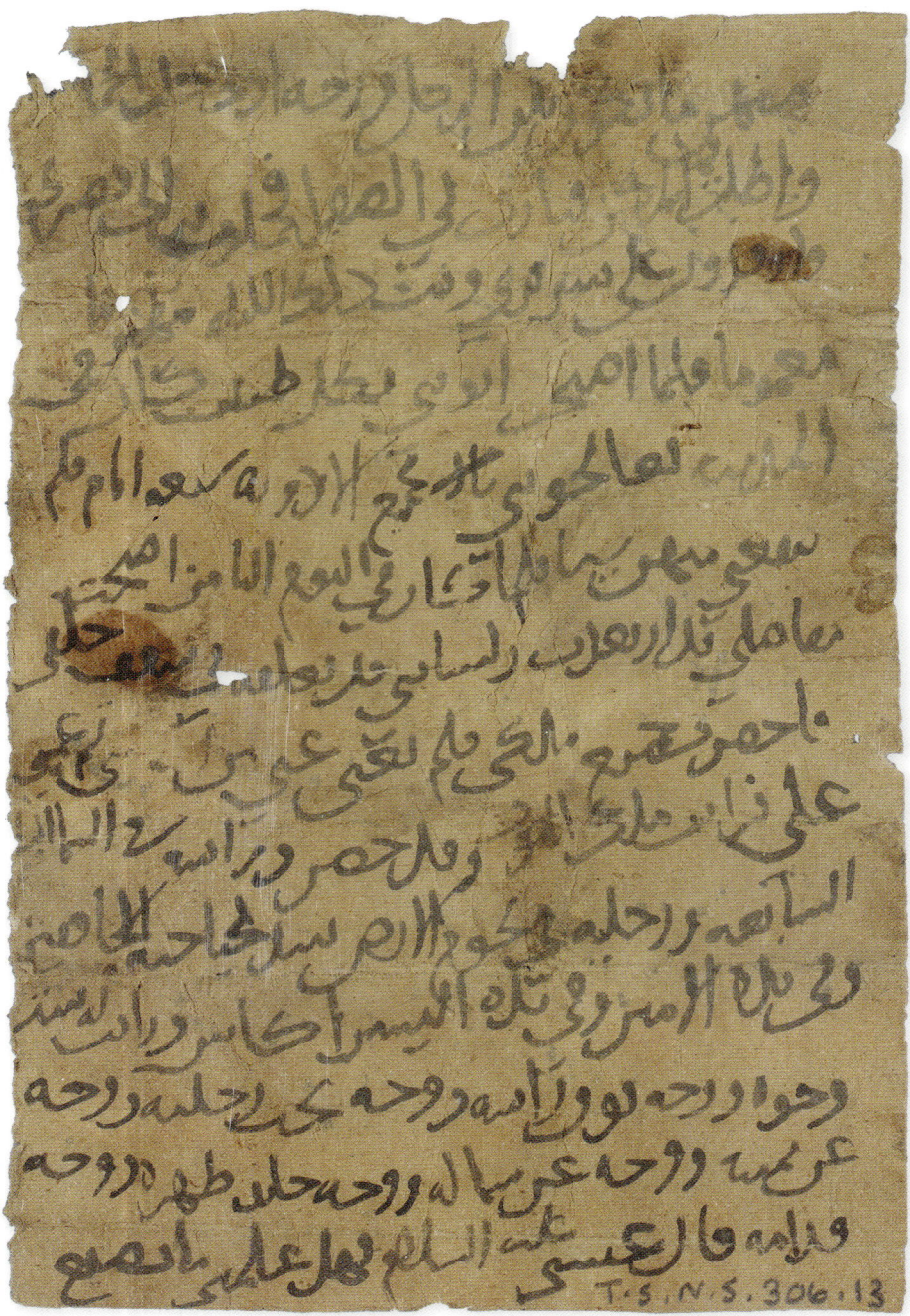

T-S NS 306.13

The Story of the Skull

The Cairo Genizah holds numerous Arabic folk tales – some Jewish, some Muslim, some Christian, and some that crossed the boundaries between religious communities. This is an Islamic version of 'The Story of the Skull', a tale also found in Jewish and Christian traditions in the pre-modern period. It tells the story of "'Isa [i.e. Jesus], the Prophet of God" and his encounter with the reanimated skull of a long-dead pagan king.[10]

Ca. 14th–16th century

Miniature Qur'an

Scrap of a miniscule Qur'an manuscript with a writing area just 2 inches wide. The image shown here is the actual size of the manuscript. Despite the space limitations, the scribe managed to fit six verses of Sura 2 (*The Cow*) onto this page. The place of origin is unclear, but the script style resembles certain Arabic manuscripts from Yemen and India.

Ca. 14th–16th century

T-S NS 183.79

Poetry for the Prophet

Classical Arabic poetry by the 14th-century Yemeni writer, ʿAbd al-Rahim al-Buraʿi. Al-Buraʿi is best known for his work in praise of the prophet Muhammad. This fragment preserves a poem embedded in a longer biographical narrative about Muhammad's life. The two columns are supposed to be read across together. This layout corresponds to the structure of Classical Arabic poetry, which often consists of blocks of half-line units forming rhyming couplets.

Ca. 15th–18th century

T-S NS 297.16

T-S Ar.42.145

Qur'anic Writing by Two Scribes

Two pages from a writing exercise containing passages from Sura 36 (*Ya Sin*) and Sura 37 (*The Ranked*) of the Qur'an. These leaves probably did not belong to a complete book, but rather were used to train a new scribe in the fine art of Arabic calligraphy. The page on the right clearly displays the consistency of an experienced hand – someone who has done this many times before. The page on the left shows heavier strokes and considerable variation in the letter shapes. This may have been a student trying to imitate the example of their teacher.[11]

Ca. 16th–18th century

T-S Ar.19.20

Biography of Muhammad

A late work of *sira* literature, a genre of Islamic writing about the biography of the prophet Muhammad. This book was copied during the Ottoman period on paper produced in Europe. It cites the earliest surviving *sira* author, the 8th-century historian Muhammad ibn Ishaq, as well as the 14th-century religious scholar Ibn Kathir al-Dimashqi.

Ca. 16th–18th century

Qur'anic Wall Hanging

Part of verse 255 of Sura 2 (*The Cow*), also known as the 'Throne Verse', intended to be hung on a wall. This verse is considered one of the most important passages in the Qur'an and is widely copied for its protective power. This fragment comes from a much larger sheet of paper that is blank on the back, suggesting it was not part of a book, but rather it had a decorative purpose. The script is a fine calligraphic *thuluth* style known from the Ottoman period.[12]

Ca. 16th–19th century

T-S Ar.19.7

Or.1080 14.60

Readings and Recitation

Table of prominent reciters of the Qur'an, beginning with the ten canonical 'readings' (known as *qira'at* in Arabic) in the righthand column. The other side of the page has excerpts about the Qur'an from two works by the renowned 15th-century scholar, Jalal al-Din al-Suyuti: his *History of the Caliphs* and his *Little Collection* of hadith.[13]

Ca. 19th century

Turkish Prayer Book

Booklet from the late Ottoman period with Turkish instructions for prayer. The Ottoman Empire conquered Egypt in 1517 and controlled Cairo for much of the remaining Genizah period. Like most Ottoman Turkish manuscripts, this one is written in Arabic script.

Ca. 19th century

T-S Ar.39.153

Notes to Chapter VII

1   Magdalen M. Connolly and Nick Posegay, 'A Survey of Personal-Use Qur'an Manuscripts Based on Fragments from the Cairo Genizah', *Journal of Qur'anic Studies* 23, no. 2 (2021): 5.

2   A potentially older manuscript is another Genizah fragment held in Budapest, known as MTA 198. See Anne Regourd, 'Arabic Documents from the Cairo Geniza in the David Kaufmann Collection in the Library of the Hungarian Academy of Sciences—Budapest', *Journal of Islamic Manuscripts* 3, no. 1 (2012): 1–19. Thank you to Athina Pfeiffer for her thoughts on the date of the script style.

3   Nick Posegay, 'Jewish Parchment, Muslim Prayer – Uncovering an Early Abbasid Palimpsest (T-S Ar.51.73)', *Fragment of the Month (June)*, Cambridge University Library: Genizah Research Unit, 2021.

4   Thank you to Kristine Rose-Beers (Head of Conservation at the Cambridge University Library) for spotting the fingerprint.

5   T-S Ar.39.83 is from the same manuscript.

6   Mohamed Ahmed has identified T-S Ar.38.3 as a small fragment of poetry from *The Unique Necklace* which may also belong to this manuscript. See Mohamed A. H. Ahmed, 'An Initial Survey of Arabic Poetry in the Cairo Genizah', *Al-Masāq* 30, no. 2 (2018): 228.

7   Thank you to Ayala Meyer Eliyahu and Sarah Stroumsa for first identifying this fragment for the Friedberg Genizah Project.

8   The other copy is T-S AS 155.397, recently identified by Alan Elbaum and Moshe Yagur, which displays an earlier form of Judaeo-Arabic writing that may date to the 10th century; https://geniza.princeton.edu/en/documents/37995/. For a full translation of the letter, see Hartwig Hirschfeld, 'The Arabic Portion of the Cairo Genizah at Cambridge,' *The Jewish Quarterly Review* 15, no. 2 (1903).

9   Colin F. Baker and Meira R.P. Polliack, *Arabic and Judeo-Arabic Manuscripts in the Cambridge Genizah Collections: Taylor-Schechter Arabic Old Series (T-S Ar.1a-54)*, Cambridge Genizah Series 12 (Cambridge: Cambridge University Press, 2001).

10 See Magdalen M. Connolly, 'Qiṣṣat al-ğumğuma: An Arabic-Script Version of the Narrative in the Cairo Genizah Collections' in *From the Battlefield of Books: Essays Celebrating 50 Years of the Taylor-Schechter Genizah Research Unit*, eds. Nick Posegay, Magdalen M. Connolly, and Ben Outhwaite. Leiden: Brill, 2024.

11 Magdalen M. Connolly and Nick Posegay, 'A Survey of Personal-Use Qur'an Manuscripts Based on Fragments from the Cairo Genizah', *Journal of Qur'anic Studies* 23, no. 2 (2021): 20.

12 Magdalen M. Connolly and Nick Posegay, 'A Survey of Personal-Use Qur'an Manuscripts Based on Fragments from the Cairo Genizah', *Journal of Qur'anic Studies* 23, no. 2 (2021): 18-19.

13 Thank you to Ayala Meyer Eliyahu and Sarah Stroumsa for first identifying this fragment for the Friedberg Genizah Project.

VIII (a).
Documents

When we talk about Genizah 'documents', we don't mean just any old piece of paper or parchment. Instead, 'document' distinguishes a genre of writing that is not literature, magical, educational, or liturgical, but is informational or evidential: most documents are legal deeds that govern relationships between individuals or facilitate record-keeping. They are often – though not always – produced by agents with communal or governmental authority. They include transaction receipts, financial records, court testimonies, business contracts, and petitions to rulers.

This chapter comes in two parts. Part (a) contains a variety of document types written both by Jews and by members of the Islamic governments in Egypt. Part (b) contains only a special type of document called a *ketubbah*, a Jewish marriage contract, one of the most ubiquitous documents in Jewish archives. Not only are ketubbot very common in the Cairo Genizah, they are often artistically distinct from other legal documents.

Recycled Ikshidid Document

Arabic fiscal document from the Ikshidid chancellory, mentioning two key figures: Muhammad ibn Tughj and Abu al-Misk Kafur. Ibn Tughj, also simply called "the Ikshid," was an Abbasid governor who established the Ikshidid dynasty as the autonomous rulers of Egypt in 935 CE. Kafur was an enslaved black servant, most likely from Nubia, whom Ibn Tughj freed and appointed to educate his two sons. He later became a military officer and a diplomat. When Ibn Tughj died in 946, Kafur assumed guardianship of the Ikshidid princes and took control as the *de facto* leader of Egypt. He ruled until his own death in 968, just one year before the Fatimids conquered Fustat. This document found its way to the Jewish community, who used it to copy liturgical poetry (specifically *yoserot*) by Solomon Sulayman al-Sinjari, even across and between the lines of the existing Arabic document.[1]

940–41 CE

T-S NS 139.65

Mosseri Ia.1.2

Judaeo-Persian Settlement

Record of a court settlement written in Judaeo-Persian (Persian in Hebrew characters). The people involved in the case were Karaite Jews, part of a growing Jewish community that rivalled Rabbinic Judaism in some parts of Iraq and Iran (☛ Chapter I). The final lines include signatures from men named Ibn Ismaʿil, Abraham ben Padawi, and Saʿid ha-Levi. This is one of the earliest dated Karaite documents and one of the earliest Judaeo-Persian manuscripts known in the world.[2]

951 CE

Illuminated Arabic Document

This manuscript is unlike any other document in this chapter. It is clearly Islamic, with oversized Arabic calligraphy repeating the phrase "sovereignty is God's" (*al-mulk lillah*) in a band along the top. The second band has drawings of three animals – a rabbit, a scimitar oryx, and what is perhaps a peacock – between floral motifs, one of which still has a bit of gold leaf at its centre. The text below is so badly damaged it has proven almost impossible to decipher, yet we are sure it begins with the *tasliya* ("may God bless our lord Muhammad, His prophet, and his family…"), a standard formula at the start of Fatimid documents. There also appear to be remnants of a witness signature near the bottom, again consistent with the layout of legal documents. These features are at odds with the expensive artistic decoration that is not typically found in Islamic documents.

The closest comparison we have found for the bands of calligraphy are the patterns in *tiraz* textiles, a type of stylised Islamicate embroidery that incorporates inscriptions into fabric. Similar patterns, including the repeated phrase "sovereignty is God's," appear in textiles commissioned by the Fatimid Caliphs al-ʿAziz (975–996) and al-Hakim (996–1021). It therefore seems likely that this document was commissioned by a high-ranking member of the Fatimid Caliphate around that time. For what purpose, we still aren't sure.[3]

Ca. 975–1025 CE

T-S K10.12

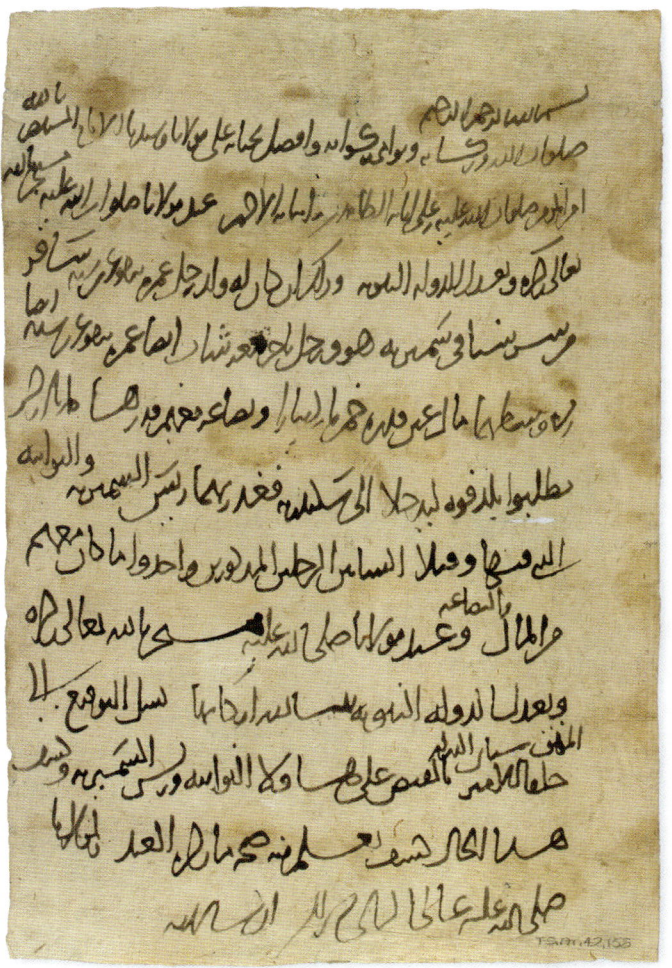

T-S Ar.42.158

Deaths on the Nile

In this petition, a grieving father asks the Fatimid Caliph al-Mustansir for justice concerning two homicides that took place on a Nile riverboat. A pair of Jewish merchants – including the son of the petitioner – were travelling to Alexandria with 500 dinars in cash and 200 more dinars worth of goods. That much wealth proved too great a temptation for the boat's crew, who betrayed and murdered both merchants before stealing their cargo. The petition requests that al-Mustansir authorise the local governor to arrest the captain and sailors for questioning.[4]

1036–1094 CE

Q: Why are chancery deeds and petitions found in the Genizah?

You wouldn't expect to find such a large cache of documents from Egypt's Islamic chanceries in a synagogue storeroom. A few petitions and government deeds might be there because they were produced by or dealt with matters concerning the Jewish community. Jews, alongside Christians, were *dhimmis* – protected minorities under Islam – and could directly petition the Islamic ruler to seek justice. Furthermore, many Jews are known to have served in the governmental bureaucracy, some even at the highest levels of the Islamic court. So it is also plausible that Jewish courtiers deposited their own documents into the Genizah chamber along with other papers. But this does not really explain the many Fatimid, Ayyubid, and Mamluk government documents in the Genizah that do not relate to Jews at all. They concern communications between different departments of the Islamic government, or their dealings with Muslim and Christian plaintiffs. How did these manuscripts find their way to the Ben Ezra synagogue?

The answer may be the value of paper and parchment as recyclable resources. Petitions were often written on large sheets with widely-spaced, grandiose lettering (petitioners didn't want the Caliph to have to squint!). After the petition had been dealt with, the government habitually disposed of them rather than maintaining a large archive. They sold them off as scrap paper, and that is how they came to be recycled for writing such things as letters, sermons, liturgical poetry, calendrical essays, and exercises for trainee scribes, before finally being consigned to the Genizah.[5]

Marriage in Jewish Egypt

Jewish marriage is formalised through a legal document known as a *ketubbah* ('marriage contract'). In the Middle Ages, Egypt's Jews also drew up other types of contracts as a relationship progressed toward marital union. Written engagement, betrothal, and pre-nuptial contracts often preceded the writing of a ketubbah, and each contract could have different legal stipulations depending on the situation of the couple. One unusual clause, preserved in ketubbot written according to the ancient Palestinian rite, entitled the bride to a divorce if she found that she 'hated' her husband.

L-G Misc. 42

Engagement Contract

This deed is the earliest known example of a Jewish engagement contract (*shetar shiddukhin*). Until the 12th century, engagement was an agreement between two families, often made years before the marriage took place while the couple were still children. Traditionally, it did not require a legally binding document. But with increasing numbers of Jewish men seeking their fortune on the long and dangerous Indian Ocean trade routes, the Egyptian community began to formalise engagement through a written deed. This allowed the bride-to-be and her family to assert her rights should her future husband deny the engagement after many years away. This fragment records the engagement of Sitt al-Kull ('Mistress of Everything') bat Perahyah and Toviyyah ben Tiqvah.[6]

1119 CE

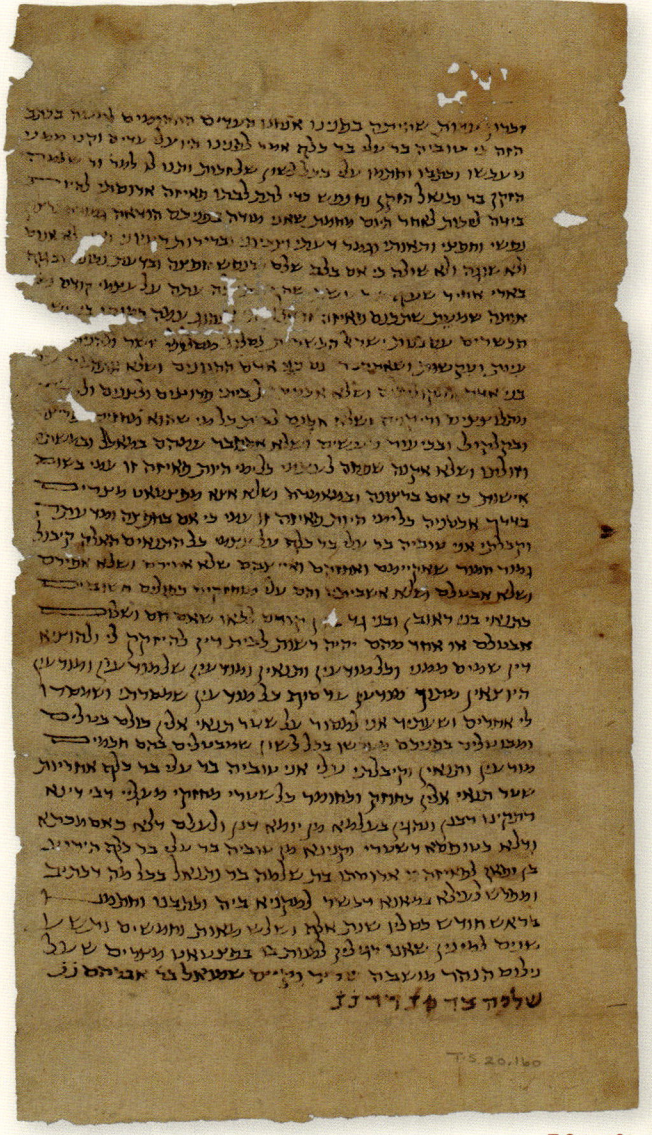

T-S 20.160

Prenuptial Agreement

Court testimony of a prenuptial agreement between Toviyyah ben Eli (known as Ibn Zaffan, 'son of the dancer') and his fiancée, Fa'iza bat Solomon. Toviyyah testified "of his own free will" to the Jewish court in Fustat: "I will not bring into my house licentious men, buffoons, frivolous jesters, and good-for-nothings … I will not associate with them for food and drink, or anything else. I will not purchase for myself a female slave, as long as Fa'iza is with me, except with her express permission…" Fa'iza's family were seemingly aware of Toviyyah's unsavoury bachelor habits, and, as he was probably marrying socially or financially above himself, he vowed – in humiliating detail – to behave himself after marriage.[7]

1048 CE

Q: Aren't prenuptial agreements a modern invention?

While modern 'pre-nups' focus on how assets should be divided in the event of divorce, the pre-nuptial contracts found in the Genizah aim to address problems that might arise during a marriage. This does sometimes include financial provisions, but as often they concern where the newlyweds should live, whether the wife should permit her husband to travel, whether she could be obliged to go with him (which could mean never seeing her family again), whether the husband could purchase an enslaved woman (for concubinage), and restrictions on the behaviour of both parties (would the husband be permitted to beat his wife and her relatives? would the wife be allowed to malign her mother-in-law?). Other clauses allow both sides to exit the marriage if promises were not kept. Most stipulations aimed to increase equality between the couple, establishing rights for the bride to which she would not otherwise be entitled. Her representatives could only negotiate terms up until the day of the wedding.

Trousseau List

Trousseau lists record the assets – jewellery, clothing, household goods, real estate, books, and enslaved servants – that a bride brought as a dowry into her marriage. This dowry (called *nedunya*) was entrusted to the groom, but the items or their equivalent cash value had to be returned to the bride in the event of divorce or her husband's death. In effect, this was an insurance policy to help ensure a woman's economic security and independence should the marriage fail. This bride's name is unknown, but her trousseau list reveals that she was fabulously wealthy – the wealthiest woman known from the Genizah. Her dowry includes a gold tiara (worth 80 dinars), a pair of peacock pins (18 dinars), an amber bowl with a gold rim (5 dinars), a crystal rooster (4 dinars), a pen-box made in China, with 2 knives, a sand sprinkler (for blotting), and an ivory plate (13 dinars), equipment for bloodletting (2 dinars), cloud-coloured festival attire consisting of a robe, a wimple, and a greyish headband (50 dinars), a green robe with gold threads and a wax-coloured wimple (5 dinars), a handbag of blue brocade (20 dinars), bedspreads, sofas and soft furnishings (198 dinars), copperware for lighting and washing (200 dinars), four enslaved women named ʿIzz, Dalal, Nusa, and Wafa (100 dinars), and 250 dinars worth of books. The total value of the bride's assets is the enormous sum of 2100 dinars.[8]

Ca. 1128–1153 CE

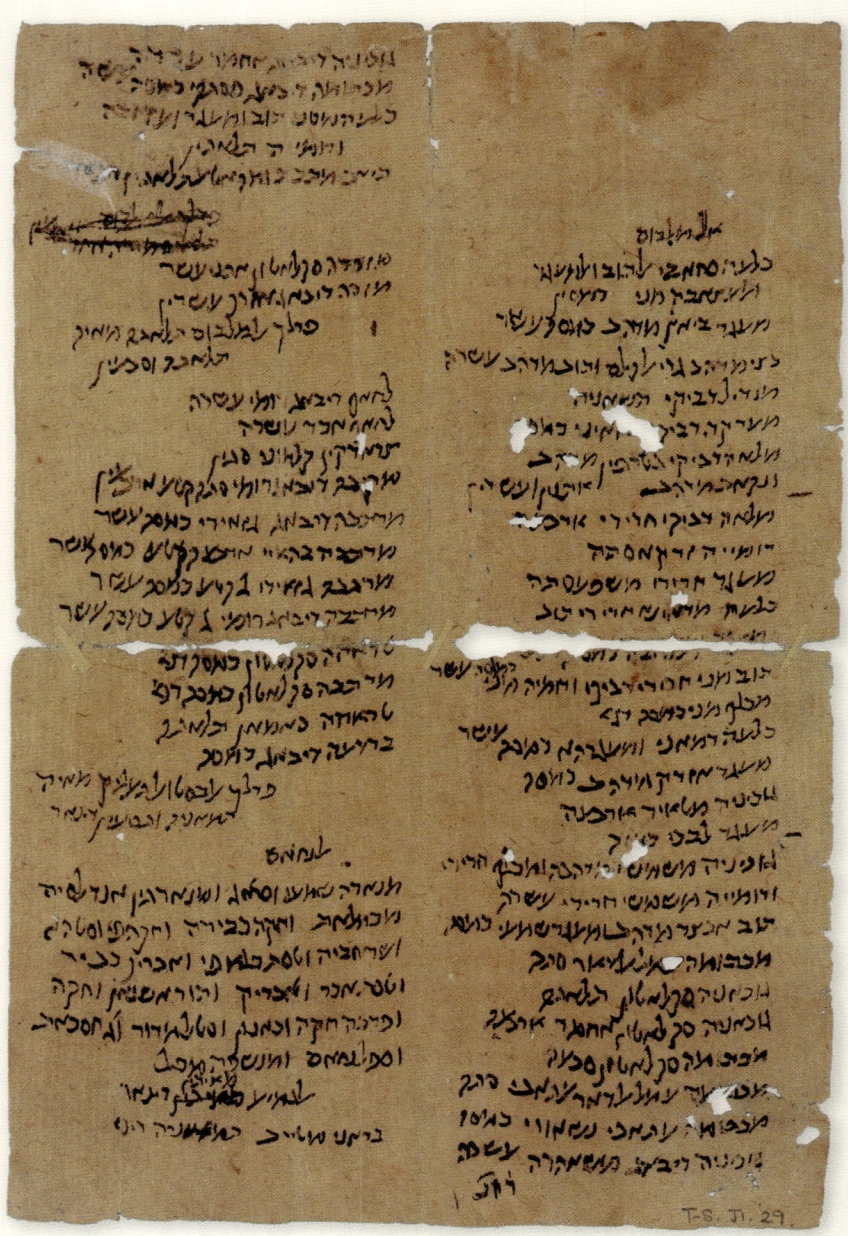

T-S J1.29

T-S 16.90

Marriage Contract

Part of a ketubbah from 1104 CE. The ceremony took place in Fustat, but the names of the witnesses and the newlyweds are lost. The fleurs-de-lis – here quite elaborate – are a common motif that scribes used to decorate the blessings at the top of ketubbot.

1104 CE

Bill of Divorce

Not all marriages lasted. This manuscript is a *get*, a Jewish deed of divorce traditionally written in Aramaic, with which Amram ha-Levi divorced his wife Mu'tazza bat 'Allun in Fustat. The large signatures at the bottom belong to David ben Shekhanyah and Muhsin ben Husayn – the document's scribe and the witness to the divorce, respectively.

1024 CE

T-S 10J2.1

A Good Christian Man?

According to this court record, two Muslim witnesses accused a Jewish woman of having an intimate relationship with a Christian doctor. They reported that they often saw her around his apothecary shop and claim to have spied on her for 40 days before informing a judge. Islamic authorities carefully supervised not only Muslim morals, but also those of their subject Christian and Jewish communities. Some citizens apparently felt justified in watching over other people's personal affairs to ensure they behaved morally.[9]

1063 CE

T-S 8.130

Or.1080 J93

A Remarkable Inventory

A list of items from Fustat's Babylonian (Iraqi) synagogue that were temporarily stored in the Palestinian (Ben Ezra) synagogue. It is written on the back of a marriage contract for a Karaite couple. The Babylonian and Palestinian Jewish congregations lived alongside each other in Egypt for much of the Genizah period, and this list shows us that they were not opposed to working together. It is also a clue. One of the items listed is 'a codex of the Torah said to be in the handwriting of Rabbi Saʿadyah." This refers to Saʿadyah ben Yusuf al-Fayyumi (d. 942), an Egyptian Jew (born in the Fayyum) who became the Gaon of the Jewish academy at Sura in Iraq. If the Torah supposedly copied by Saʿadyah was later deposited in a genizah, then it is possible that there are fragments of it somewhere in the Cairo Genizah collections. However, with only this vague description to go on, we would be unable to identify those fragments as his work, as no known examples of Saʿadyah's handwriting have ever been found.[10]

1080 CE

The Famous Murder Case

Top portion of a court record referring to "the famous murder case" of Sitt al-Husn bat Isaac and her mother, Sitt al-Bayt bat Mevorak. Sitt al-Husn's husband, Ummar, killed them both, but the court needed to determine who had died first. Why? The second victim would have inherited the entire estate of the first, and competing heirs were now claiming both estates. In the end, the two parties agreed to split the inheritance equally. This copy is in the hand of the prolific Genizah court clerk and scribe, Halfon ben Manasseh.

Ca. 1100–1138 CE

T-S 8.111

T-S Misc.8.25

Arabic Bread Lines

List of Jewish community members who received charitable distributions of bread, including a number of clearly European and Byzantine immigrants to Egypt. The list refers to "the orphans of the astrologer," "the mother-in-law of the son of the woman from Palestine," "the female washer of the dead of the Rum," "the acquaintance of the dyer," and "a semi paralysed woman." In one month, the total amount of bread distributed was around 3600 pounds (1633 kilograms), and cost the community 18 dinars. The list is in Judaeo-Arabic, and there's a formula used in Arabic letter writing on the back.[11]

1107 CE

Draft Document on Spare Parchment

Notes for the sale of part of a housing compound, valued at 220 dinars, featuring "an arched doorway, two corridors, a living room, a recess with a bench in it, marble columns, a ceiling, and a fountain," again written by the court clerk Halfon ben Manasseh. The homes bordering the property – which helped to place its exact location in legal terms – were inhabited by a scribe, a man with a "long neck," a Jewish woman, a Christian man, and a Muslim man. Living in an era when writing materials were sometimes in short supply, Halfon used this spare scrap of oddly-shaped parchment for his first draft of a deed of sale. He would have recopied it onto a more regular sheet later. Hundreds of legal documents and letters in Halfon's handwriting are preserved in the Genizah, as well as letters between him and his merchant brother, Yefet. Their entire family bore the nickname Ibn al-Qata'if, which means 'son of the pastries' (specifically, the crepe-like dessert also known as *kunafa*). This name may have reflected an ancestor's sweet nature – or sweet tooth![12]

Ca. 1120–1130 CE

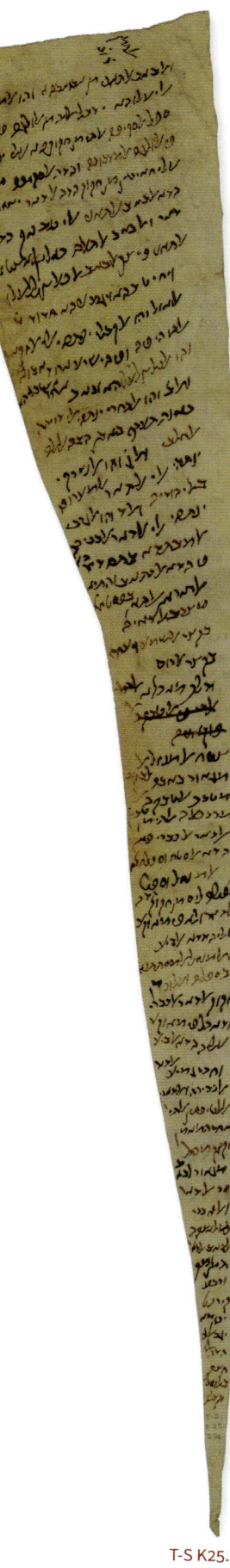

T-S K25.284

T-S Misc.29.24

Rental Agreement

Arabic legal document from July 1115 when Abu al-Futuh, a government clerk, leased a plot of land in Fustat to Ephraim ben Eli "the Jew." It notes that the plot borders the cemetery and another plot of land rented by a woman named Adwa bint ʿAskar. Witness signatures appear at the bottom. The back of the page was recycled for another document, written in May 1138, when Ephraim's son transferred the lease to his own son, Eli. Notice the holes in the parchment along the creases where the contract was constantly refolded over many years.

July 1115 – May 1138 CE

The Court of Public Opinion

Yom Kippur, the Jewish day of atonement, is normally a day of forgiveness, but Fustat's Babylonian Jewish community once used it to publicly shame a prominent woman by throwing her out of their synagogue. Karima bint 'Ammar – better known by her nickname al-Wuhsha ('the one without whom one feels lonely') – is mentioned in several Genizah manuscripts as a self-made businesswoman with a knack for flouting convention. Her crime in the eyes of her community? Having an affair with a married man and giving birth out of wedlock.

This document records the testimony of witnesses years later, in a court case where her 'illegitimate' son, denied by his father, attempts to prove his parentage before his own wedding. With typical foresight, Wuhsha had contrived to allow herself to be discovered *in flagrante* with her lover, by two upstanding members of the community. It is they who give their testimony in this document, thereby asserting her son's legitimacy in law. Wuhsha died five years after her excommunication. In her will, she left large sums of money to the synagogues of Fustat – including the one that excommunicated her – ensuring they would have to pray for her memory. To her hapless boyfriend, Hassun of Ashqelon, she left nothing besides forgiveness for the debts he owed her.[13]

Ca. 1129–1135 CE

T-S 10J7.10

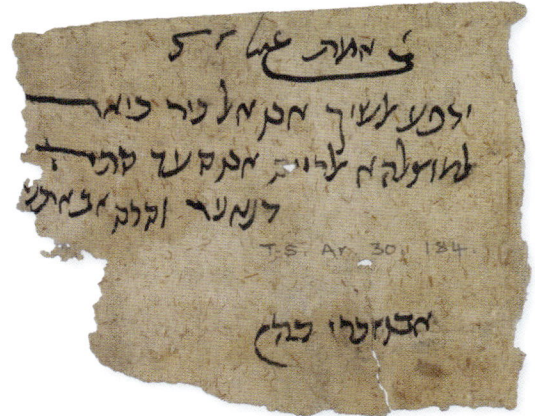

T-S Ar.30.184 P3

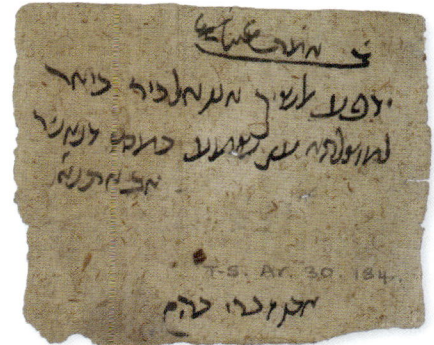

T-S Ar.30.184 P5

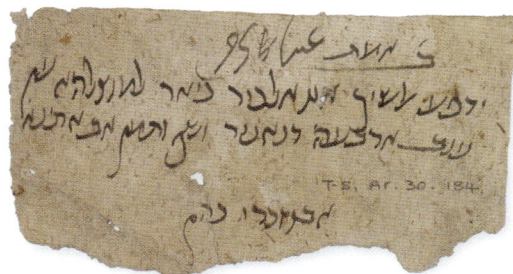

T-S Ar.30.184 P10

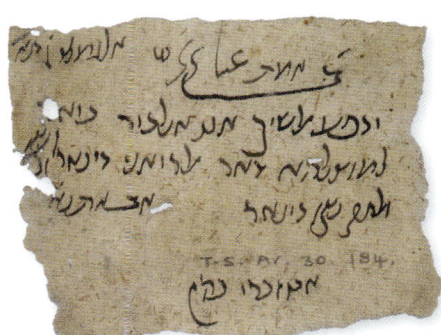

T-S Ar.30.184 P12

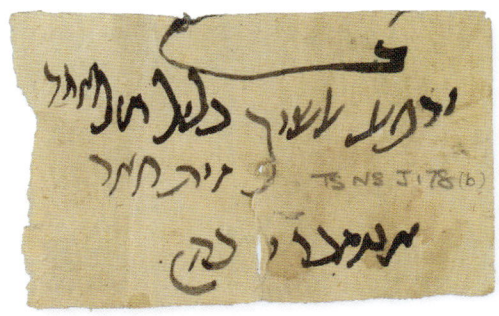

T-S NS J178(b)

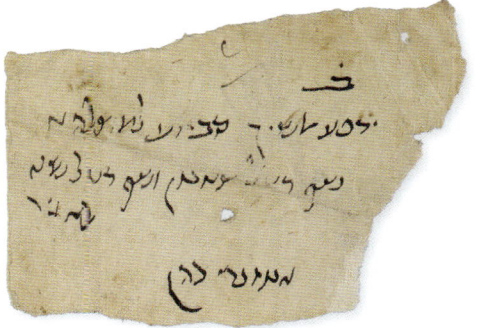

Mosseri II.158.3

Personal Cheques

These are some of the oldest cheques in the world. Orders of payment like this functioned as early 'paper money', allowing wealth to travel long distances w thout actual bags of gold making the dangerous journey. Coins, especially silver, were often in short supply in Egypt, and it was more convenient to write a note instructing your banker to pay out funds on your account. All of the cheques here were written by Abu Zikri Ko en, a prominent Jewish merchant, in the 1130s and 1140s. His cheques are for relatively small sums, such as five dinars to pay for an order of wax candles or one and a quarter dinars for an order of gum mastic.

Ca. 1130s–1140s CE

A Sweet Deal

Deed of sale in Judaeo-Arabic for one half of a sugar factory in Minyat Zifta, an important trade hub located in the eastern Nile Delta. The text notes that the surrounding properties had a mix of occupants of different faiths, including a Muslim *qadi* ('judge') and a Jewish "son of the Rav." Many manuscripts in the Cairo Genizah can be traced back to the Jewish community in Minyat Zifta.

Ca. 1140 CE

T-S 8.4

T-S 13J22.2

A Wealthy Woman's Last Will

When Sitt al-Husn, wife of Nathan ben Samuel, felt her death was imminent, she summoned witnesses to her bedside. It was Shabbat – Saturday – so nothing could be taken down in writing, but she was keen to make her wishes known. She was a woman of substantial wealth, and bequeathed most of her estate to her husband while arranging to sell part of it to cover her funeral expenses. She also freed her two enslaved maidservants – Dhahab and Sitt al-Samar – and bequeathed them a portion of her property "providing they remain of Jewish faith." After the Sabbath had passed, a local clerk drew up this will based on the testimony of those whom Sitt al-Husn had called.[14]

Ca. 1151 CE

Petition to the Fatimid Court

Petition sent by someone named Ja'far to the Fatimid government in Egypt, asking that they not withdraw support from him. Official petitions like this are fairly common in the collection, identifiable by their wide spacing and often monumental script. After they were processed in the state chancelleries, many petitions were repurposed as scrap paper. In this case, a Jewish writer used the back to list payments owed to a physician.[15]

12th century

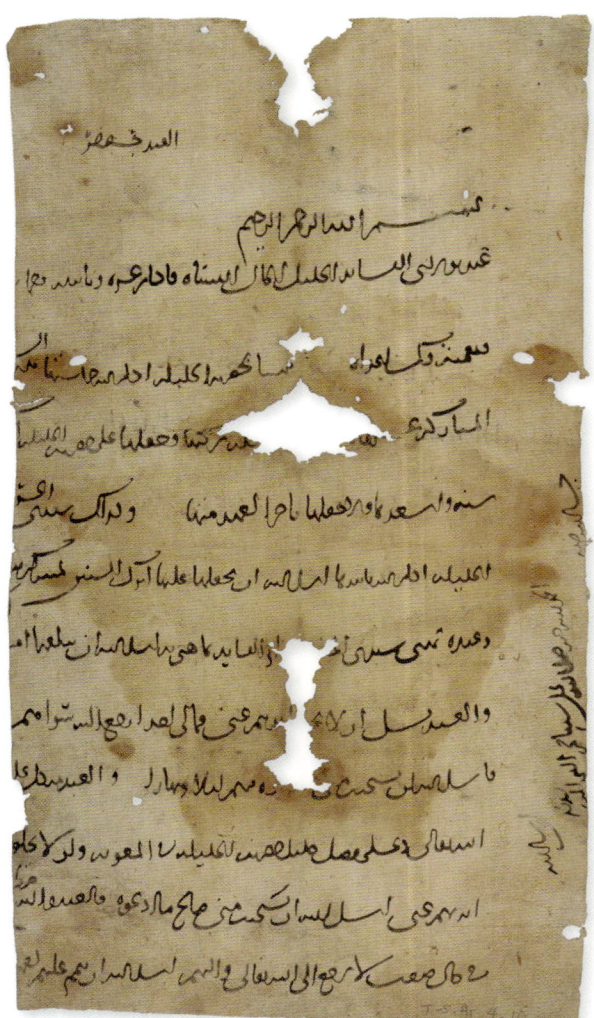

T-S Ar.4.10

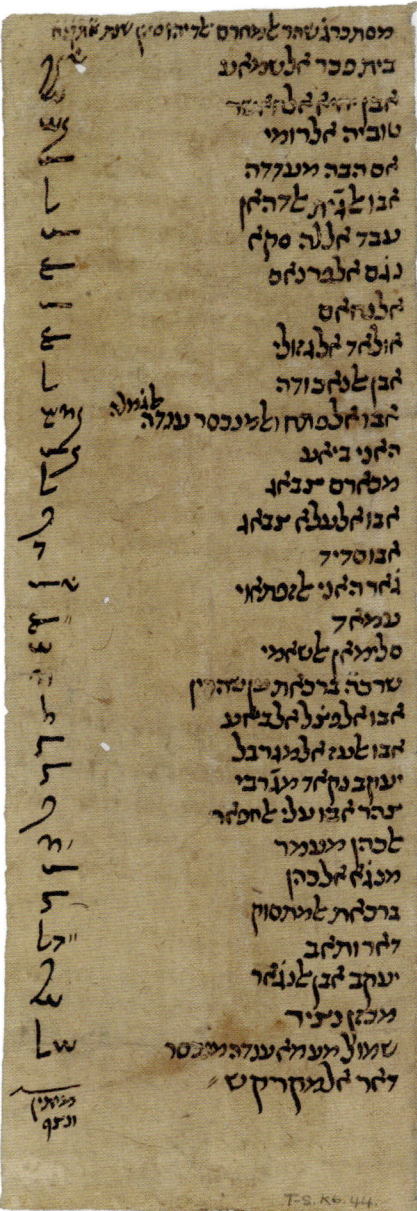

T-S K6.44

Charitable Accounts

Financial records for a Jewish charitable foundation, noting incomes and expenses, including some money accrued through renting out properties. The symbols in the left column frequently appear in accounting documents. They are called *zimam* numerals (sometimes also called 'Coptic' or 'Rumi' numerals, though those are in fact slightly different things). While they are mainly derived from the Coptic and Greek alphabets, they achieved widespread use among merchants and traders of various faiths and languages in medieval Egypt.[16]

1247 CE

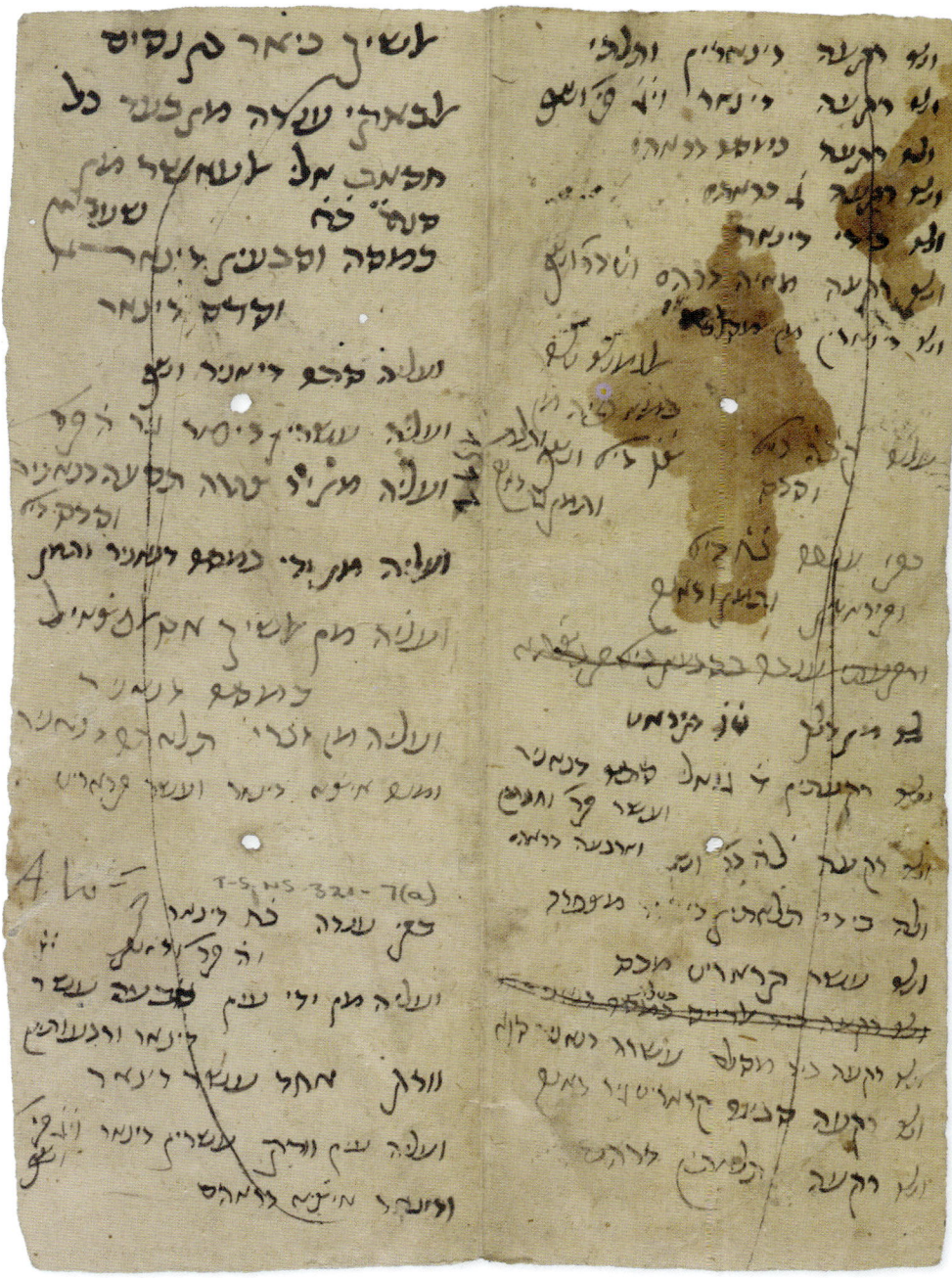

T-S NS 321.7a

Double-Entry Book-Keeping

Before the discovery of bankers' accounts in the Genizah, it was thought that the system of double-entry book-keeping was popularised in the Italian city-states of the 14th century. However, 'bilateral accounts' (separate columns for debits and credits) are widely attested in the Genizah from at least the 12th century, showing that modern accounting practices probably have much older roots.

12th century

Draft Contract for a Polygamous Marriage

Although most Jewish marriages were monogamous, some men did take multiple wives.
This is a rough draft of a ketubbah for a woman who was captured and held as a sex-slave,
most likely when Mamluk forces retook Acre from the Crusaders in 1291. A wealthy Egyptian
Jew, Abraham ben Solomon, paid her ransom and brought her back to Egypt. He waited
90 days to make sure she was not pregnant by her rapists, then offered to marry her as his
second wife – providing she would let him marry other women later on. Because of the
unusual circumstances of this 'match', the scribe made many changes to the document
before settling on the exact wording.[17]

Ca. 1291–1292 CE

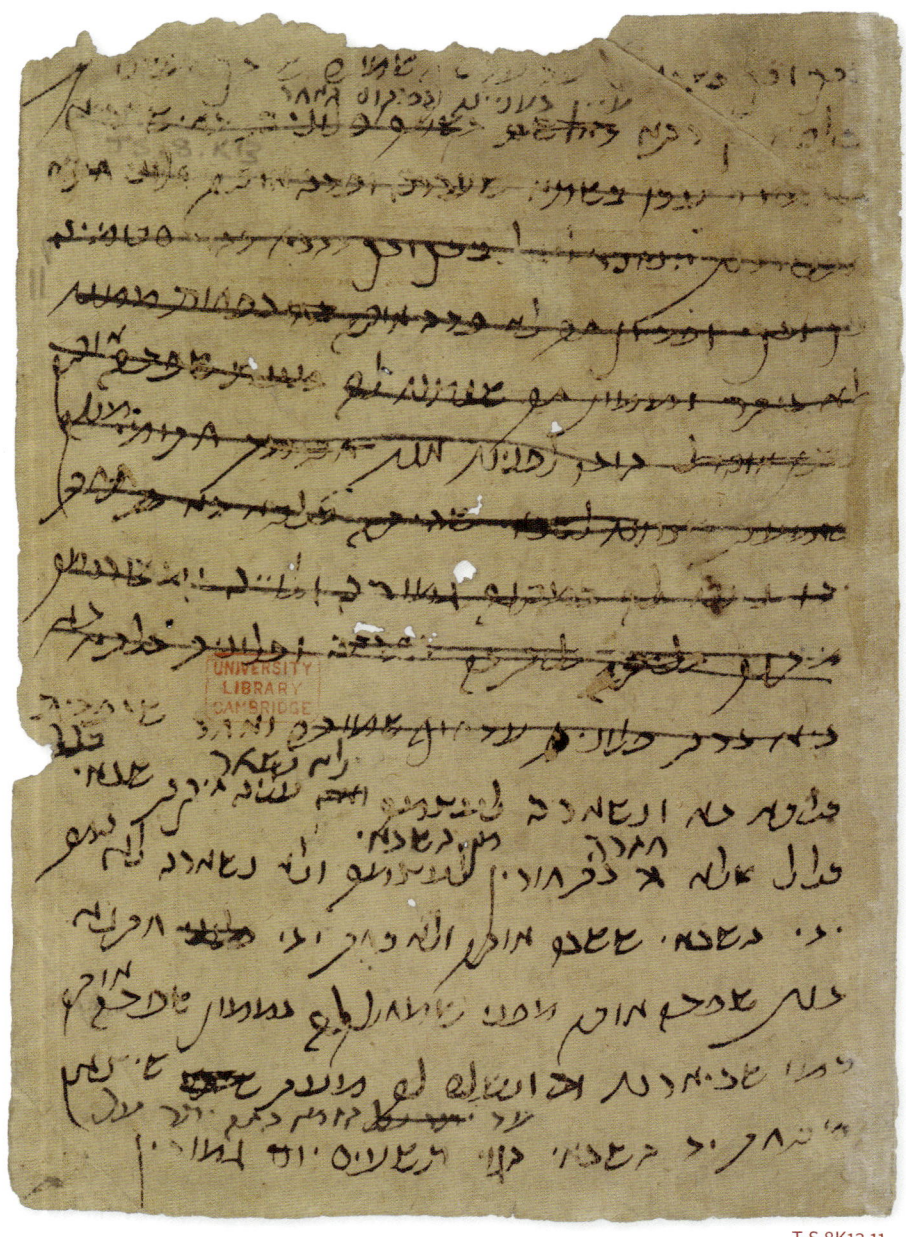

T-S 8K13.11

Climbing the Property Ladder

Arabic legal deed relating to the sale and resale of a house, the upper floor of which was in ruins (with the stairs removed). The initial buyer was a Jew named Ishaq ben Mansur, who purchased the property in 1317, but the document records at least eight additional sales, including one as late as 1349. If you look closely, you can see two red stamp seals used to approve the contents. Also notice the numerous horizontal creases where the parchment was folded up for easy storage or delivery between parties.[18]

Ca. 1317–1349 CE

T-S Ar.53.73

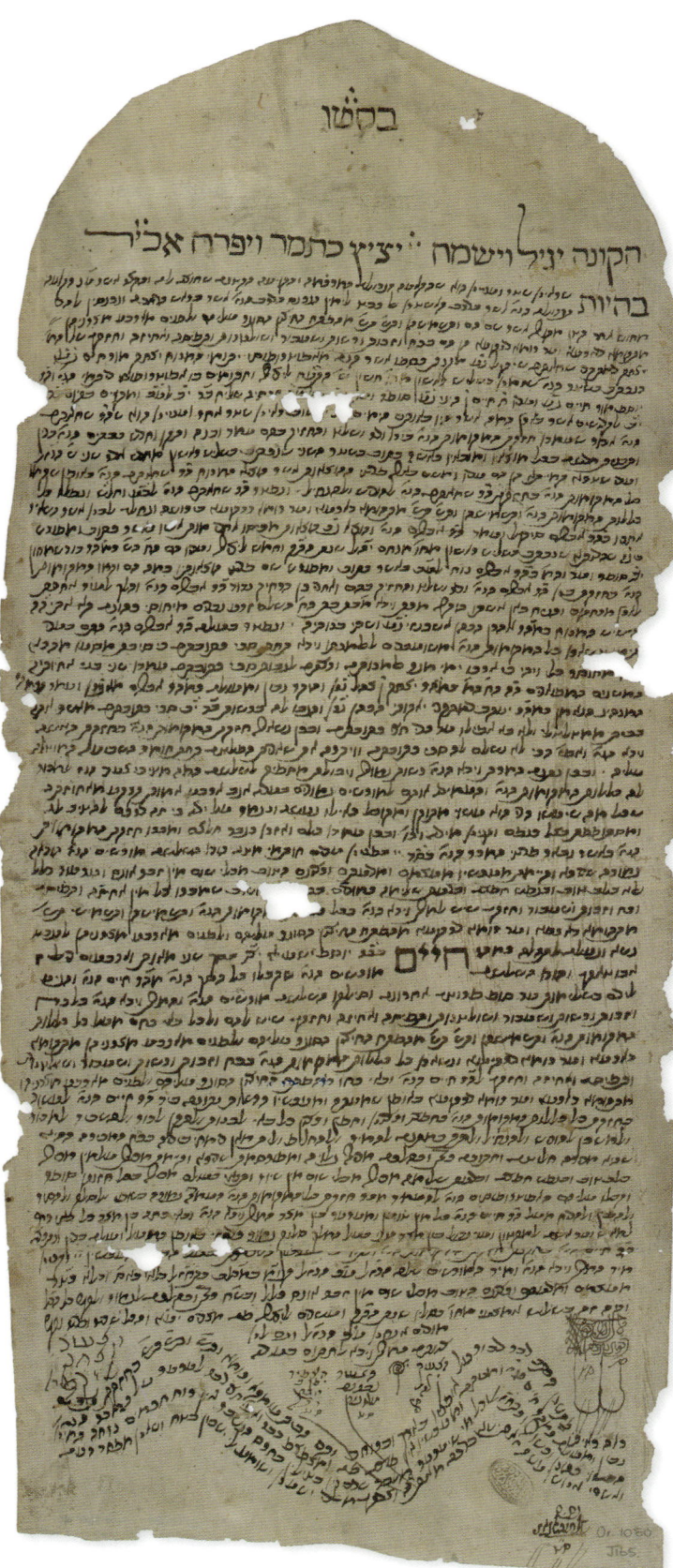

Artistic Hall Marks

Hebrew deed of sale for a large hall in Fustat, adorned with an Ottoman-era stamp seal and elaborate signatures. Interestingly, the shape and decoration of this document evoke the artistic designs of contemporaneous ketubbot (☛ Chapter VIIIb). Such a level of ornamentation is unusual for most legal documents in the Genizah.[19]

1759 CE

Or.1080 J165

Romantic Investment

Contract in Hebrew stating that a woman, Mercada bat Jacob Arubas, will invest money in the business of Samuel Elyon. The agreement was signed in Cairo. Mercada's name suggests her family originally came from a Romance-speaking country, likely Spain or Portugal. The top right corner has a stylised Hebrew abbreviation B''H, standing for *Barukh ha-Shem* ('blessed is the name [of God]'), a common feature in later Jewish documents. At the bottom, Samuel Elyon's decorative signature appears twice, using an elaborate style that became popular during the Ottoman period.

1761 CE

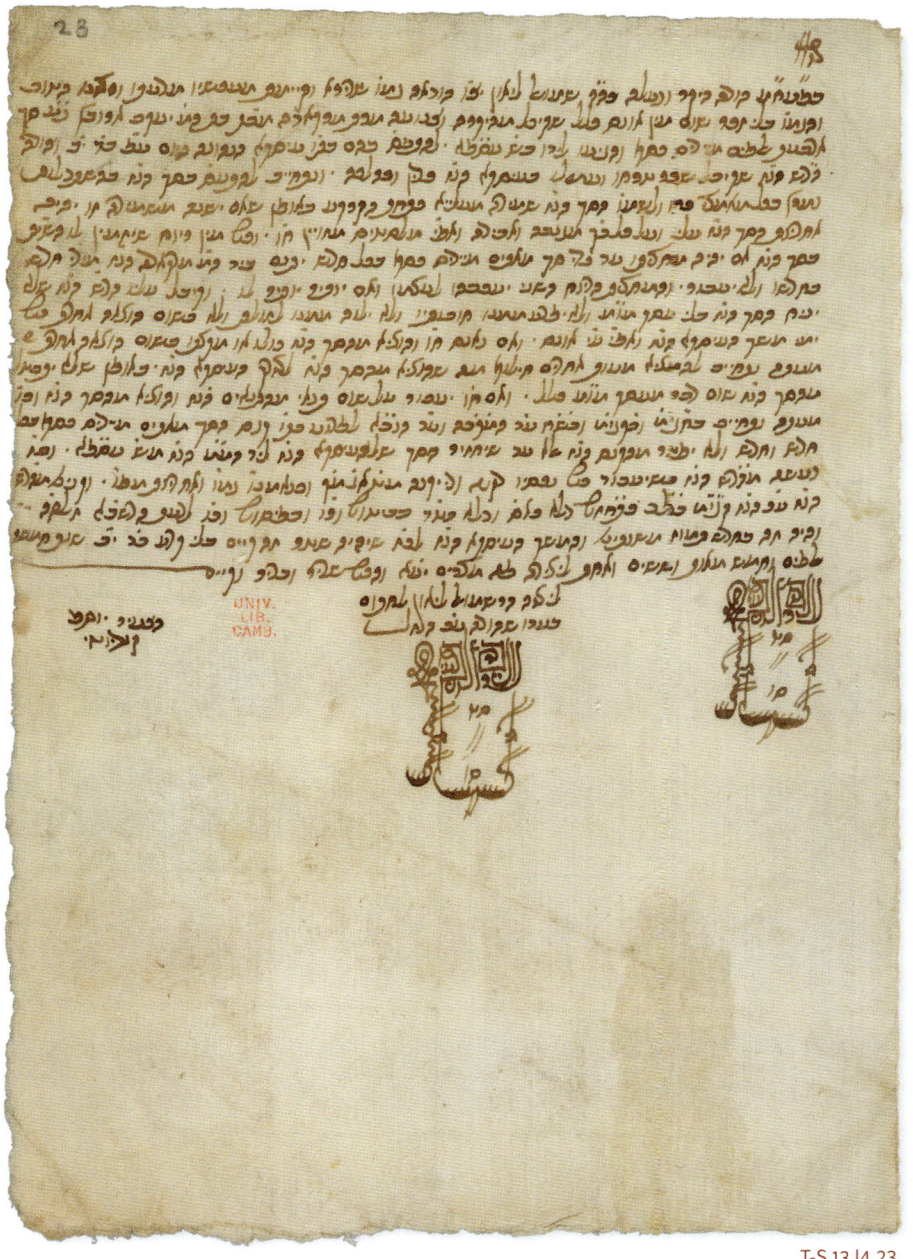

T-S 13J4.23

Notes to Chapter VIIIa

1   Identification and information in part from Alan Elbaum of the Princeton Geniza Project (https://geniza.princeton.edu/en/documents/23643/). Thank you to Dr Elbaum for suggesting this document for inclusion in this book.

2   Shaul Shaked, 'An Early Karaite Document In Judaeo-Persian', *Tarbiz* 41, no. 1 (1972): 49–58.

3   Bernard O'Kane, 'The Egyptian Art of the Tiraz in Fatimid Times', in *The World of the Fatimids* (Exhibition Catalogue), ed. Assadullah Souren Melikian-Chirvani (Toronto: Aga Khan Museum, 2018), 178–89.

4   Geoffrey Khan, *Arabic Legal and Administrative Documents in the Cambridge Genizah Collections*, ed. Stefan C. Reif, vol. 10, Genizah Series (Cambridge: Cambridge University Press, 2006), 33–331.

5   See Marina Rustow, *The Lost Archive: Traces of a Caliphate in a Cairo Synagogue* (Princeton University Press, 2020).

6   Identified by Amir Ashur. Translated by Amir Ashur and Ben Outhwaite in *Discarded History: the Genizah of Medieval Cairo*, exhibition catalogue (2017). https://doi.org/10.17863/CAM.13917.

7   Published by Mordecai Akiva Friedman, 'Pre-Nuptial Agreements with Grooms of Questionable Character: Two Documents from the Cairo Geniza' *Diné Israel* 6 (1975), CV–CXXII.

8   Shelomo Goitein, 'Three trousseaux of Jewish brides from the Fatimid period,' *AJS Review* 2 (Cambridge, United Kingdom: Cambridge University Press, 1977), 77–110.

9   Additional information, including the date and join, from Marina Rustow and Alan Elbaum of the Princeton Geniza Project (https://geniza.princeton.edu/en/documents/4020/).

10 See Amir Ashur, 'On Autographs of Saadya Gaon Attested in the Genizah: CUL Or.1080 1.85 and T-S 8D.1', *Fragment of the Month (January)*, Cambridge University Library: Genizah Research Unit, 2018.

11 Information in part from the Princeton Geniza Project (https://geniza.princeton.edu/en/documents/4643/); S.D. Goitein, *A Mediterranean Society*, Vol. 2, p. 443; and quotations from Mark Cohen, *The Voice of the Poor in the Middle Ages* (Princeton, New Jersey: Princeton University Press, 2005), no. 65.

12 S.D. Goitein, 'Geniza documents on the transfer and inspection of houses', *Revue de l'Occident musulman et de la Méditerranée*, 13–14 (1973), 406–410.

13 T-S Ar.4.5 is Wuhsha's will. In it, she leaves money for various purposes, including the education of her young son (though not enough to turn him into a scholar).

14 S. D. Goitein, 'Wills and Deathbed Declarations from the Cairo Geniza' (Heb.), in Meir Benayahu (ed.), *Izhak Ben-Zvi Memorial Volume* (*Sefunot* 8), vol. 1 (Jerusalem: Ben Zvi Institute, 1964), pp. 105–126; Moshe Gil, *Documents of the Jewish Pious Foundations from the Cairo Geniza* (Leiden: Brill, 1976), 270–274.

15 Geoffrey Khan, *Arabic Legal and Administrative Documents in the Cambridge Genizah Collections*, ed. Stefan C. Reif, vol. 10, Genizah Series (Cambridge: Cambridge University Press, 2006), 390–391.

16 See Stephen Chrisomalis, *Numerical Notation: A Comparative History* (Cambridge: Cambridge University Press, 2010), 150–175.

17 Mordechai Akiva Friedman, *Jewish Polygyny* (Heb.) (Tel Aviv: Bialik, 1986), 95–106.

18 Information from Alan Elbaum of the Princeton Geniza Project and Shelomo Goitein's notes (https://geniza.princeton.edu/en/documents/8319/).

19 Information in part from the Princeton Geniza Project (https://geniza.princeton.edu/en/documents/19792/).

VIII (b).
Ketubbot

One of the most distinctive types of Jewish document is the ketubbah (plural: *ketubbot*, from the Hebrew and Aramaic root *k-t-b* meaning 'to write'), the marriage contract that specifies the legal and financial arrangements of a marriage. The signing of the ketubbah represents the formal completion of the marriage process, which would have begun with engagement and betrothal.

The traditional ketubbah text was formulated in Aramaic, with roots that likely go back to the Second Temple period. The ketubbah specifies the traditional marriage gift (*mohar*) of 200 *zuz* (silver coins) the bride would receive (but only half if she had previously been married), as well as an additional financial gift promised by the groom. Most of this additional gift would only be paid on divorce or after the husband's death. The value of the bride's dowry – her trousseau, and any other assets she was bringing into the marriage – was specified, as well as a series of stipulations and mutual obligations enjoined upon the couple. The ketubbah contract is a fixed text today, but in the Middle Ages the formulae were still in flux and differences between communities are reflected in their writing of their ketubbot. The ancient Palestinian customs that lived on in some Egyptian Jewish communities included the husband's ketubbah obligation to pay his wife's ransom should she be kidnapped (from his own funds and not from her dowry), and grant the wife a right to receive a *get* (deed of divorce) if she 'hates' her husband. The ketubbah's legal status is validated by the signatures of at least two witnesses.

Ketubbot are one of the most common types of document preserved in the Cairo Genizah, since every married Jewish couple, no matter their status, would have had one. Unlike the legal documents in the first half of this chapter, scribes often decorated these contracts with calligraphic superscriptions with good wishes for the couple, joyful biblical verses, vibrant colours, artistic designs, and illustrations. As ketubbot are so visually unique, they have earned themselves a separate section in this book.

A Right to Divorce

It might seem odd to start a chapter on marriage contracts by discussing divorce, but part of a ketubbah's purpose was to secure a woman's legal and financial position in a marriage. For Jewish marriages contracted according to the Babylonian custom, which became the dominant tradition in Judaism, only the man could make the decision to divorce his wife. In Jewish marriages contracted according to the Palestinian custom, as was practised among the congregation that used the Genizah synagogue, women also had the right to request a divorce on no more grounds than that they disliked their husband. This is the surviving middle part of a large and nicely written ketubbah for a bride and groom named Maliha and Saʿid, containing the end of Maliha's dowry (valued at 456 and ⅓ dinars) and the stipulations for their marriage according to Jewish law. Since the couple wed according to the Palestinian custom, it specifies that Maliha will be entitled to a divorce if she 'hates' her husband and wants to leave his home: "If this Maliha hates this Saʿid, her husband, and desires to leave his home, she shall lose her ketubbah money, and she shall not take anything except that which she brought in from the house of her fathers alone; and she shall go out by the authorisation of the court and with the consent of our masters, the sages." The parchment was later recycled and the Hoshaʿnot liturgy for the end of the festival of Sukkot was written on the back.[1]

10th century

T-S 24.68

T-S.16.374

Jewish Marriage in the Byzantine Empire

This ketubbah documents a Jewish wedding that took place more than 1000 years ago in Mastaura, a Byzantine town on the banks of the River Meander (Maiandros) in Asia Minor. It includes the names of the newlyweds – Evdokia bat Caleb and Namer ben Elqana – along with the names of several witnesses. Evdokia's dowry is listed in a mix of Greek and Hebrew, including a pair of gold earrings, a small tablecloth, a 'double red' silk dress, a scarf, and a bag for bathing accessories. The irregular curve on the right side is probably from a natural curve around a limb of the animal whose hide was used to make the parchment.[2]

1022 CE

T-S 16.123

On Again, Off Again

Sarwa bat Mevorakh and Marwan ben Toviyya had a tumultuous relationship. This is the ketubbah for their second marriage, drawn up in Ramla in 1052. Like their first marriage to each other, this one also seems to have ended in divorce – the vertical lines drawn through the contract marked it out as officially cancelled after the marriage was dissolved. The fold lines and rows of sewing holes suggest that a bookbinder later recycled this parchment to reinforce the cover of a book.[3]

1052 CE

T-S 16.73

A Marriage in Tatters

A badly torn fragment of a decorated ketubbah, preserving some of a monumental superscription in red and gold with fleurs-de-lis and other foliate designs. Few details are preserved, but we think it was written by Hillel ben Eli, the leading scribe of the Fustat Bet Din (Rabbinical court) in the second half of the 11th century. Our classmarks that begin with just a number (8, 12, 16, 20, 24, etc.) indicate the size (in inches) of glass plates that were originally used to hold the fragments in the early 20th century, so this is a large fragment from what would have been an even larger document.

Ca. 1080 CE

T-S 24.1

A Mixed Marriage

This ketubbah is a rare example of a mixed marriage. Although they were both Jewish, the bride, Nashiyya bat Moses, was a Karaite, while the groom, David ha-Nasi ben Daniel, was a mainstream Rabbanite. Since customs varied greatly between the two denominations, the ketubbah sets out in detail how the couple will manage their differences: David will not force his wife to sit in candlelight on Shabbat (Karaites did not approve of the rabbis' accommodations to biblical law) and they will both respect each other's festivals. Many witnesses signed at the bottom of the contract that marked the political union between two powerful families: David was the son of the Head of the Jerusalem Academy who would later assume the title of Exilarch ('Head of the Diaspora'). Nashiyya was the daughter of a leading Karaite courtier, Moses ha-Kohen ben Aaron. The dowry was more than 1100 dinars.

1082 CE

Karaite Micrography

Fragment from the superscription of a decorative ketubbah, with ornamental geometric shapes drawn with minutely-written biblical verses (a technique known as 'micrography'). Freehand flowers at the centre of each square have been embellished with blobs of gold paint. The marriage was probably Karaite, as the biblical verses chosen (like Ruth 4:9) are also used in other Karaite ketubbot.[4]

Ca. 11th–12th century

T-S 8.90

A Half-Price Bride

A near-complete ketubbah from Fustat for Sittut bat Tahor and Meshullam ben David, dated Kislev 1414 according to the Seleucid calendar (= November 1102 CE). A note between the lines says that Sittut was the divorcee of Yefet ben Khiyyar, so her *mohar* (the money paid by the groom) is listed as 12 and a half *zuz*, only half the amount expected had she been 'a virgin' entering her first marriage. At the end of the document, the scribe states that he inserted the note about Sittut's ex-husband, ensuring that it would not be mistaken for an unauthorised change. The document also notes that Sittut produced her *get* ('deed of divorce') from her ex-husband and it was ritually shredded in front of the witnesses.

1102 CE

Or.1080 J289

T-S 16.52

Fustat Fleurs-de-Lis

Ketubbah for a wedding in Fustat between a divorcée, Turfa bat Nathan, and a cantor, Sedaqa ben Yefet. Turfa's dowry was quite meagre, consisting of clothing worth just 5 dinars. This makes her one of the poorest women whose ketubbah we still have. Despite her tenuous financial situation, her ketubbah – written by the prolific court clerk, Halfon ben Manasseh – is on a large piece of parchment and even has some decoration.

January 1124 CE

T-5,16,107

Jewish Marriage in Aleppo

Part of a ketubbah from a wedding that took place in Aleppo, Syria in 1107 CE. The names are mostly lost, but the bride was known as Bat Menahem and a man called Josiah ben Yivhar witnessed the ceremony. It seems that the couple must have emigrated from Aleppo to Egypt afterwards, as the ketubbah found its way into the Genizah. Someone used the back of the document to practise writing the Hebrew alphabet, perhaps one of the couple's children.

1107 CE

T-S 16.107

Remarried in the 12th Century

Part of a ketubbah for a divorcee, Sitt al-Ma'ali bat Hesed, who is marrying David ben Tahor. The date is lost, but signatures of several witnesses survive, including some people we know were alive during the early 12th century. Probably copied in Fustat, Egypt.

Ca. 1125 CE

Lyrical Calligraphy

Part of a large and highly artistic ketubbah for the marriage of Sitt al-Sada bat Obadiah and Nathan ben David, in Cairo. This fragment is from the upper lefthand side of the manuscript, and other pieces from the contract's superscription are found among the Genizah manuscripts in Oxford's Bodleian Library. The original would have been visually stunning, with ornamental borders in blue and gold, calligraphy, and micrographic poetry by the 11th-century poet Yinnon bar Semah. The high standard of decoration is similar to the elaborate 'carpet pages' found in prestigious Bible codices (so much so that the Cambridge fragment was originally thought to be a page from a Bible).

Ca. 12th century

T-S K10.4

T-S 20.62

A Seven-Year Itch

Two fragments of a ketubbah for the marriage of Sitt al-Ahl ('Mistress of the Family') bat Yefet and Joshua ben Samuel ben Judah. It was written in Fustat in 1125 CE by the clerk of the Jewish court, Halfon ben Manasseh ha-Levi. Two notes on the back reveal more about the marriage: Sitt al-Ahl's mother gave a gift to the newlyweds the next year, and seven years later, Joshua swore an oath to divorce Sitt al-Ahl. He soon changed his mind, but since an oath had been sworn, he was obliged to go through with the divorce and a remarriage ceremony in 1132 CE.

1125 CE

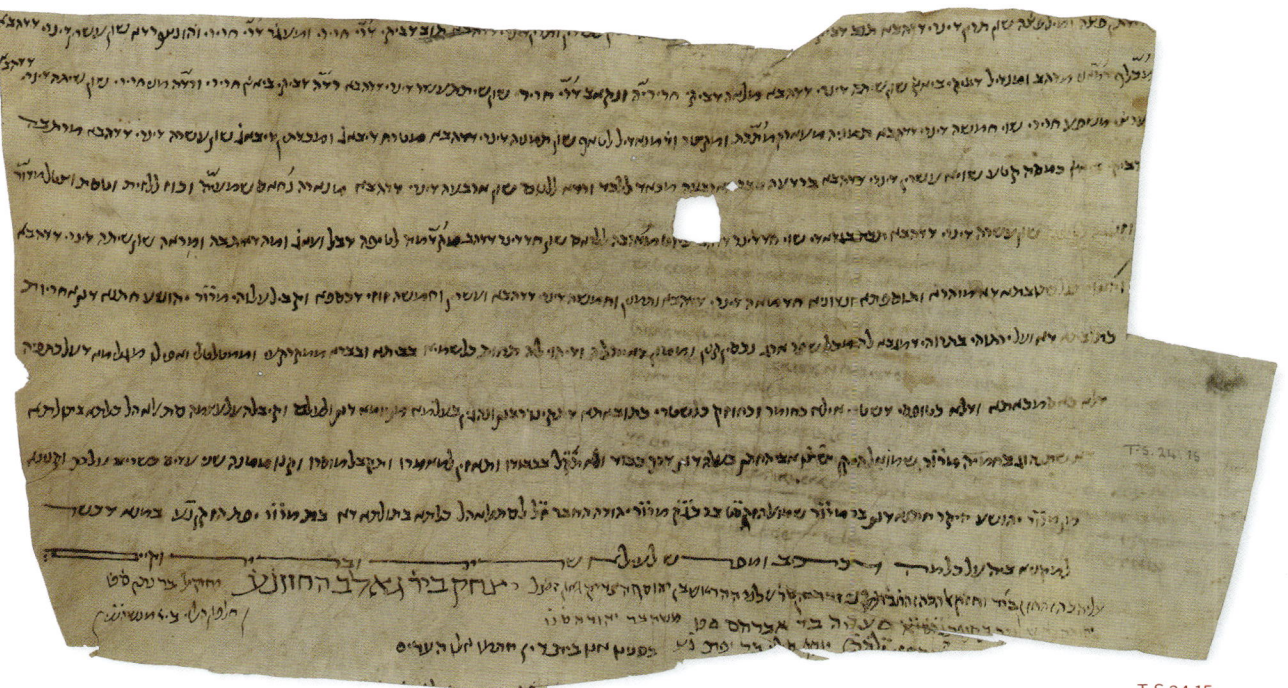

T-S 24.15

Delayed Matrimony

Part of an elaborately decorated ketubbah, written by the scribe Joseph ben Samuel ben Saʿadyah ha-Levi in Fustat in the late 12th century. Much of the text is lost, but the bride's name was Khibaʾ and her husband was one of the two sons of Levi ha-Levi the Cantor. The scribe changed the surviving portion of the date from "Tuesday the 10th" to "Wednesday the 11th." Did something delay the ceremony?

12th century

T-S 24.17

Red and Gold and a Gaon

Fragments of a beautiful ketubbah commemorating a wedding in Fustat for an unknown couple. The date is also missing, but the marriage was contracted under the authority of Gaon Sar Shalom ha-Levi, head of the Jews in Egypt at the time of Moses Maimonides.

Ca. 1170 CE

T-S NS 324.100

T-S 16.104

T-S 16.76

Marriage in the Time of David Maimonides

Fragmentary ketubbah documenting the marriage of Ratab bat Isaac
ha-Kohen ha-Sar and Yeshua ha-Kohen. It was written in Fustat under
the jurisdiction of David Maimonides, grandson of the famous Jewish
philosopher, Moses Maimonides. The Maimonides family led the
Egyptian Jewish community for five generations.

1292 CE

A Widow and an Italian Groom

Part of a ketubbah from the Ottoman period for a wedding "in the city of Cairo" between a widow named Rachel and the son of one Michael Viroti. Their full names and the names of the witnesses are lost. Part of the dowry gives values in *bunduqs*, a type of Venetian gold coin also known as *ducats* or *sequins*.

1567 CE

T-S 16.113

Or.1080 J83

A Habsburg Dowry

Parchment ketubbah for the marriage of Judah Mas'ud ben Moses Mas'ud and Sitt al-Bayt ('Mistress of the Household') bat Abraham Me'ir, dated 14 Nisan 5532 (= 1772 CE), in Cairo. The border is decorated with gold and tulip designs, and the parchment is cut and shaped at the top. The bridal payment, like the couple's names, is given in large letters to make it stand out: 300 *abu taqa riyyals*. The term *abu taqa*, literally 'father of the little window', was the Egyptian Arabic nickname for the Austrian *thaler* that began circulating in Cairo during the 18th century (given for the resemblance of the Habsburg crest to a window frame!).

April 17th, 1772 CE

Ottoman Love Birds

A painted ketubbah for the wedding of Esther Tantan bat Elijah Reuben and Raphael Tortosh ben Mercado, dated 30 August 1816 CE. They married in Cairo and Esther had a dowry listed as 110,000 silver *medins*. Three witness signatures appear at the end of the text.

August 30th, 1816 CE

T-S 16.332

Zodiacs and a Portrait

A ketubbah in a late Sefardi hand for the
marriage of Hayy Dayyan ben David Dayyan and
Mazal Tov bat Judah Dayyan, dated April 1821.
The wedded couple were probably paternal
cousins. The paper is cut in the shape of a
dome, with a design depicting birds, trees,
and a building overseen by a sun and
an eye. The bride and groom sit
within one room, holding
hands. The 12 signs of the
zodiac line the border.

April 16th, 1821 CE

Or.1080 9.21

Add.3124b

Vine Art

Decorated ketubbah for the marriage of Moses ben Abraham and Esther Aziza bat Joseph, both Karaites, in Cairo on 12 Adar 5612 (= 3 March 1852 CE). The border has a leafy vine design in red and green, with a quote from Genesis 49:22 at the bottom that continues the agricultural theme: "Joseph is a fruitful branch, a fruitful branch by a spring." We aren't exactly sure how this fragment came to Cambridge. It is conserved with another ketubbah (Add.3124a) from the 13th century that was purchased from the Jerusalem bookdealer, Solomon Wertheimer, in 1893. This later ketubbah could have come from Wertheimer or been mixed up with the other after it arrived in Cambridge.

March 3rd, 1852 CE

Notes to Chapter VIIIb

1   M.A. Friedman, *Jewish Marriage in Palestine: A Cairo Geniza Study. Volume II: The Ketubba Texts* (1981), 53–58.

2   J.G. Krivoruchko, 'Code-switching in medieval Judeo-Greek texts from Cairo Genizah', *Studies in Modern Greek Dialects and Linguistic Theory* (2011), 282–283.

3   M.A. Friedman, *Jewish Marriage in Palestine: A Cairo Geniza Study*. Volume II: The *Ketubba* Texts (1981), 155–165.

4   Judith Olszowy-Schlanger, *Karaite Marriage Documents from the Cairo Geniza: Legal Tradition and Community Life in Mediaeval Egypt and Palestine* (Leiden: Brill, 1998), 323.

IX.
Education

Cairo Genizah manuscripts offer a rare glimpse into the Jewish schoolrooms of medieval Egypt. They reveal a literate society where most Jewish children – girls as well as boys – were given at least a basic education, if not at school then with private tutors. The Hebrew Bible formed the focus of this education, and Hebrew was taught so that the children would be equipped with the skills to enable them to take part in the synagogue service and read the Torah. As writing material became more plentiful through the introduction of paper to Egypt, all children gained the means to practise writing Hebrew as well as simply reading it. Hundreds of their writing exercises now survive in the Genizah. Children first studied the Hebrew alphabet and vowel signs, copied while sitting cross-legged on the floor and balancing writing boards on their knees. Once they conquered the alphabet, they progressed to passages from *Vayyiqra*, the biblical book of Leviticus. Books were a precious commodity, so they were often shared between several pupils in the schoolroom. Children learned to read upside-down or sideways so they could follow the lesson from wherever they sat.

Letters from the Genizah often show parents expressing concern about their children's education, fretting about the quality of their lessons, bursting with pride at their accomplishments, or worrying about their teacher's fees. The education of the poor or orphaned children was usually the responsibility of Jewish charitable organisations, which paid their school fees, sometimes at a reduced rate. Educating children was a key aim for the community. On top of basic schooling in literacy and Jewish texts, it was considered important for many children to learn a useful trade. Parents paid apprenticeship fees – sometimes for years – to ensure older children could train with an expert craftsperson.

School Bullies Break a Tablet

A Jewish teacher sent this note home to the father of a victim of school bullying. The children mentioned are Jewish, but are referred to by their Arabic *kunya* (nickname): "I would like to inform my lord the shaykh… that Abu al-Hasan, no sooner had he been given over into my care, than his eye was on his schoolwork… But another child called Abu al-Hasan ibn Wuhayb rose up and broke his writing-board with the full knowledge of the other boys!" The writing-board in question would have been a small piece of wood laid across the knees – a portable table.[1]

Ca. 11th–12th century

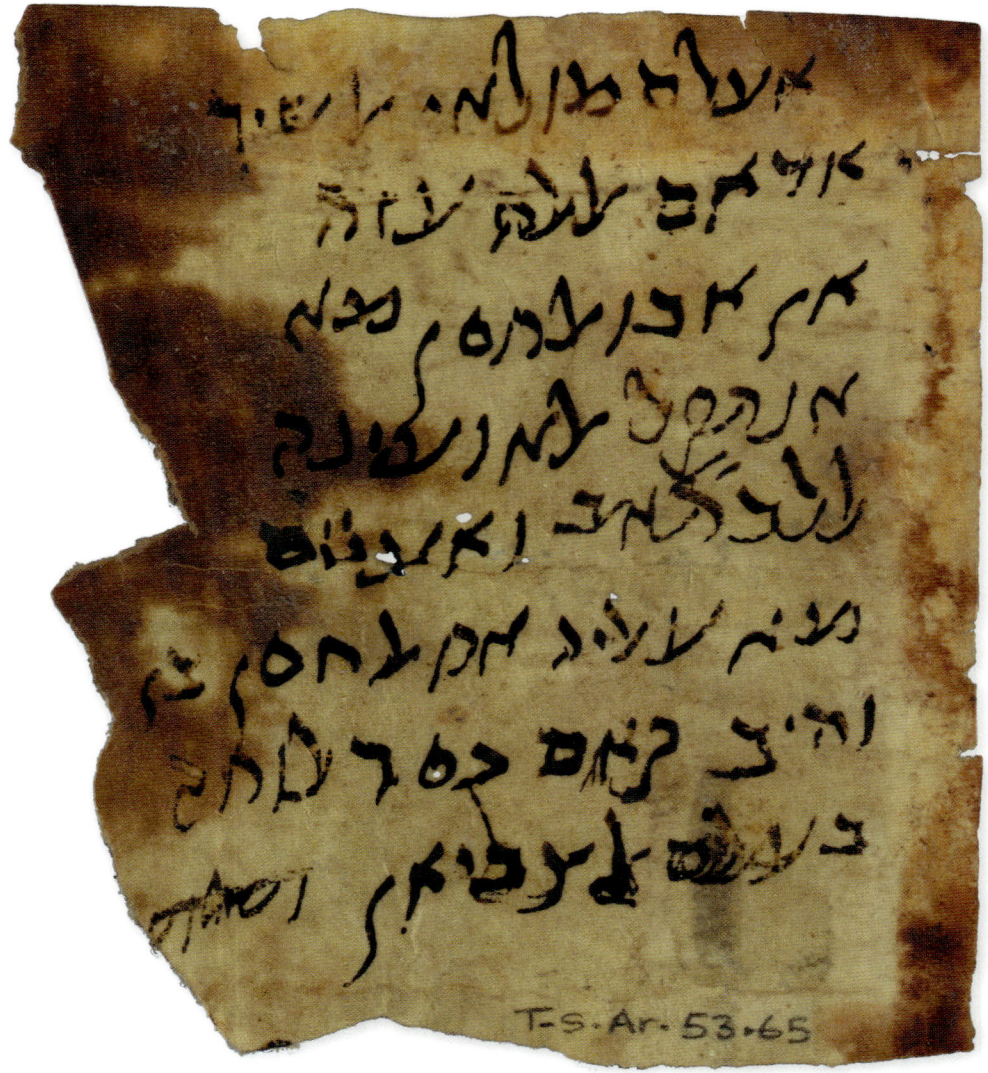

T-S Ar.53.65

T-S Ar.5.58

Arabic Biblical Glossary

Glossary of Hebrew words from the biblical book of Samuel (chapters 17–19). The first and third columns (from the right) give the Hebrew words, while the second and fourth columns give Arabic translations. The Arabic is written in Hebrew characters with full vowel signs, preserving its exact pronunciation in the writer's Egyptian dialect. Most Cairene Jews were native Arabic speakers, so Hebrew-Arabic glossaries such as this helped them learn to read the Hebrew Bible.[2]

Ca. 11th–12th century

Corresponding about Curricula

Much of what we know about medieval children's educational curricula comes from correspondence between teachers, pupils, and their families. Students boasted about their newfound knowledge while parents fought to ensure that their children received the best quality teaching available. Their messages tell us that, in addition to Hebrew literacy, Jewish students also learned Arabic, mathematics, and calligraphy. These skills were useful for anyone pursuing careers in business, law, science, medicine, or government administration. Two of these fragments (T-S 13J23.20 and T-S NS J401L) were copied by the Fustat court clerk and scribe, Halfon ben Manasseh.

Students in Libya

This long letter – sent from a young man in Tripoli to his uncle in Alexandria – carries greetings and news about various family members. The writer was proud of his education, stating plainly: "I am writing you this letter with my own hand!" He was also proud of his brother: "Nabat still attends school; he is now thirteen. You mentioned in your letter that your boys studied the Sacred Law, Arabic, and Hebrew calligraphy. We thanked God for this."[3]

1089 CE

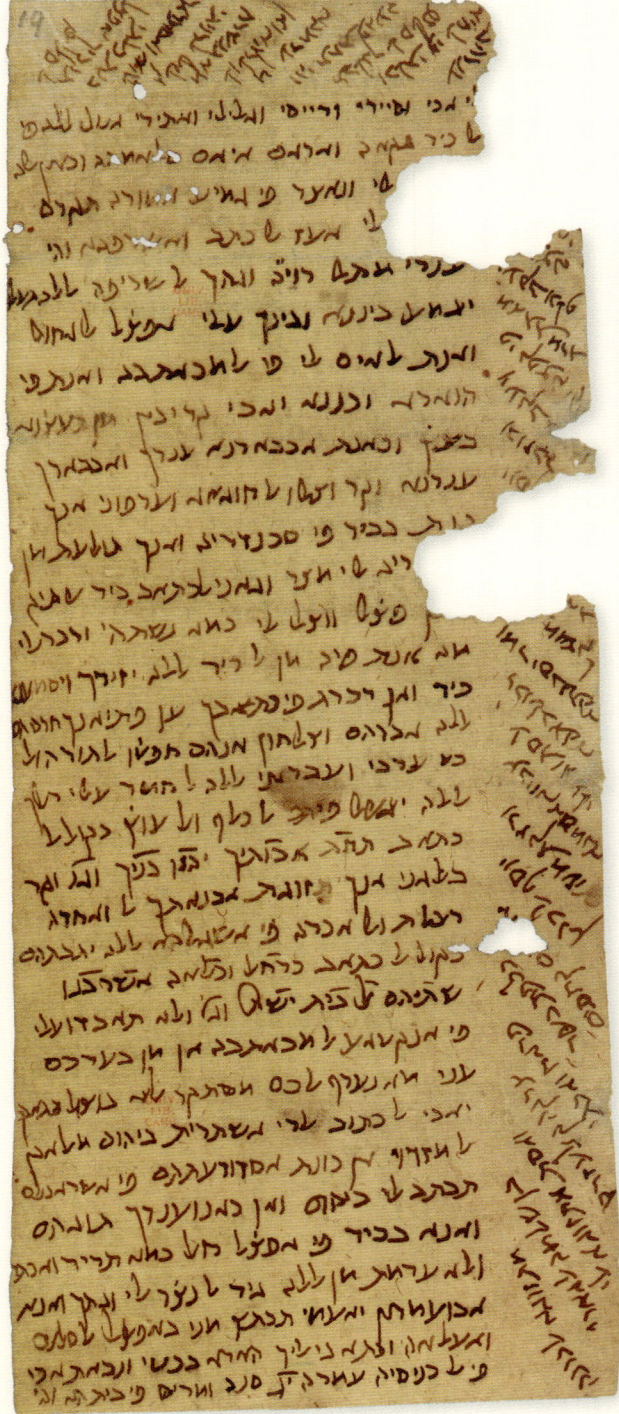

T-S 18J3.19

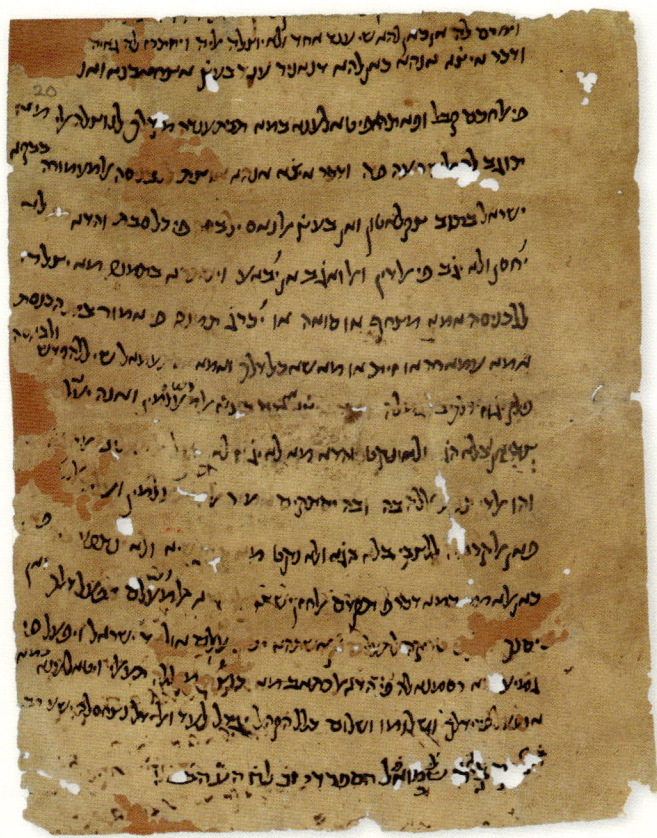

T-S 13J23.20

Back to Basics

Isaac ben Samuel "the Spaniard," a judge in 12th-century Fustat, had strong opinions on the right way to teach children. When a cantor from the Egyptian countryside asked for his opinion about the controversial reading method of 'whole word recognition', favoured by a local schoolteacher, Isaac was greatly disturbed. "You first mentioned that a teacher in your place instructs the boys without [first teaching them] the alphabet and the vowel signs. This is by no means permissible, for the alphabet and the vowel signs are the basis of all teaching; through the alphabet, God has given us His message; through it, the pupils get a firm grounding, and on it, everything rests." If the teacher wants to continue in his post he must change his method immediately. Isaac instructs the cantor to keep an eye on the situation and report back to Fustat.[4]

Ca. 1100–1130 CE

A Contract to Teach

Maliha, the widow of Abu Sa'd, was determined to get value for her money. She contracted this agreement with Abu al-Fadl "the elder" (likely not a professional teacher), guaranteeing exactly what her son, Hiba, would learn from him. Hiba will study Arabic script, so as to "be able to write a letter in his own hands without blemish in spelling… and be able to write anything dictated to him." He will also learn arithmetic, "mastering the use of the abacus" and "tens" or "decimals." In return, Abu al-Fadl will receive 2 dinars, a decent fee.[5]

Ca. 1100–1138 CE

T-S NS J401L

241

Lost Work of Arabic Grammar

This is *The Book of Arabic Inflexion According to the System of the Greeks*, a book for studying Classical Arabic using ancient Greek methods. Its author was Hunayn ibn Ishaq, a 9th-century Syriac Christian and famed translator of Greek texts into Arabic, but here the text is transliterated into Hebrew characters for the benefit of Jewish readers. Classical Arabic was important for Egyptian Jews to learn if they wanted to pursue careers in fields like science, medicine, philosophy, or government. This book was thought to be lost to history until just a few years ago, when one of our researchers identified it in the Cairo Genizah.[6]

Ca. 11th–12th century

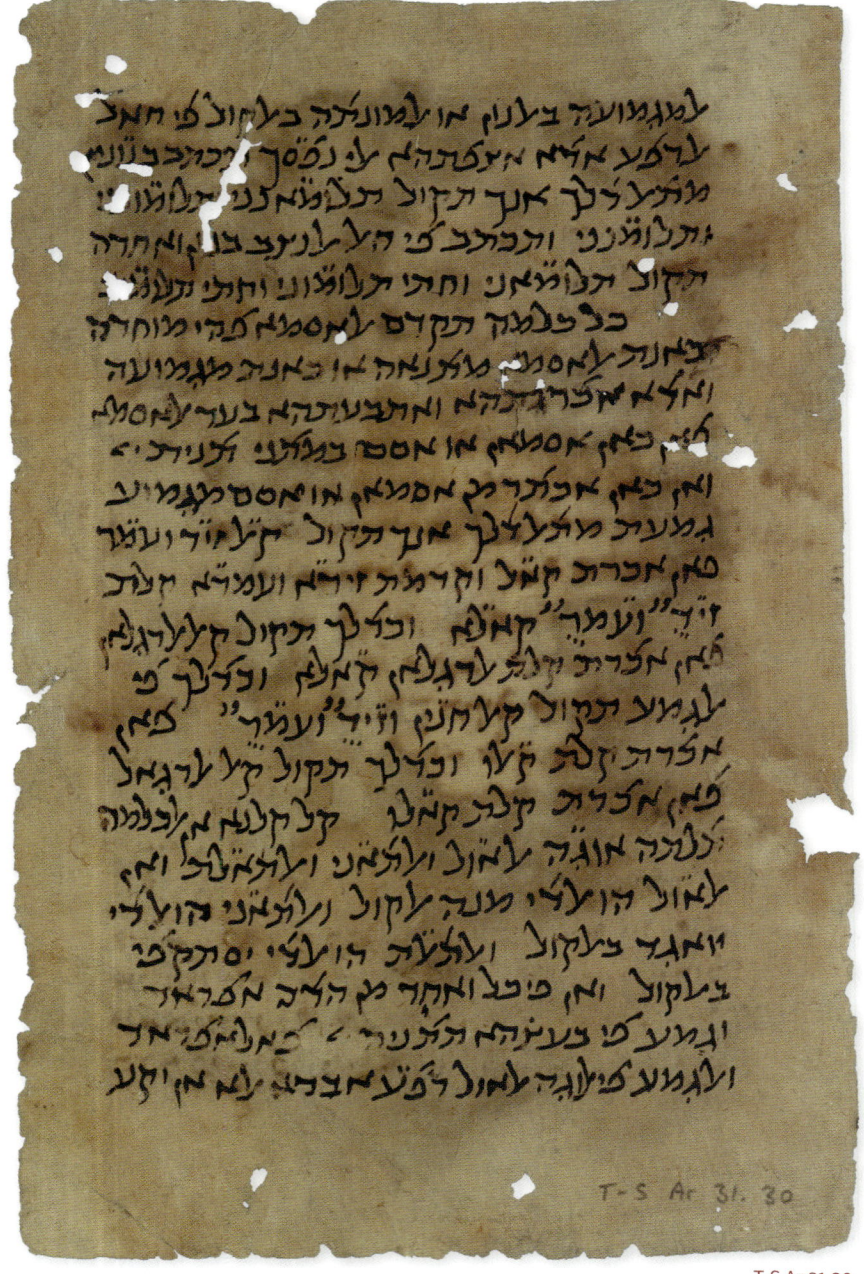

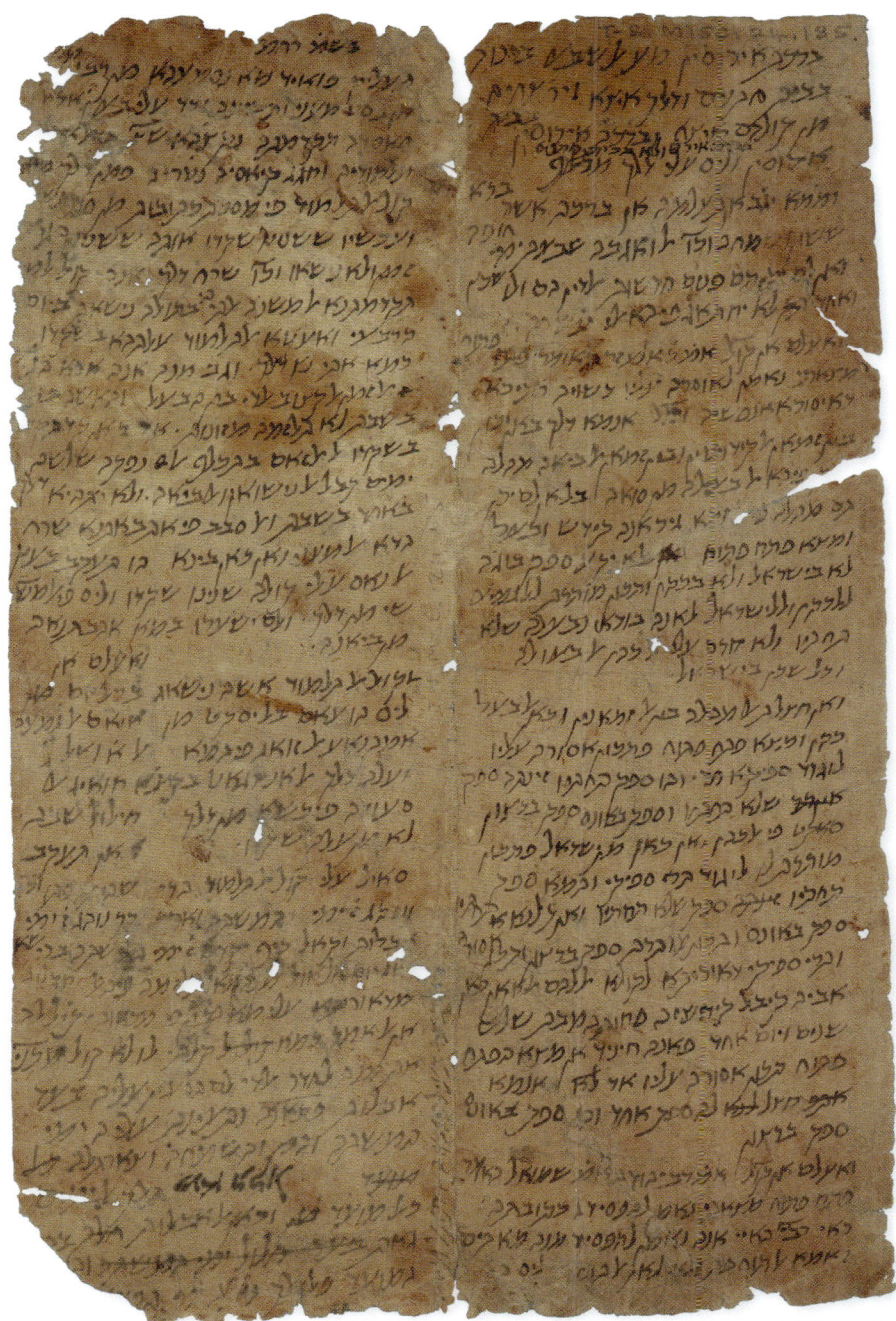

T-S Misc.24.185

Notes on a Maimonidean Lecture

What was it like to study Talmud with Moses Maimonides? In addition to his responsibilities in leading Egypt's Jews and his work as a physician in the Sultan's court, Maimonides also lectured to students, teaching Talmud and medicine. A student took these cramped and detailed notes as they sat listening to Maimonides speak about the first chapter of the talmudic tractate *Ketubbot* (probably taught using the compendium of Isaac al-Fasi).

Ca. 1168–1204 CE

מא יקולוﬡ רבותﬨנו הד﬩ﬨﬦ הﬠולם החﬥﬤ﬩ ס המﬠﬧﬥﬡﬦ
ﬞﬞﬞﬞﬞ

T-S G1.21

Medieval Labour Relations

Document with two separate legal enquiries posed to Maimonides – one each on the front and back – asking whether teachers who swore not to teach anymore could get out of their oaths. In the first case, a teacher went to a party and tipsily complained about how little money he made. The father of some of his students was present, and when the partygoers asked how much he paid the teacher, he did not give a great answer. The teacher swore not to teach any of his children again. Once he sobered up, he argued he should be released from the oath since he was inebriated when he made it. In the second case, a teacher got into a fight with a man and swore to stop teaching his daughters. He regretted the oath, seeking to retract it on the grounds that his livelihood was at risk and there was no one else to teach the girls.[7]

Ca. 1168–1204 CE

Alphabet Scroll

Fragment of a long scroll featuring the Hebrew alphabet in three different orders. The first is the primary *aleph-bet* order (*aleph, bet, gimel, dalet*…) written in large letters, perhaps to be hung as a banner in a classroom. The back has the alternative 'atbash' order (*aleph*, *tav*, *bet*, *shin*), often used in Hebrew ciphers, and the *aleph-yod* order (*aleph*, *yod*, *qof*, *bet*) used to represent numerals. Notice also the two little birds drawn above the letters in red ink.

Ca. 11th–13th century

T-S K10.26

Lessons from the Two Masters

Two pages from the Judaeo-Arabic *Book of Differences* by the 11th-century scholar of the Hebrew Bible, Mishael ben Uzziel. He lists the differences between how the two 10th-century 'masters' of the Tiberian biblical tradition – Aharon ben Moses ben Asher and Moses ben Naftali – pointed the text of the Hebrew Bible. The differences are numerous, but mostly reflect minor variations in notation and pronunciation. This section contains lists for Ezekiel and Chronicles. Someone has studied this book and added their own notes in the margins.

Ca. 11th–13th century

T-S D1.56

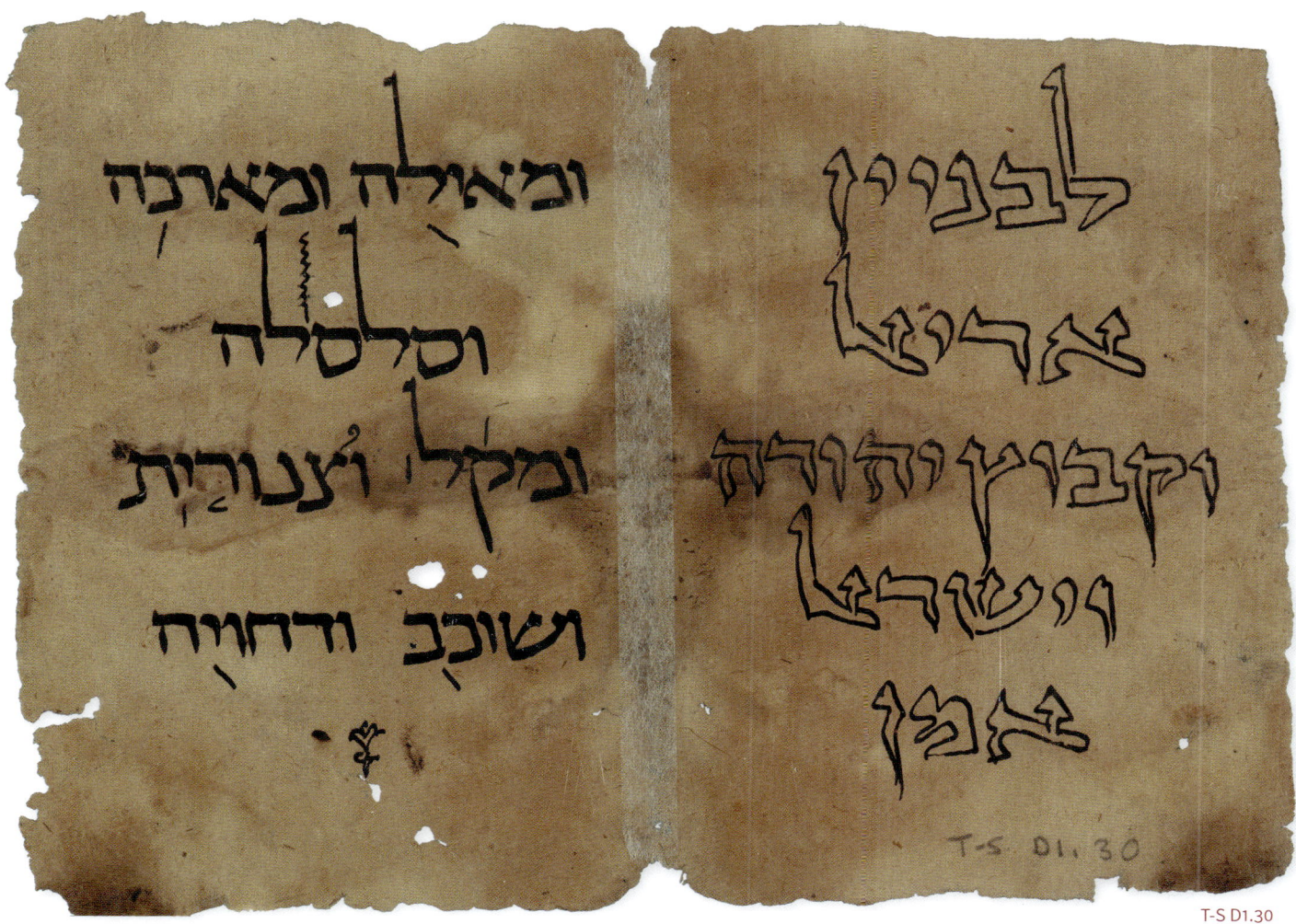

T-S D1.30

Hebrew with an Arabic Accent

This booklet was made by a professional scribe but would have served as a reference for someone learning to recite the Hebrew Bible. The right side is part of a blessing in fancy hollow letters (☛ Chapter X), while the left is a list of the accents used to chant the Hebrew Bible. The scribal sign for each accent accompanies its name, including the jagged zig-zagging line of the *shalshelet* ('chain') accent, here translated into Arabic as *silsila*.

Ca. 11th–13th century

Illuminated Hebrew Textbooks

Medieval textbooks like these were often elaborately decorated with images and bright colours to keep the attention of young readers.

T-S K5.13

Illuminated carpet page and exemplar Hebrew text featuring a lamp and menorah interspersed with Star of David designs. The letters *aleph*, *bet*, and *gimel* repeat with each of the Tiberian Hebrew vowel signs as an example for new learners to copy.

Ca. 11th–13th century

T-S K5.2

L-G Glass 11

Another primer for teaching the Hebrew alphabet, this time presented in the 'half-and-half' order (*aleph, lamed, bet, mem…*).

Ca. 11th–13th century

More Hebrew letters copied with the Tiberian vowel signs, this time surrounded by a micrographic border of Hebrew text.

Ca. 11th–13th century

Practice Hebrew phrases and alphabetic lists in red and green ink. The right page also has decorative Stars of David. It appears that someone – perhaps a bored student – traced over some of the letters with a darker black ink.

Ca. 11th–13th century

T-S K5.3

Another child's exercise book for learning Hebrew writing. The lower left corner has a colophon identifying the writer as Solomon ben Saʿadyah ha-Levi, a Jewish cantor. He makes a few mistakes in his Hebrew!

Ca. 12th–13th century

T-S 16.378

Textbook page with the end of the Hebrew alphabet and a Hebrew prayer. The reverse has the text of the first chapter of Leviticus for students to copy.

Ca. 12th–13th century

T-S K5.10

Doodle Boat

The other side of this fragment has the *'amidah* (Eighteen Benedictions) prayer for Rosh Hashanah, the Jewish new year, but this side seems like more fun. On the left is a child's exercise in writing the Hebrew alphabet. The bottom right is practice writing Arabic script. The top right is a drawing of a boat with a sail and multiple rows of oars. Doodling on schoolwork is an ancient art.[8]

Ca. 12th–13th century

T-S AS 108.130

Doodles by a Jewish Student

Pages from a small notebook that a child used to practise the Hebrew alphabet. This student apparently had some trouble focusing and added several doodles, including a menorah and a camel (or is it a medieval robot?).

Ca. 12th–13th century

T-S K5.19

Trope Trainer

Hebrew text of Genesis 1 in a haphazard grid and rough script style. Above the biblical text, the same hand has written the name of the accent that should be used to recite each word. These accents dictate the cadence and musical features of Hebrew cantillation (also called 'trope') for the public recitation of the Bible in a synagogue service. The ritual cantillation of biblical passages was something that all Jewish males were expected to learn. Perhaps this manuscript was copied by a boy preparing for his Bar Mitzvah?[9]

Ca. 12th–13th century

T-S Misc.22.264

Alphabet Exercises

Exercises by someone practising the Hebrew alphabet in forward and reverse order. The style of the script is quite rough, suggesting that a child or someone just learning to write was responsible. The flowers and heart patterns on the left side are 'pseudo' micrography, mimicking the scribal art of drawing borders with Hebrew characters (☛ Chapter X) without actually saying anything coherent.

Ca. 12th–13th century

T-S K5.50

Introduction to Arabic

Hebrew wasn't the only language that Egyptian Jews were interested in studying. This fragment comes from *The Book of All Things in Grammar*, an introduction to Classical Arabic by the 10th-century scholar Abu al-Qasim al-Zajjaji. This page has been transliterated into Hebrew characters, but it still records the Arabic language. Interestingly, the Hebrew letters are vocalised with Arabic vowel signs. It may even be an exercise that a Jewish student undertook to practise adding vowels to Classical Arabic.[10]

Ca. 12th–13th century

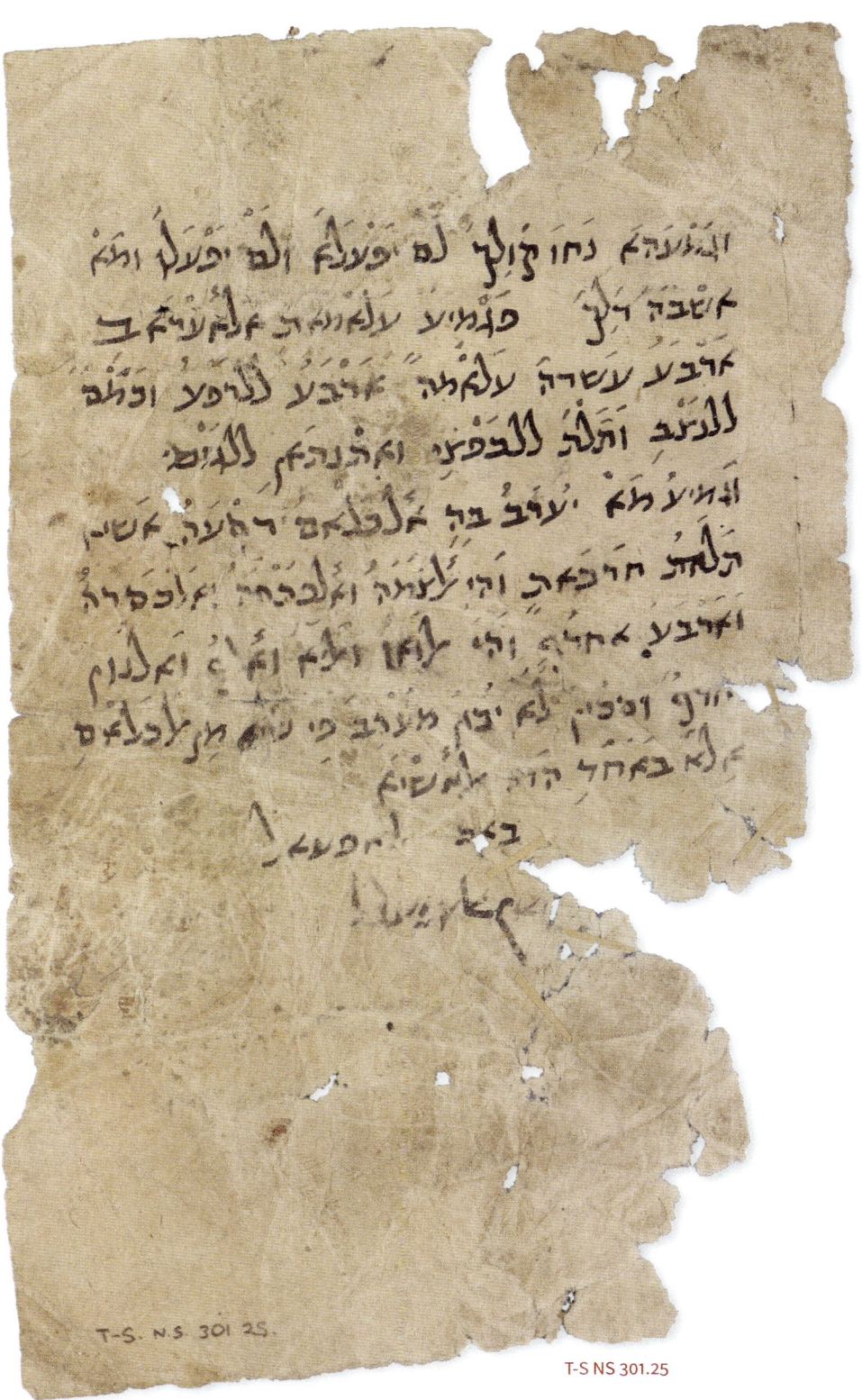

T-S NS 301.25

Letter About an Unruly Student

A Jewish teacher sent this note home from school: "…my lord, I have not been successful in educating this boy… Whenever I spank him, I do so excessively; but as soon as I begin, the mistress rushes along and, having smacked him four or five times, releases him… As soon as he comes in, he starts fighting with his sister and cursing her incessantly… Perhaps you could threaten him with a little spanking and tell him to be reasonable." Besides showing that corporal punishment was a fact of life for children at that time, this letter is also clear evidence that some Jewish girls attended schools alongside their brothers, and female schoolteachers taught alongside male teachers.[11]

Ca. 12th–13th century

T-S 8J28.7

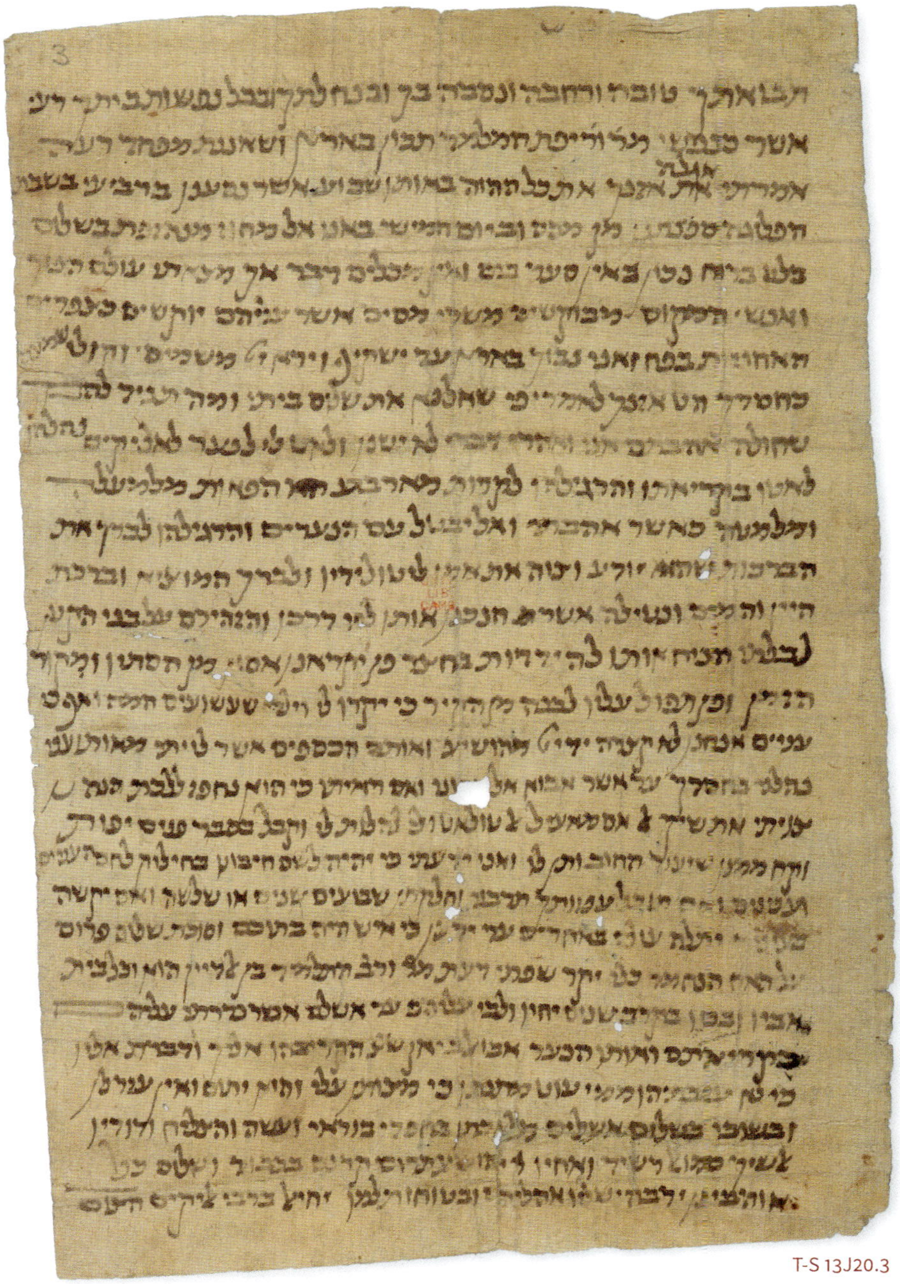

T-S 13J20.3

Reading from All Sides

When Yehiel ben Elyaqim, a Byzantine Jew who settled in Egypt, had to travel down the Nile, he worried about his children back home in Fustat. He wrote this letter to a close friend, asking him to keep an eye on their education, as he wanted his son to learn to read from "all four sides, from above and below." Such a skill was valuable when books had to be shared among several children sitting in a circle in the schoolroom. Yehiel also fretted about hygiene – "tell his mother to wash his hands" – and even expressed the worry that a tile might fall from the roof and injure his youngest son as he toddled outside, "for they are precious to me and are my darling children."

13th century

Ketubbah Homework

Jewish children needed materials to practise Hebrew writing, but not every household could afford to provide them spare paper. One thing that all Jewish parents would have had at home was a ketubbah, a marriage contract, traditionally on parchment (☛ Chapter VIIIb). Some thrifty families evidently let their children practise writing in the empty space on their ketubbot. Here the Hebrew alphabet appears between the lines of the marriage contract.[12]

Ca. 13th century

T-S 8.91

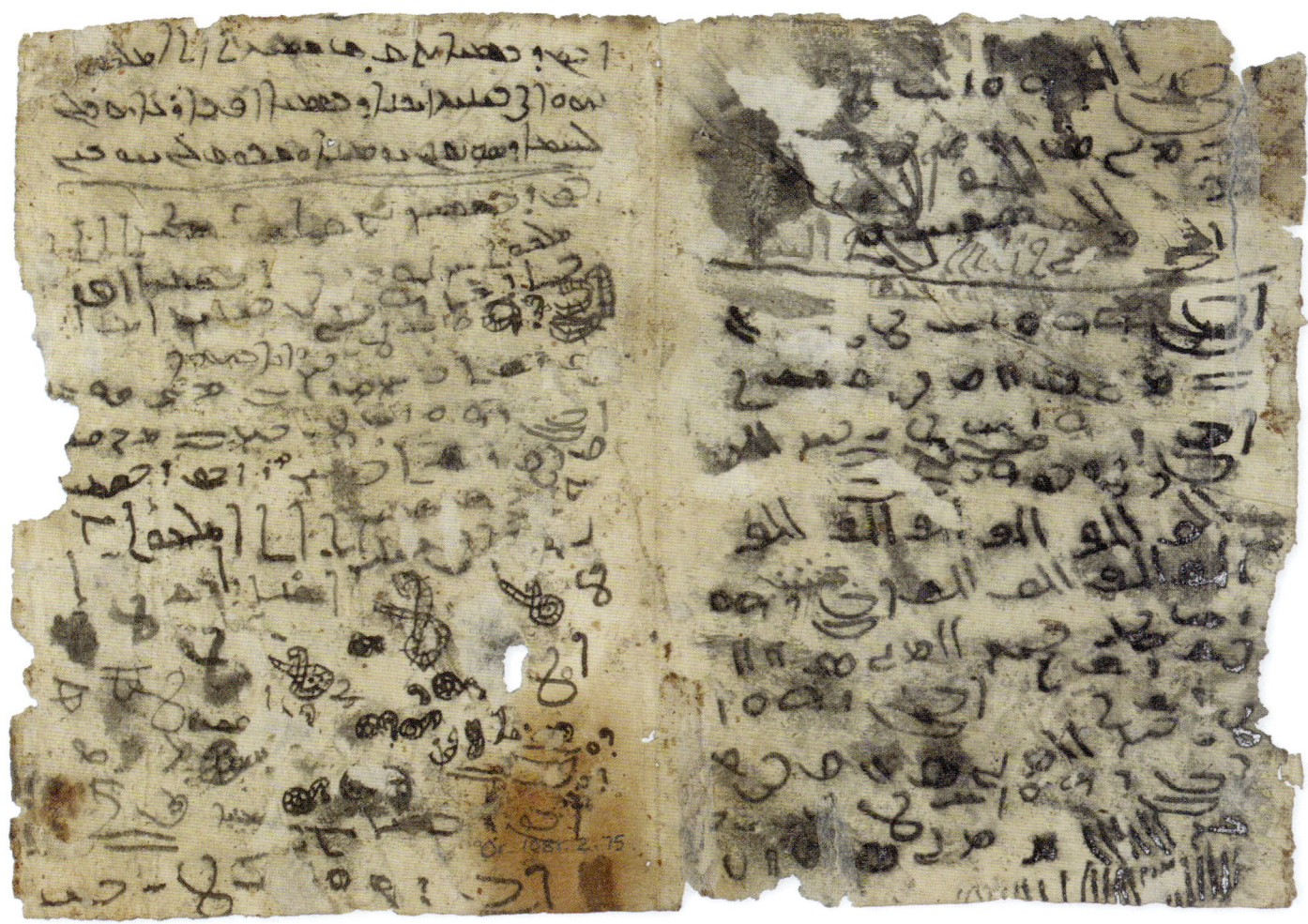

Or.1081 2.75.6

Syriac Writing Exercises

Pages from a booklet of writing exercises in Syriac and 'Garshuni' (Arabic language written in Syriac script). The letters of the Syriac alphabet and Christian religious vocabulary – "God," "Christ," and "Israelites" – appear, as well as two exercises copying the Lord's Prayer. Syriac is a dialect of Aramaic used by Middle Eastern Christians from the 2nd century CE up to the present day. Cambridge University Library purchased this fragment, as well as many others in the Or. Collection, in the early 1890s from the Jerusalem bookdealer Rabbi Solomon Wertheimer. Many of Wertheimer's manuscript wares originated from the Ben Ezra Synagogue in Fustat, but not all. It is possible that he collected this one in Palestine.

Ca. 16th–17th century

Modern French Primer

Illustrated page of vocabulary from *A New Method Simplifying the Teaching of Reading*, a French primer by Pierre Régimbeau. Egyptian students began learning French as a 'prestige' language following the European colonial occupations of the 19th century.[13]

1868 CE

T-S AS 190.21

Modern Biblical Hebrew Primer

One of more than a dozen fragments in the collection from the second edition of *Education for the Youth*, a primer for learning to read Biblical Hebrew. This section divides Hebrew text into syllables to make it easier to recite. Faraj Mizrahi, an Iranian Jewish immigrant, printed this copy at his publishing house in Alexandria. It proved so popular among Egypt's Jews that he reprinted it eight times before his death in 1913.[14]

1887–1888 CE

T-S NS 85.96

Modern Arabic Primer

Two pages of *The Method of Spelling and the Practice of Reading in the Arabic Language*, an educational primer for teaching reading and writing in different calligraphic script styles. It is attributed to ʿAli Mubarak Pasha (d. 1893), Egypt's Director of Education and a major reformer who championed public schools in the 1860s and 70s. This copy belonged to someone who called himself Shaykh ʿAbd l-Barr(?).[15]

1886 CE

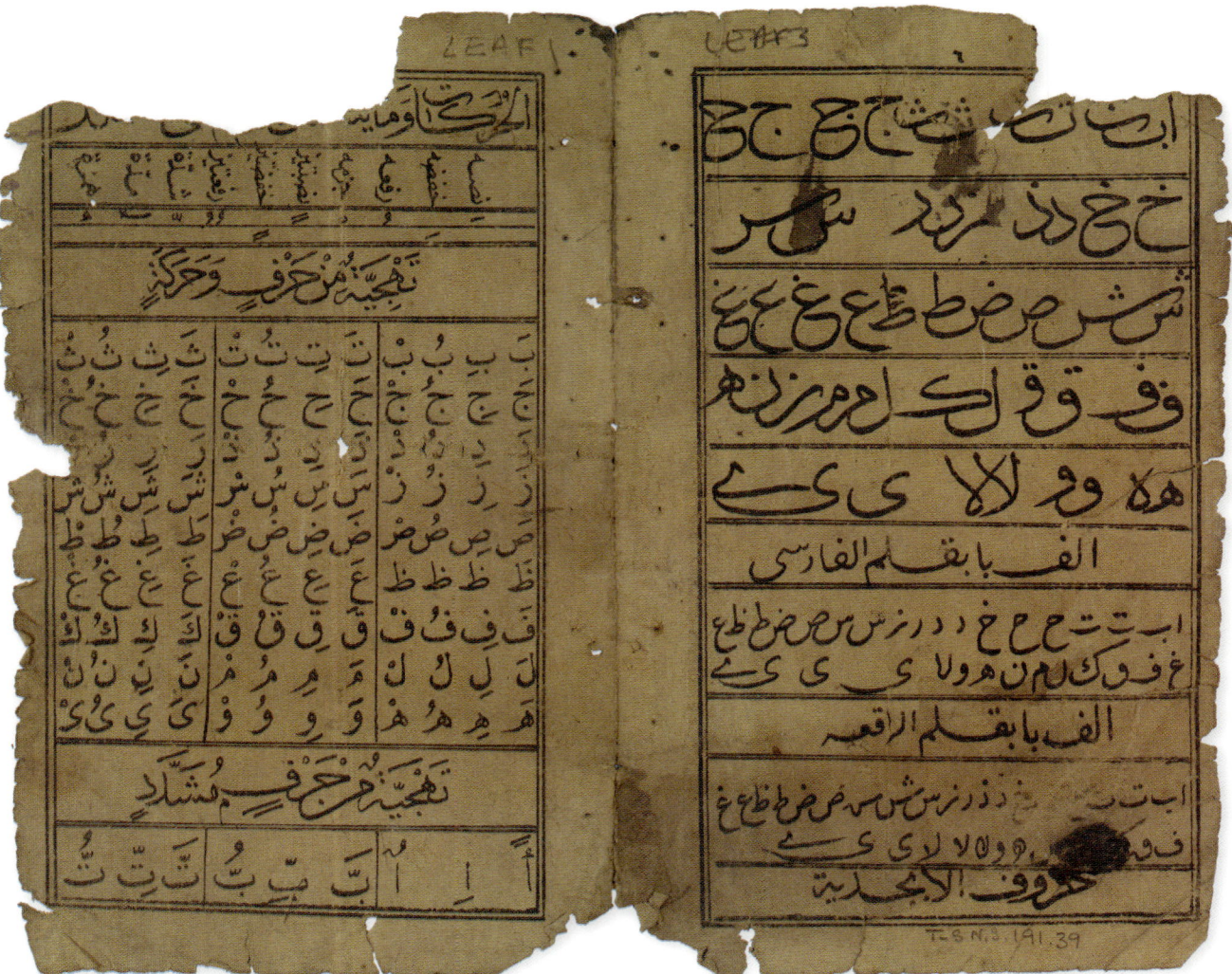

T-S NS 191.39

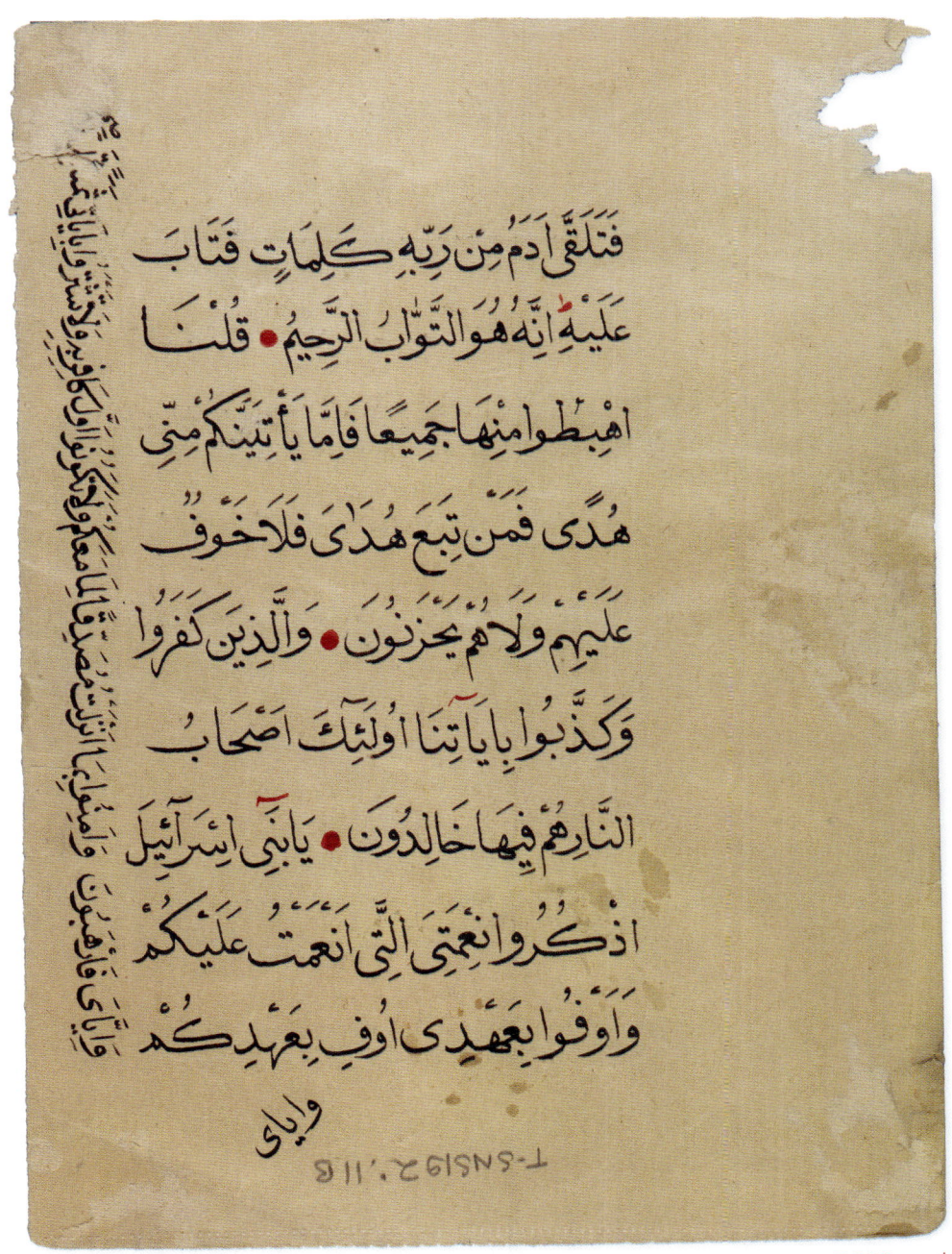

T-S NS 192.11b

Qur'anic Exercise from a Public School

Final draft of a calligraphic writing exercise for Sura 2 (*The Cow*) of the Qur'an. An attached note indicates that it came from *Madrasat al-Qarabiyya*, a public school in Cairo in the late 19th century. The student who wrote it was well-trained and even included the full set of Arabic vowel signs that are typically omitted in writing. Given that al-Qarabiyya was a public school, we cannot rule out the possibility that the student was a Jew practising Arabic calligraphy. That could explain how this fragment reached the Cairo Genizah.[16]

Ca. 1872–1897 CE

Notes to Chapter IX

1   Translation by Ben Outhwaite.

2   Nick Posegay, 'A Judaeo-Arabic Biblical Glossary as a Source for Arabic Historical Dialectology', *Journal of Arabic and Islamic Studies*, no. 20 (2020): 33–52.

3   S.D. Goitein, *A Mediterranean Society*, Vol. 2, p. 174.

4   S.D. Goitein, 'Side Lights on Jewish Education from the Cairo Geniza,' in Isidore David Passow and Samuel Tobias Lachs, eds., *Gratz College Anniversary Volume: On the Occasion of the 75th Anniversary of the Founding of the College* (Philadelphia: Gratz College, 1971), 93–94.

5   S.D. Goitein, 'Side Lights on Jewish Education from the Cairo Geniza,' in Isidore David Passow and Samuel Tobias Lachs, eds., *Gratz College Anniversary Volume: On the Occasion of the 75th Anniversary of the Founding of the College* (Philadelphia: Gratz College, 1971), 97–98.

6   Nadia Vidro, 'A Book on Arabic Inflexion According to the System of the Greeks: A Lost Work by Ḥunayn b. Isḥāq', *Zeitschrift Für Arabische Linguistik* 72, no. 2 (2020): 26–58. This manuscript was most likely copied by Hillel ben Eli. Thank you to Amir Ashur for identifying the hand of the scribe and estimating its date.

7   M.A. Friedman, 'New Fragments of Maimonides' Responsa,' in Shelomo Morag, Issachar Ben-Ami, and Norman Stillman, eds., *Studies in Geniza and Sephardi Heritage Presented to Shelomo Dov Goitein on the Occasion of His Eightieth Birthday by His Students*, Colleagues and Friends (Jerusalem: Misgav Yerushalayim, 1981), pp. 118–120 [Hebrew].

8   Thank you to Amir Ashur for helping to date this manuscript.

9   Marc Michaels, 'T-S Misc.22.264 – a trope trainer from the Cairo Genizah', *Fragment of the Month (July)*, Cambridge University Library: Genizah Research Unit, 2022.

10 Nadia Vidro, 'Arabic Vocalisation in Judaeo-Arabic Grammars of Classical Arabic', in *Semitic Linguistics and Manuscripts: A Liber Discipulorum in Honour of Professor Geoffrey Khan*, ed. Nadia Vidro et al. (Uppsala: Uppsala University Library, 2018), 350. The Arabic title of this book, *Kitab al-Jumal fi Nahw*, is actually a pun. It can be translated as *The Book of All Things in Grammar* or *The Book of Sentences in Grammar*.

11 S.D. Goitein, 'Side Lights on Jewish Education from the Cairo Geniza,' in Isidore David Passow and Samuel Tobias Lachs, eds., *Gratz College Anniversary Volume: On the Occasion of the 75th Anniversary of the Founding of the College* (Philadelphia: Gratz College, 1971), 90–91.

12 The scribe who wrote this ketubbah was most likely Solomon ben Samuel ben Sa'adyah ha-Levi in the first half of the 13th century. Thank you to Amir Ashur for this identification.

13 Nick Posegay, 'Searching for the Last Genizah Fragment in Late Ottoman Cairo: A Material Survey of Egyptian Jewish Literary Culture', *International Journal of Middle East Studies* 54, no. 3 (2022): 435.

14 Mosseri IXa.8.9 belongs with this classmark.

15 An ownership note appears on T-S NS 269.321, which is the title page of this book. See Nick Posegay, 'Searching for the Last Genizah Fragment in Late Ottoman Cairo: A Material Survey of Egyptian Jewish Literary Culture', *International Journal of Middle East Studies* 54, no. 3 (2022): 433–434 (although that goofus misread the name in the note).

16 Magdalen M. Connolly and Nick Posegay, 'A Survey of Personal-Use Qur'an Manuscripts Based on Fragments from the Cairo Genizah', *Journal of Qur'anic Studies* 23, no. 2 (2021): 21–22.

X.
Bookmaking & Scribal Arts

Before the introduction of the printing press, every part of a book had to be made by hand in a process that involved tanners, weavers, stationers, chemists, scribes, bookbinders, and leatherworkers. Before writing could even begin, scribes needed writing materials. The most common materials for Genizah manuscripts were parchment, made from dried animal skins, and rag paper, made from textile pulp spread into thin sheets. Ink was also mixed by hand using pigments from charcoal, metallic compounds, and plant extracts. Professional scribes trained for years in the arts of calligraphy to give their customers a high-quality reading experience, often including creative marginal designs alongside works of both science and religion. Before or after writing, bookmakers sewed pages together into units called 'quires' (usually 6–10 pages), then bound all the quires together into a 'codex' – what we today would recognise as a 'book'. Such codices were often bound between hardcover boards and wrapped in leather that was tooled with artistic patterns. A well-made book was a valuable, treasured possession.

The fragments in this chapter demonstrate the handiwork of artisans at every stage of this process. Most of them are anonymous, but their labour survives through a history of use, and often re-use too, that eventually landed them in the Cairo Genizah.

Qur'anic Recycling

Torn pages from a tiny Qur'an, just three inches wide. Sura 1 begins at the top right: "In the name of God, the Compassionate, the Mercifu…." Much of the text has rubbed off, likely because this fragment was sewn into the binding of another book. There is an extra fold along the bottom with six pairs of holes where the binder stitched them together. It was common for medieval bookbinders to cut up and recycle old manuscripts to reinforce new bindings, and Muslims often saved retired Qur'ans by putting them to use in this way.[1]

Ca. 10th–11th century

T-S NS 327.46

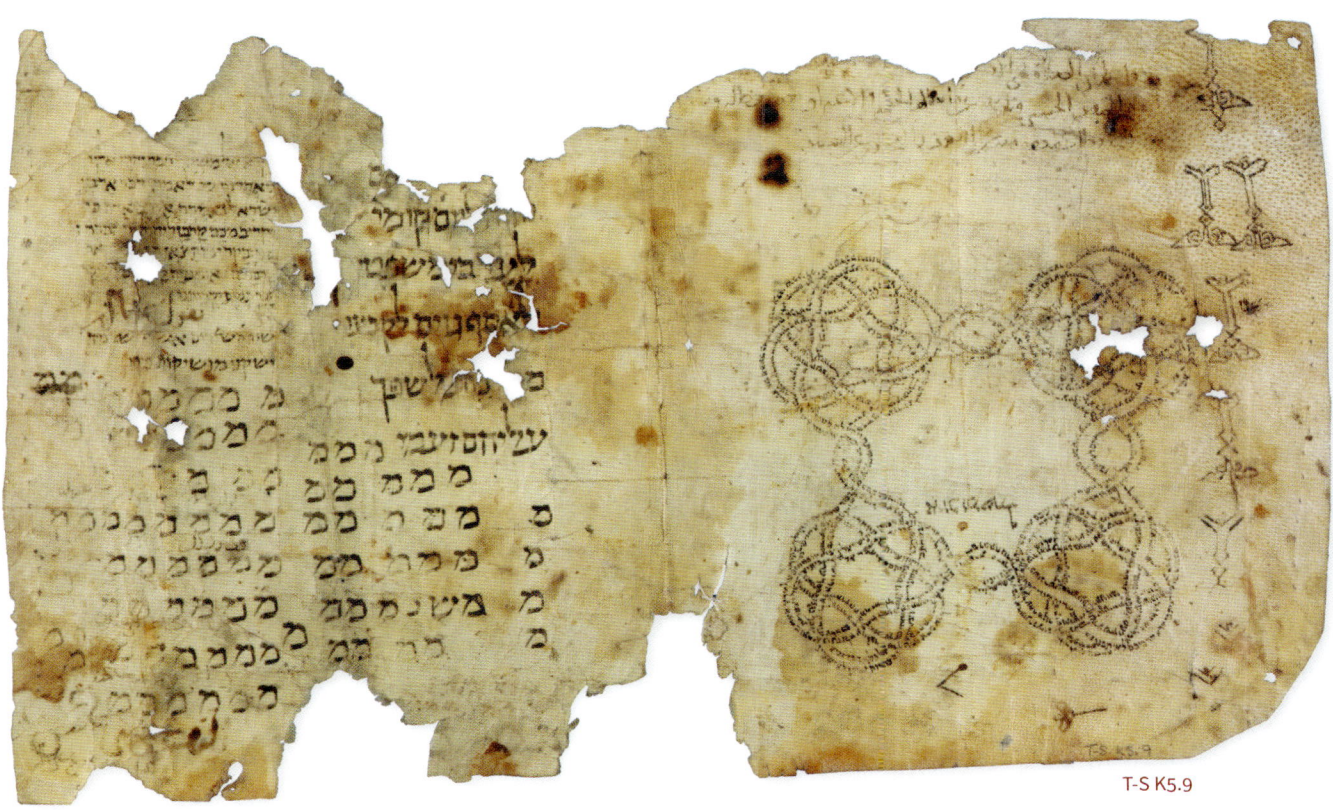

T-S K5.9

Scribal Notebook

Even the best-trained scribes need to practise. This is a spare b t of parchment that a professional scribe used to perfect their letters and experiment with 'micrography', a method of making intricate shapes with tiny Hebrew writing. A faded Arabic text also appears at the top, suggesting that either the Hebrew scribe or the person they got this parchment from also wrote in Arabic. Hair follicles are still clearly visible in the top right corner from the animal skin – usually sheep in the Genizah world – used to make the parchment.

Ca. 10th–12th century

Two Types of Calligraphy

A scribe used this blank page from a book of Hebrew liturgical poetry to practise two forms of calligraphic writing. Larger 'hollow' letters were often used for the title and dedication pages of longer manuscripts. Smaller micrography – making designs with tiny letters – was used to embellish the margins and decorative 'carpet pages' of expensive books.

Ca. 10th–12th century

T-S K25.28

T-S K25.220

Layers of Re-use

This leaf is one layer of a parchment book cover. The original stitching is intact, but only a few fragments of the next layer are still attached to the top left corner and righthand edge. The manuscript also reveals several 'layers' of use, including both Arabic and Hebrew jottings on the back as well as magical characters with geomantic patterns (used for divination, ☞ Chapter V). Much of the ink has worn off, most likely from rubbing against the adjacent layer, which suggests it was written before the binder sewed the cover together.

Ca. 11th–12th century

Latin Fragmentology

This tiny parchment fragment contains the poem *Ilias Latina*, a Latin version of Homer's *Iliad* composed in the 1st century CE. This section covers the events of the fifth book of the Iliad and was probably copied in France in the 11th or 12th century. Old manuscripts were sometimes torn into thin strips like this and used to reinforce the binding of other books. Latin manuscripts are rare in the Cairo Genizah – it's possible that a Crusader or a member of a Crusader's household originally carried this one from Europe to Egypt.

Ca. 11th–12th century

T-S Misc.27.2d

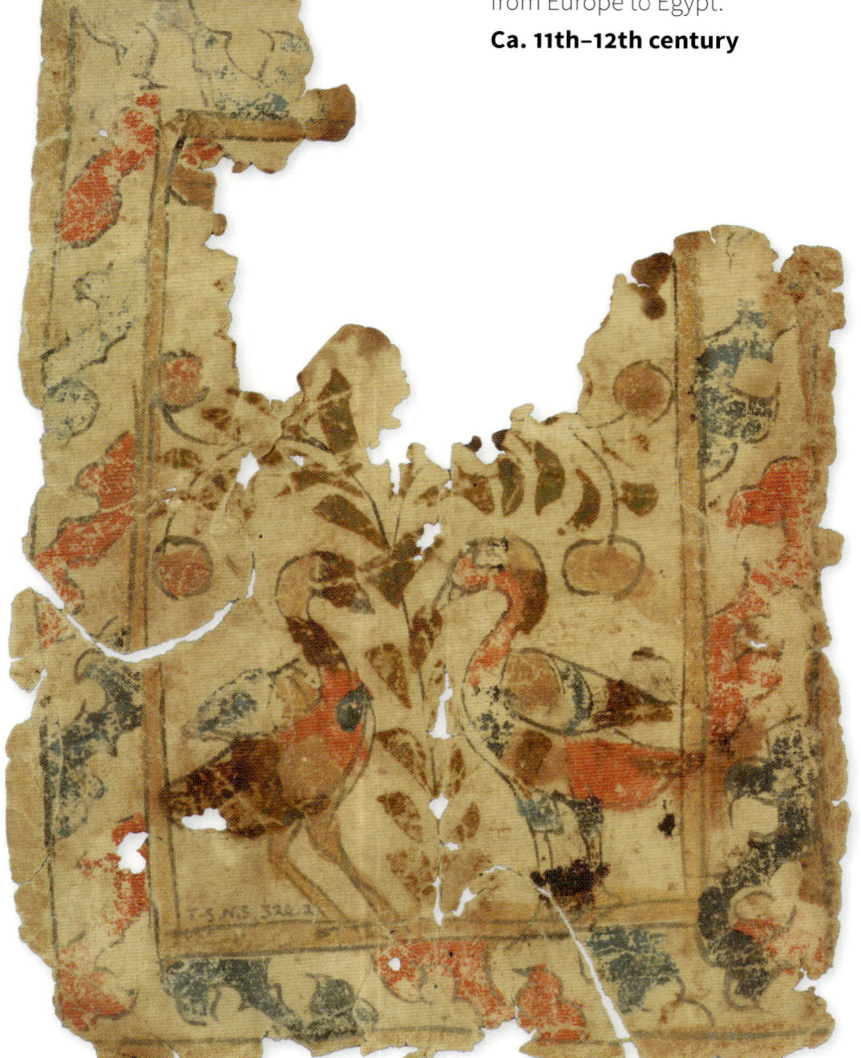

T-S NS 324.2

Egyptian Love Birds

Illuminated page depicting two Egyptian geese, a species of waterfowl native to the Nile valley. Ancient Egyptians considered them sacred messengers between heaven and earth. They can now also be found along the River Thames and in East Anglia. We've even seen them on the River Cam here in Cambridge. As is so common in the Cairo Genizah, a child used the back of this page to practise the Hebrew alphabet.

Ca. 11th–13th century

T-S K5.1

Textbook Dragons

Dragons and intricate knotwork decorate this child's Hebrew textbook, which contains the text of Leviticus 1. Hebrew primers like this were often richly decorated with bright colours to hold the attention of easily distracted children. Leviticus was the first piece of biblical text that young students copied after they mastered the Hebrew alphabet (☛ Chapter IX).

Ca. 11th–13th century

North African Arabic Calligraphy

North African Qur'an fragment containing portions of Suras 77–80. The scribe copied it in what's known as a *maghrebi* ('Western') script style, used in the region between present-day Libya, Morocco, and Spain. One of the tell-tale signs of a *maghrebi* script is the long looping letter tails that reach back up towards the baseline. The scribe also used gold ink and a more archaic style for the chapter headings. The fragment is made of parchment and has a 'horizontal' orientation (i.e. 'landscape'). These two features tend to indicate that a Genizah manuscript is relatively old, but both remained in vogue later in the Maghreb than they did in Egypt.[2]

Ca. 11th–13th century

T-S Ar.38.64

T-S NS 19.28

Bible Codex Destroyed by Rust

Most Genizah manuscripts are written with one of two types of ink: carbon or iron gall. Medieval carbon inks were mostly made from charcoal, but iron gall inks were made by mixing acid from gall nuts – growths on oak trees made by the larvae of wasps – with chemical compounds containing iron. Iron gall tends to stick to parchment better than carbon ink, but over time, the iron can oxidise and eat through the writing surface. The main text of this Bible (Numbers 14–18) has been destroyed by iron gall ink corrosion, but the marginal notes, written in carbon ink, survive intact.[3]

Ca. 11th–13th century

Draft Knotwork and Jottings

A scribe's practice notebook, with geometric figures and interlocking patterns that were probably a planned outline for the Hebrew micrography of another manuscript. The other side of this page has jottings in Arabic and excerpts of Hebrew liturgy.

Ca. 11th–13th century

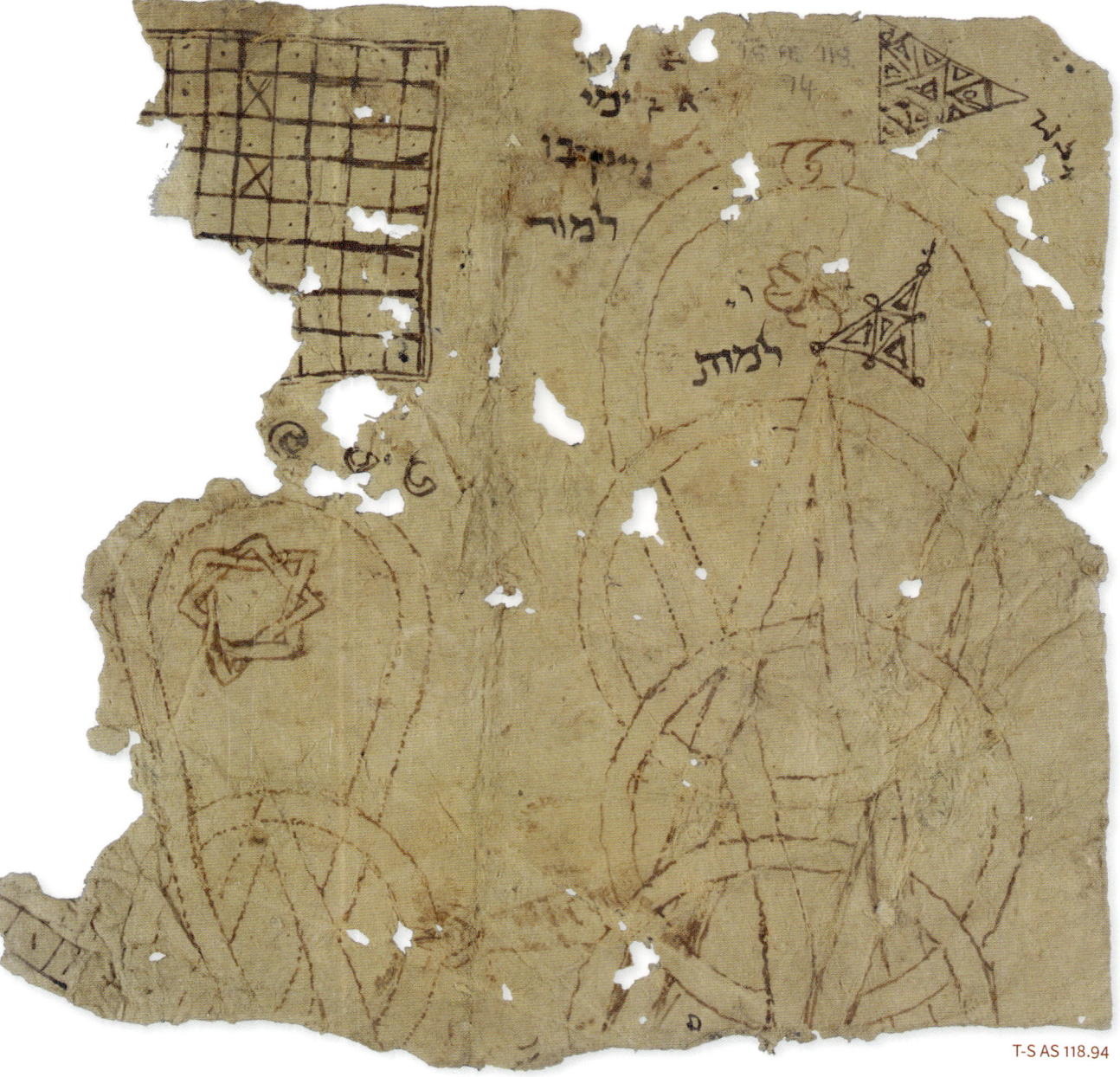

T-S AS 118.94

T-S K11.54

Complete Medieval *Mastara*

A very rare find – this is a fully intact medieval *mastara*, a 'ruling board'. A *mastara* is a scribal tool for writing neatly. It is made of several layers of paper glued together and sewn through with strings, creating a durable surface with raised lines. Scribes would press a fresh piece of paper against the ridges of a *mastara* to mark straight lines and margins before writing. The lines are numbered with Hebrew letters, but the jottings around the edges and on the back include both Hebrew and Arabic script.

Ca. 11th–13th century

Ornamental Fragments

One of the most complex projects that a scribe or artist could undertake was the decoration of an ornamental page, often the borders of a ketubbah (☛ Chapter VIIIb) or the 'carpet page' of a prestigious Bible codex (☛ Chapter II). Such ornamentation often requires large calligraphy, careful repeated geometric designs, and vibrant ink colours. These pages were not cheap to make, so in the Genizah collection we mostly see them in expensive Bibles and other important texts. The following fragments (all most likely from ketubbot) were torn from larger decorated pages that have since been lost.

T-S K10.6

Decorated fragment quoting Psalms 20:2. The outlined shapes are made with Hebrew micrography and the upper left contains a blessing for the writer.

Ca. 11th–13th century

Perhaps the most ornate of the bunch, this scribe combined red, blue, and gold inks in geometric patterns, floral motifs, and a Star of David. The text alludes to Isaiah 56:5.

Ca. 11th–13th century

T-S K10.14

T-S K10.2

Elaborately painted page with Hebrew script in a Sefardi style, most likely produced by a Jewish scribe from Western Europe.[4]

Ca. 13th–14th century

Draft Wedding Present

A large Star of David formed with Hebrew micrography. The text offers well wishes for a bride and groom whose names may be scrawled in Arabic on the lower left, including a man called Ibn al-Ra'is ('son of the leader'). This page was probably a scribe's draft and not the final version meant to be given to the newlyweds, otherwise it would've made a poor wedding gift! On the back is an excerpt from the introduction to Judah ben David Hayyuj's 10th-century dictionary of Hebrew verbs.

Ca. 12th–13th century

T-S K6.125

T-S K6.195

Two Generations of Scribes

Scrap paper where a scribe practised drawing geometric shapes with Hebrew micrography. The outer circle consists of lines from a liturgical poem for Yom Kippur (a *qerova* by the 10th century poet Solomon Sulayman al-Sinjari) while its inner spokes are the text of Genesis 49:18. Verses from Psalm 91 form the Star of David, and the triangles are made from Song of Songs 1:1 and Psalms 1:1–2. The Arabic phrase "when it finally reached him" repeats several times. A Judaeo-Arabic translation of Jeremiah 2:33–37 appears on the back of the page above large, rough letters of the Hebrew alphabet – perhaps copied by the scribe's child?

13th century

Draft Colophon by a Doctor

Scribes were often (rightly) proud of their work and composed elaborate 'colophons' to show off their skills. A typical colophon might describe the contents of a book, name the author or scribe, and give the date when they completed it. A Jewish scribe drafted these congratulatory words in large hollow letters: "I, Yedutun ha-Levi, the Doctor, son of Levi ha-Levi, wrote this." Dr Yedutun is known from several other Genizah sources dating to the first half of the 13th century, including a note on T-S K6.195, earlier in this chapter.

13th century

L-G Misc. 99

Mosseri I.35

Poetic Repetition with Judah ha-Levi

Scribal exercise repeating the openings of poems by the famed Andalusian poet, Judah ha-Levi. The scribe wrote Z"L (an abbreviation meaning 'may his memory be a blessing') after ha-Levi's name, indicating that he was already dead at the time of composition. Judah ha-Levi died in 1141 CE, and based on the handwriting of this scribe, we estimate the date of this manuscript is at least a century later.

Ca. 13th–14th century

Syriac Flap

This is one of only a handful of Genizah fragments written in Syriac, an ancient dialect of Aramaic that many Middle Eastern Christians used as a liturgical language. The text is an East Syriac hymnary for the second Sunday after Nativity. It is not always clear how such Christian manuscripts came into the possession of Egypt's Jews, but we have a hypothesis. Someone deliberately cut the edges of this leaf in a pentagonal shape reminiscent of the Islamicate 'flap' binding type that was popular in Mamluk and Ottoman Egypt (see T-S AS 176.book cover below). It is possible that Jewish binders recycled this Christian fragment to reinforce the cover of a new book.[5]

Ca. 13th–14th century

T-S AS 204.352

Mosseri I.101

Mamluk Petition, Practice, and Page Marker

Arabic letter written to a high-ranking official of the Mamluk Sultanate. A scribe-in-training re-copied some of the formulaic phrases in the last three lines for practice. After passing through the Mamluk chancellory, this page was discarded and a member of Cairo's Jewish community recycled it. The opening letters of the Hebrew alphabet are scribbled between the Arabic lines, and an excerpt from the Passover Haggadah appears on the back. The thread tied through one side is probably a page marker.[6]

Ca. 13th–15th century

Watermarks

In the late 13th century, Italian papermakers invented a new method for imprinting images onto sheets of rag paper. By attaching shapes to a metallic wire mesh, they could add unique 'watermarks' to identify their products, prevent counterfeiting, and build up a professional brand. Watermarks are nearly invisible when their paper is laid flat, but they readily appear when a light is shone behind them.[7]

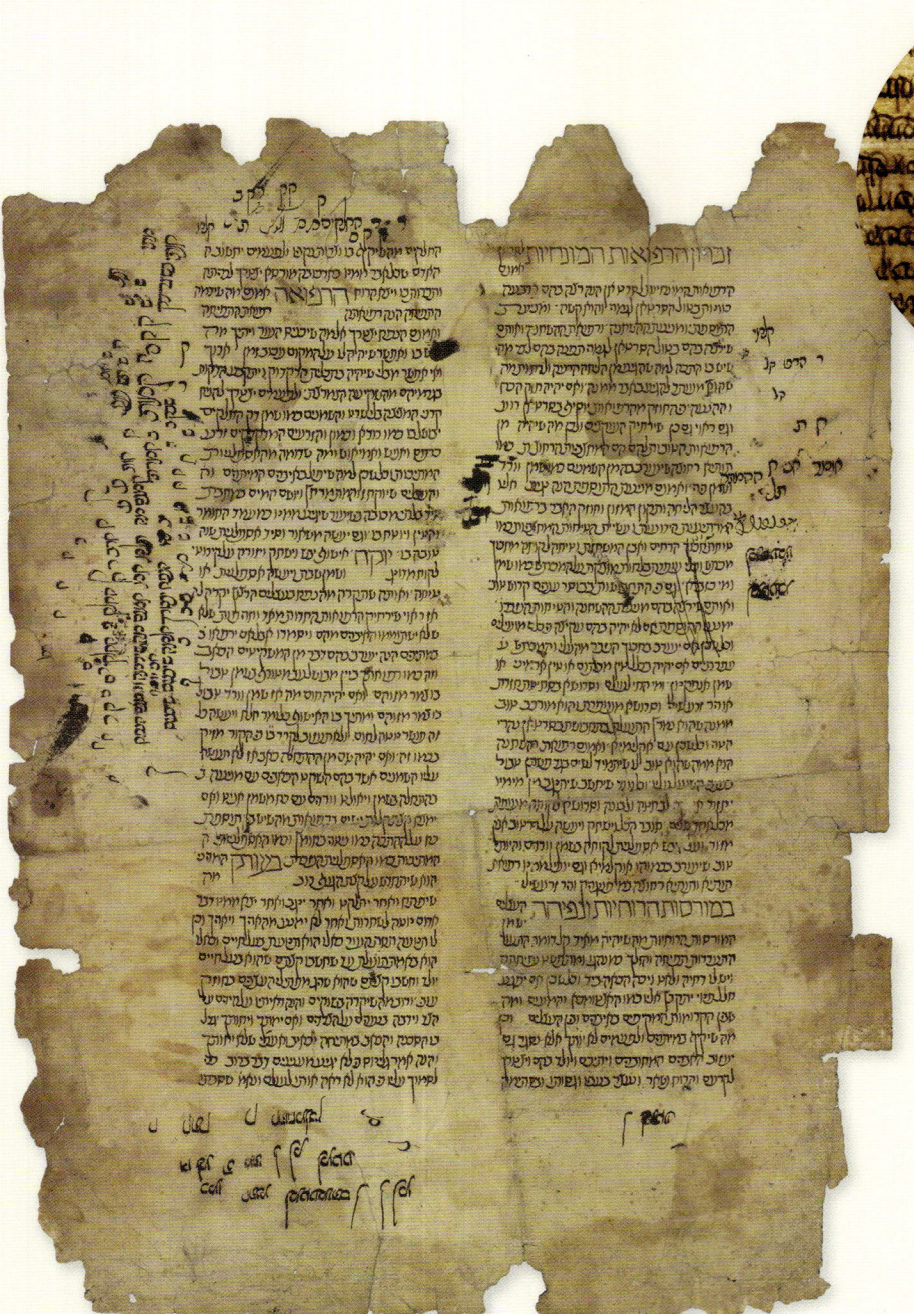

A Hebrew medical text on the composition of drugs, copied in Western Europe towards the end of the 15th century. The watermark is a ring with a gemstone and 6-pointed flower – a near-perfect match for a watermark used in Genoa in 1483. It's likely that this paper was made in northern Italy around that time.

Ca. 1483–1509 CE

L-G Misc. 1

T-S K9.17

T-S Misc.19.107

This mermaid marks a page used to copy a Hebrew grammar by the famous Provençal scholar, David Qimhi (d. 1235). Mermaid watermarks have been documented from many sources, and this one reveals that the paper was made in the mid-15th century, most likely in France.

Ca. 1430–1500 CE

Page from the Babylonian Talmud tractate *Hagigah* printed by Solomon ibn Alkabes in Guadalajara, Spain, around 1480 CE. This watermark has also been documented in Barcelona around the same time, so a local Spanish artisan may have manufactured the paper. This book probably came to Egypt with a Jewish refugee after Christian authorities expelled Jews and Muslims from Spain in 1492.[8]

Ca. 1480 CE

Sefardi Haggadah with Human-Headed Snakes

Decorated Passover Haggadah, most likely from Spain. The scribe embellished the text with 'zoomorphic' letters in the form of red- and blue-striped snakes. The use of parchment is unexpected for a manuscript this late, as paper was already in widespread use around the Mediterranean at this time.
Ca. 14th–16th century

T-S K10.1

Q: What are Genizah fragments made of?

Most Genizah fragments are made of rag paper, a dried mash of cotton or linen fibres mixed with water, derived from recipes invented in ancient China. Many are also written on parchment, made from the skins of animals – especially sheep or goats – that have been scraped, stretched, and dried. Jewish law specifies that certain items, such as Torah scrolls, mezuzot, and tefillin, must be written on parchment from a kosher (ritually pure) animal. Some twelfth-century letters, sent from India where paper was apparently in short supply, are written on cloth. Papyrus, made from the reeds of the *Cyperus papyrus* plant, is perhaps the writing material most commonly associated with Egypt in popular imagination, but it is extremely rare among Genizah fragments. Most manuscripts in the collection were produced after the 10th century when paper had already overtaken papyrus as the most common Egyptian writing material.

Leather Book Cover

Although most of the books from the Cairo Genizah have fallen apart or were dismantled for one reason or another, a few original book covers survive largely intact. The front of this one is made of leather tooled with a rectangular border and a rounded geometric design, similar to others known from the middle Ottoman period. The second fragment is a flap that was attached to this cover and folded closed like an envelope. Flaps like this are very common in Islamicate bookbinding.

Ca. 15th–16th century

T-S AS 176.book cover

Notes to Chapter X

1. Magdalen M. Connolly and Nick Posegay, 'A Survey of Personal-Use Qur'an Manuscripts Based on Fragments from the Cairo Genizah', *Journal of Qur'anic Studies* 23, no. 2 (2021): 10–11.

2. Magdalen M. Connolly and Nick Posegay, 'A Survey of Personal-Use Qur'an Manuscripts Based on Fragments from the Cairo Genizah', *Journal of Qur'anic Studies* 23, no. 2 (2021): 9–10.

3. On ink composition in the Cairo Genizah, see Zina Cohen, *Composition Analysis of Writing Materials in Cairo Genizah Documents*, vol. 15, Cambridge Genizah Studies Series (Leiden: Brill, 2021).

4. Thank you to Noam Sienna for helping to identify and date this fragment.

5. Sebastian Brock, 'Some Further East Syrian Liturgical Fragments from the Cairo Genizah', in *Oriens Christianus*, vol. 74 (Wiesbaden: Otto Harrassowitz, 1990), 44–61.

6. Identification by Marina Rustow, Alan Elbaum, and Yusuf Umrethwala for the Princeton Geniza Project (https://geniza.princeton.edu/en/documents/36156/). Thank you to Kristine Rose-Beers and Andrea Strongwater for their suggestions regarding the purpose of the thread.

7. On watermarked paper in the Cairo Genizah, see Nick Posegay and Orietta Da Rold, 'Following the Mediterranean Paper Trail: A Study of European Paper in Late Medieval Cairo (ca. 1350–1600)', *The Library*, forthcoming 2024. Posegay would like to take this moment to remember the loss of Watermark Wednesday in the hopes that future generations will honour its legacy.

8. This imprint is ISTC no. it00015200.

XI.
Printing

Almost all the fragments we have shown so far have been handwritten 'manuscripts' (from the Latin for 'hand writing'). The Cairo Genizah is best known for its manuscripts, but the Egyptian Jewish community also stored thousands of printed books in their genizot. They offer us a glimpse into the physical history of Jewish literary culture between 1450 and 1897 and help us answer an important question: where did Egyptian Jews get their books?

There are two main types of printing among the fragments in the Cairo Genizah: block prints and prints from movable type. The first kind is older, appearing in the Middle East first around the 9th or 10th century (and even earlier in East Asia) among artisans who carved wooden blocks to create text and images. A carved block of this type is known in Arabic as a *tarsh*. Printers coated *tarsh* blocks with ink and pressed them onto paper sheets, stamping them with images. For some artefacts, such as single-leaf amulets, this could be easier and cheaper than paying professional scribes. By about 1300 CE, people in Europe began making wood-block prints, a few of which also survive in the Genizah. The second kind of printing – that done with a printing press and movable type – first appeared in Europe during the 15th century. Within a few decades of Johannes Gutenberg's death (d. 1468), Egyptian Jews could acquire Hebrew books from printers in Spain, Portugal, Italy, and Constantinople. Most imprints that survive in the Genizah therefore come from outside Egypt, but there are also some that preserve the lost art of Egyptian Hebrew printing.

Tarsh Woodblock Amulets

The Cairo Genizah preserves several amulets produced with *tarsh* blocks, carved pieces of wood that Egyptian printers used to stamp text and images onto paper. Most of these prints are magical amulets, meant to provide blessings and protection to whoever carried them. They take the long, vertical format typical of handwritten Egyptian amulets (☛ Chapter V) and, somewhat surprisingly for the Genizah, they are mostly in Arabic. Many even contain passages from the Qurʾan. This suggests that the popularity of Arabic block-printed amulets was so great that they could transcend religious boundaries, even circulating in Egypt's Jewish community.[1]

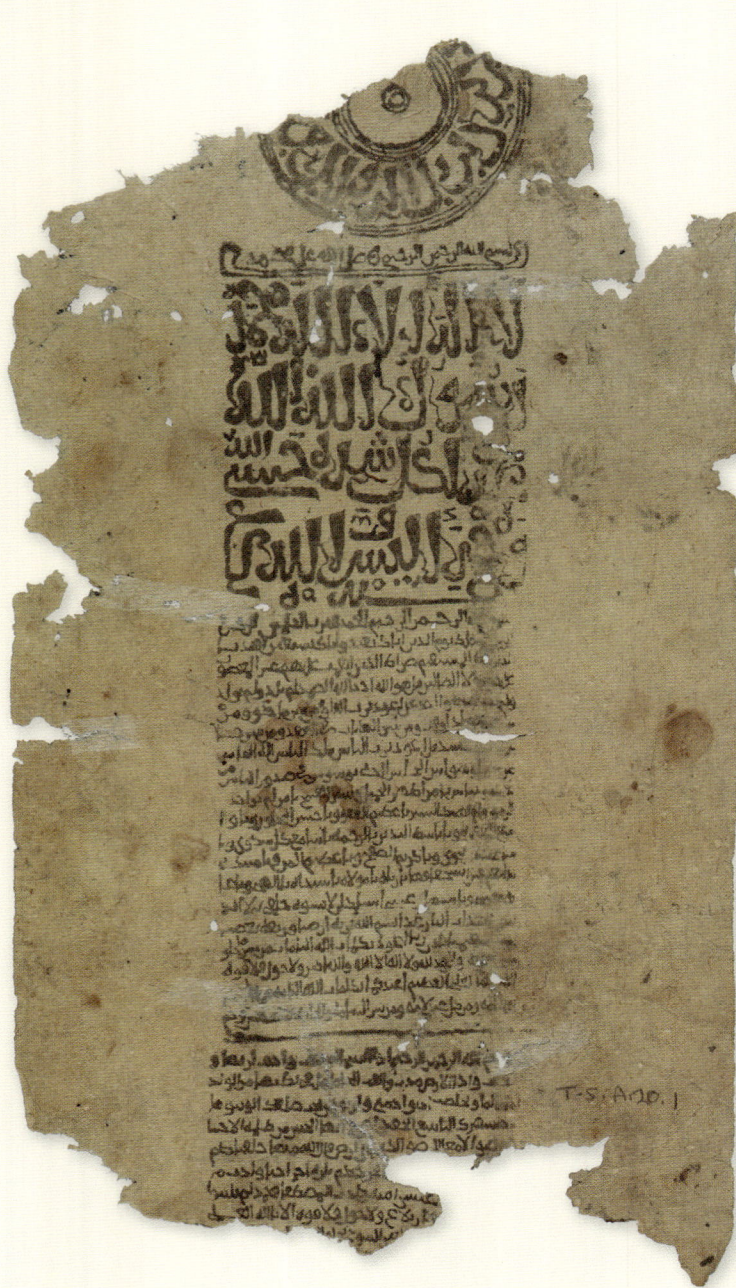

A block-printed talisman entirely in Arabic, including Qurʾanic quotations from suras 1, 112, 113, and 114.
Ca. 10th–11th century

T-S Ar.20.1

An exceptionally long amulet, consisting of two strips of paper glued together in a similar way to the papyrus rolls of ancient Egypt. The text includes a prayer and lists the names of God in Arabic.

Ca. 10th–11th century

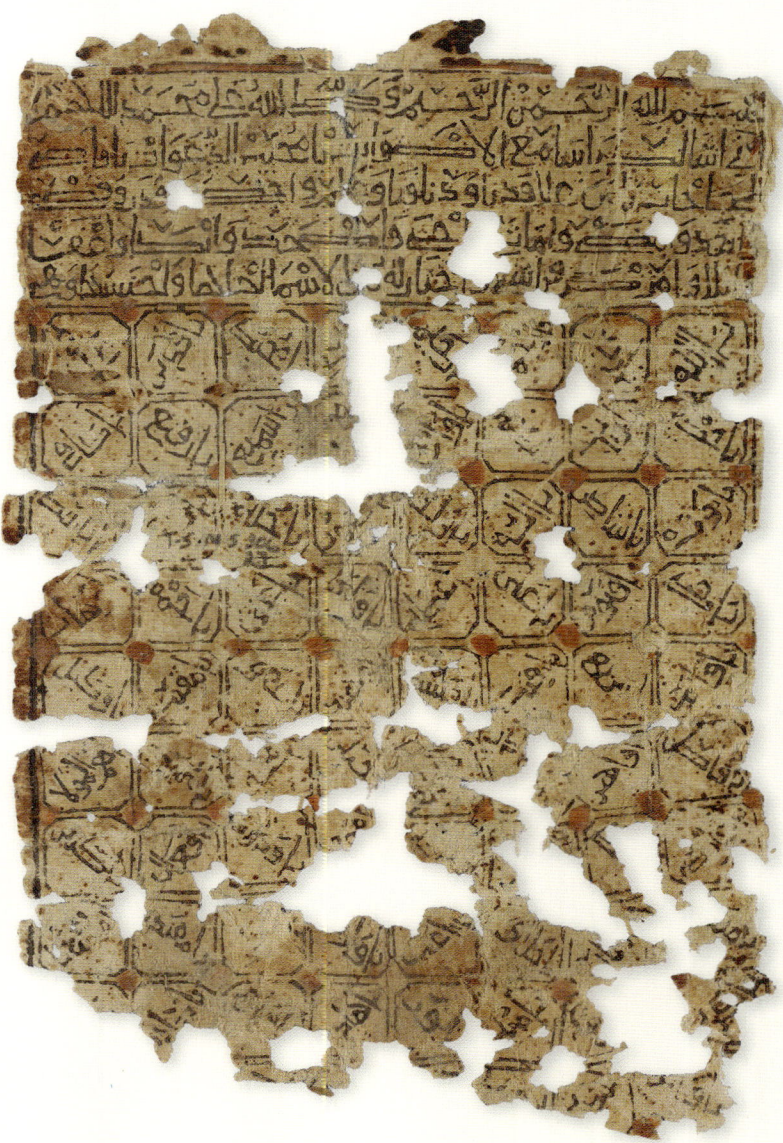

T-S NS 306.27

An Arabic amulet with a blessing for the prophet Muhammad. It lists the Arabic names of God in a matrix that resembles a magic square.[2]

Ca. 11th–14th century

T-S Ar.38.135

Block-Printed Hebrew Amulet

Although the Cairo Genizah is ostensibly a Jewish corpus, printed Arabic amulets are more common than Hebrew ones. This is the only block-printed Hebrew amulet in the collection. It reads "blessed are you coming in and blessed are you going out" (Deuteronomy 28:6). The back is blank, so the whole page was probably meant to be hung over a doorway. It's probably not later than the 14th century, but its origins are uncertain: it could have been printed in Europe, Egypt, or somewhere else.

Ca. 13th–14th century

Or.1080 J50

T-S 20.188

Northern European Biblical Broadsheet

Large broadsheet with block-printed illustrations of biblical history, running from Adam and Eve (with a human-faced serpent) in the top right, to the Assyrian King Sennacherib on the bottom left. The figures are depicted in European dress, suggesting this page was printed in Europe before being brought to Cairo. It is stylistically similar to Christian woodcuts from Germany and the Netherlands in the late 15th century.[3]

Ca. 1450–1500 CE

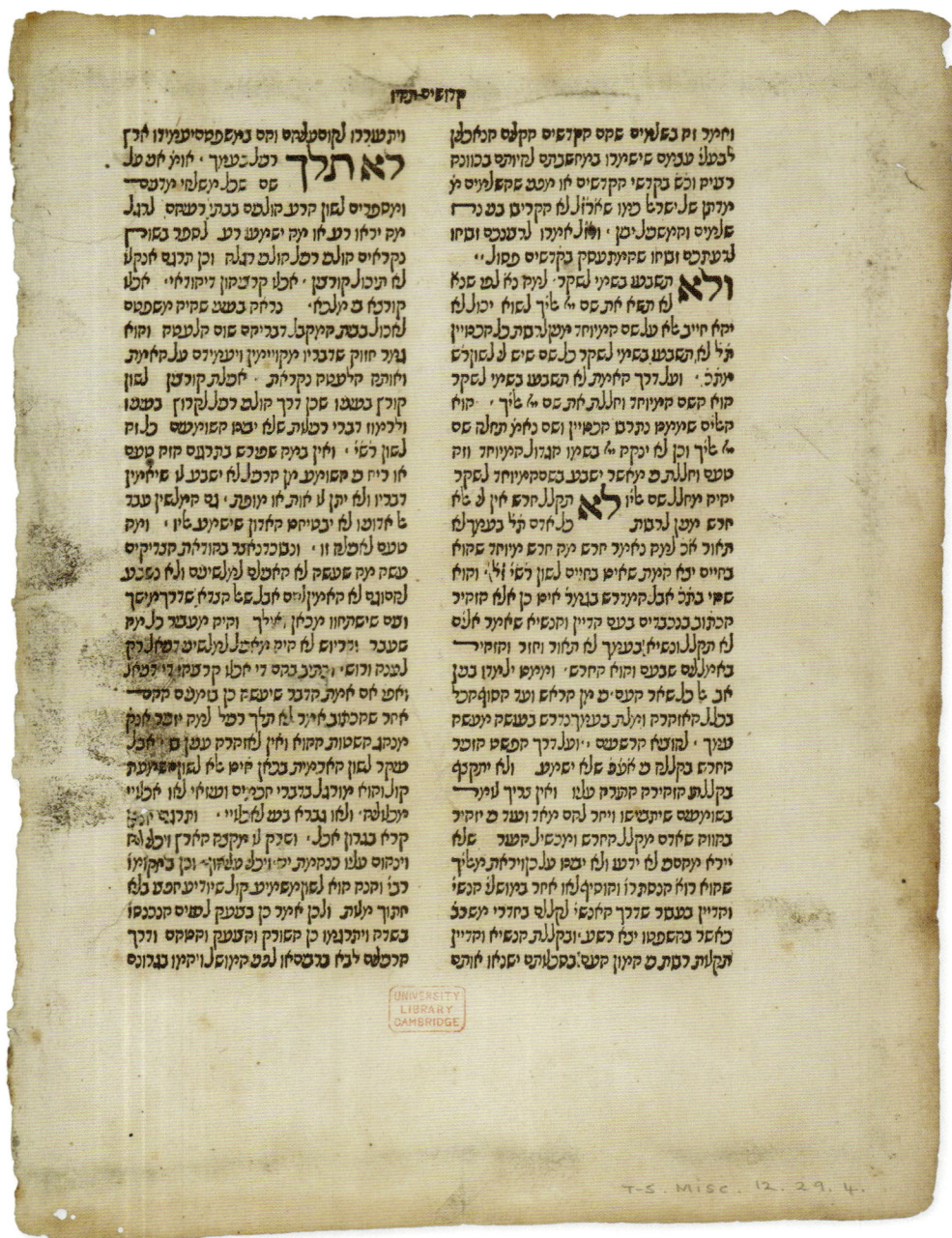

T-S Misc.12.29.4

Hand-Printed Portuguese Incunable

Incunable edition of Moses Nahmanides' commentary on the Torah. The word 'incunable' comes from the Latin for 'cradle', indicating a book published during the infancy of the printing press in Europe. For book scholars, that means anything published before 1500 CE. The Jewish printer Eliezer Toledano printed this incunable in 1489 at his press in Lisbon, Portugal. You'll notice that someone – maybe Eliezer, maybe his assistant – slipped in ink and left their handprint on the page.[4]

1489 CE

Pentateuchal Printing on Parchment

Eliezer ben Abraham Alantansi published this Pentateuch with Targum Onqelos and Rashi's commentary in 1490 at his press in Híjar, Spain. It demonstrates a strange phenomenon for those of us used to modern paper books. Some early printers actually printed on parchment, even alternating between paper and parchment folios within a single quire. The Cairo Genizah preserves several examples of this type of printing.[5]

July-August 1490 CE

T-S Misc.12.33.9

Neapolitan Woodcuts from a Jewish Press

Even after the widespread adoption of the movable-type printing press, European printers decorated their books by integrating woodcut images alongside typography. This is the earliest known Passover Haggadah printed with illustrations. The text was most likely printed by the Jewish brothers Samuel and David ibn Nahmias in Constantinople around 1506 CE. The woodcuts, however, were carved in Naples at a workshop famous for illustrating an early edition of Aesop's Fables in 1485.[6]

Ca. 1506 CE

T-S Misc.19.61

Ottoman Printing by a Portuguese Refugee

One of the first pages of an early printed edition of *Sha'are Teshuvot* (*The Gates of Repentance*), an ethical work by the 13th-century Spanish Rabbi Jonah Gerondi. It was printed in 1528/29 in Salonika, at that time part of the Ottoman Empire, by the publishing house of Don Judah Gedaliah (d. ca. 1526). Gedaliah was a Portuguese refugee who fled the expulsion of Jews from the Iberian Peninsula in the 1490s. His press was the first Hebrew printer in Salonika, and his sons and daughter continued to operate it for almost a decade after his death.

1528/29 CE

T-S NS 295.212

Soncino Polyglot Bible

During the 16th century, the main competitor of the Christian Hebrew printers in Italy was the Jewish Soncino family in the Ottoman Empire. In 1546, Eliezer Soncino printed this polyglot (multi-language) Pentateuch at the press his father founded in Constantinople. The central column is the Hebrew text, surrounded by (clockwise from top) the (Judaeo-)Arabic translation from Sa'adyah Gaon's *Tafsir*, the Aramaic translation of Targum Onqelos, Rashi's commentary, and a Judaeo-Persian translation. This is the first ever book known to be printed with Judaeo-Arabic text.[7]

1546 CE

Bomberg Colophon

Due to legal restrictions against Jewish printing, most 16th-century Hebrew printers in Italy were Christians. The most successful of these Christian printers was Daniel Bomberg, a native of Antwerp who established the gold standard for Hebrew printing at his publishing house in Venice. He is particularly famous for issuing the first complete edition of the Talmud between 1519 and 1523, several fragments of which survive in the Genizah. After Bomberg's death, other printers, including some of his former employees, competed to match the high quality that he set, though none ever quite reached it. This is the title page from Bomberg's edition of *The Binding of Isaac*, a commentary on the Torah by Isaac ben Moses Arama.

1546/47 CE

T-S NS 192.83

Talmudic Survivor of a Book Burning

Even Christian printers struggled with papal prohibitions against Hebrew printing. In 1553, the Pope banned Hebrew printing in Venice and ordered the Talmud to be burned across Italy. Daniel Bomberg's press had closed several years before, but his successors attempted to fill the vacuum left by the loss of Venetian Hebrew printing. One of them was his assistant, Israel Cornelio Adelkind, who joined the publishing house of Tobias Foa in Sabbioneta. They printed this edition of Talmud tractate *Qiddushin* shortly before the papal ban took effect, making sure to thank the local duke: "Published under the rule of Vespasiano Gonzaga." It seems that this copy escaped burning by reaching the relative safety of the Jewish community in Cairo.

1553 CE

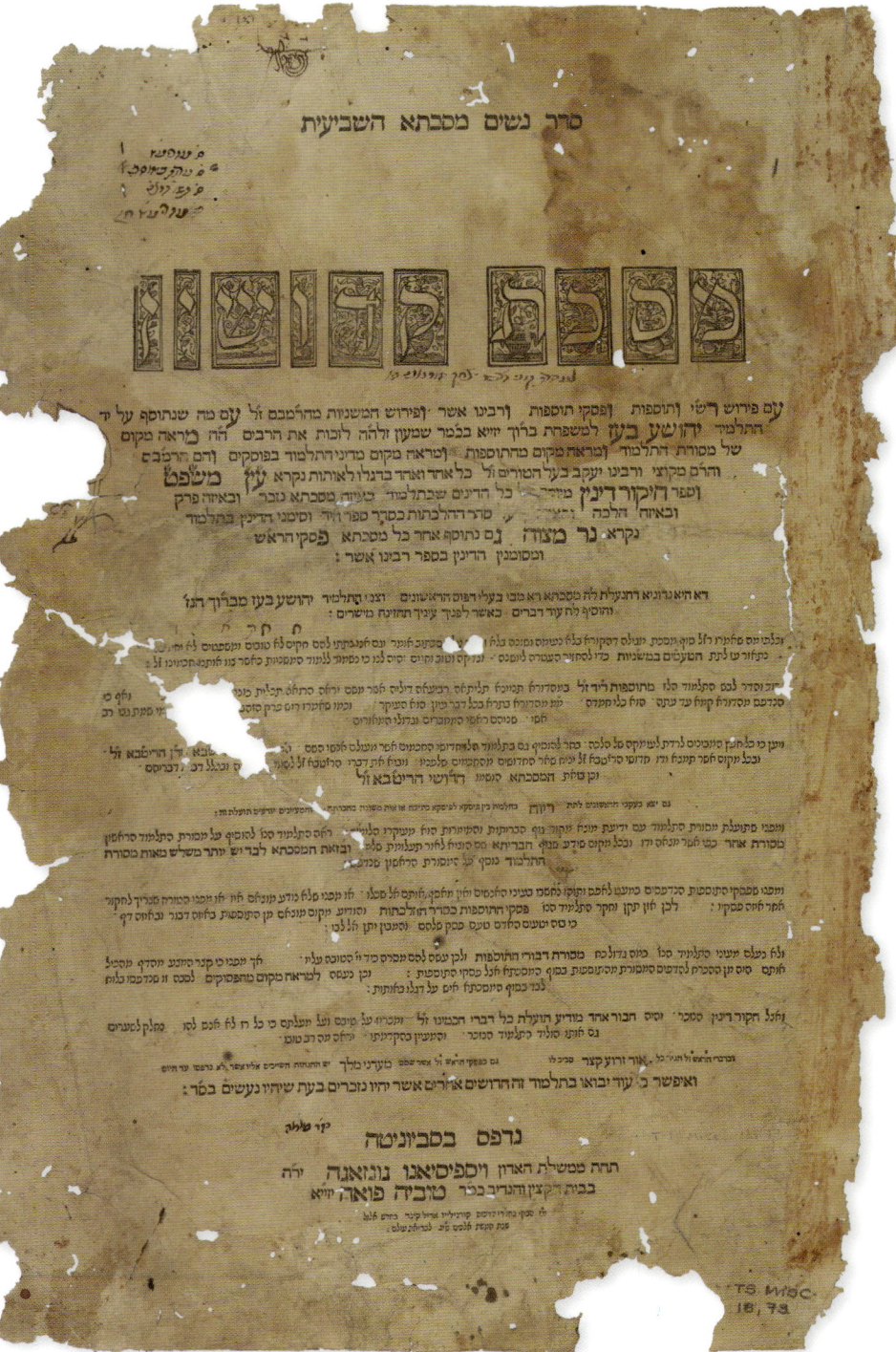

T-S Misc.18.73

The First Book Printed in Egypt

This is the 1557 edition of *Pitron Halomot* (*Interpretation of Dreams*) by Hai Gaon, the first book ever printed in Egypt with movable type. Its printer was Gershom ben Eliezer Soncino, a member of the famous Soncino family of Jewish printers. He founded the first Cairene printing press in the 1550s during the papal ban against Hebrew printing in Venice, but it only issued three books before his death in 1562.[8]

1557 CE

T-S Misc.17.5

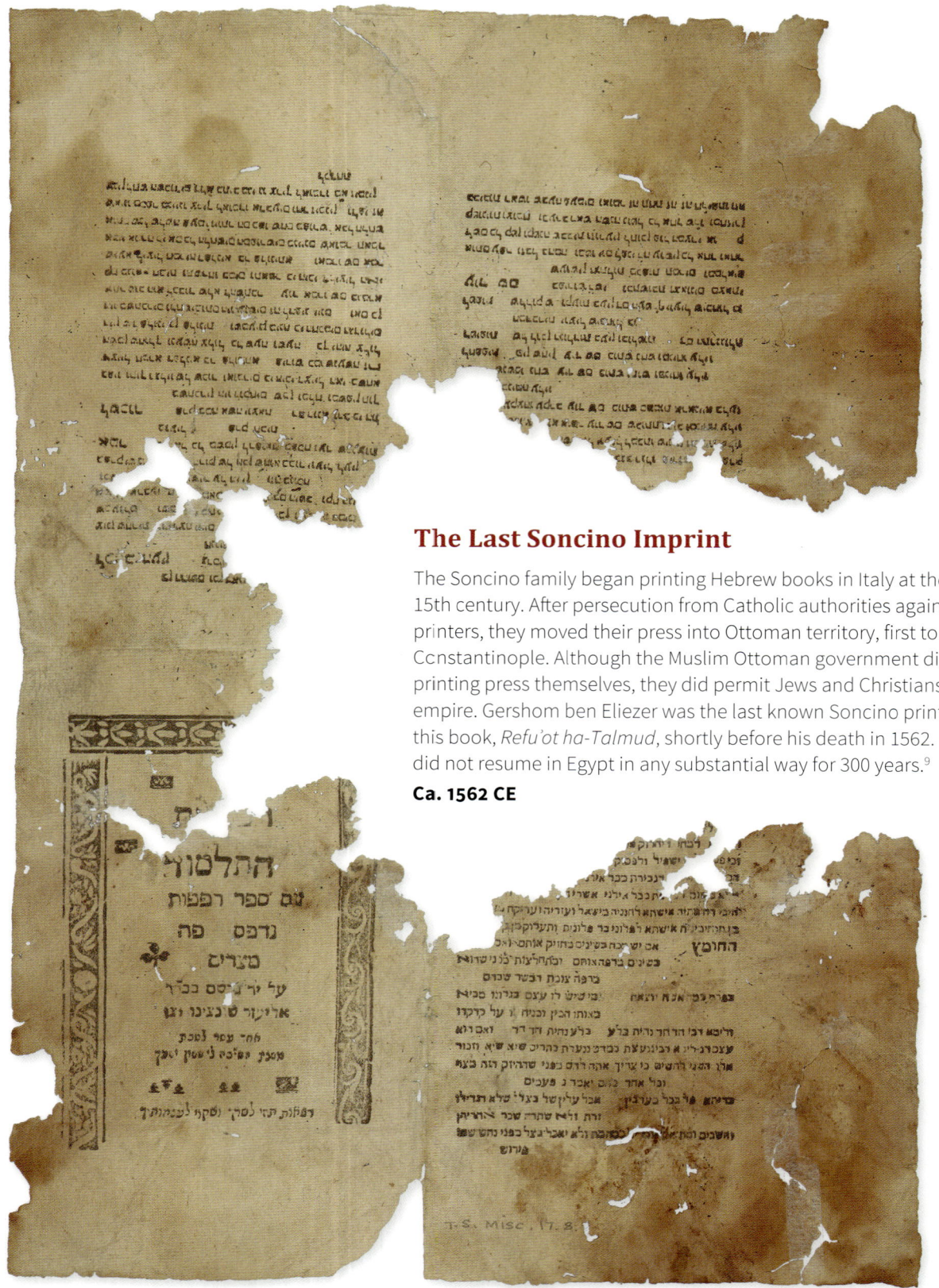

The Last Soncino Imprint

The Soncino family began printing Hebrew books in Italy at the end of the 15th century. After persecution from Catholic authorities against Jewish printers, they moved their press into Ottoman territory, first to Salonika, then to Ccnstantinople. Although the Muslim Ottoman government did not adopt the printing press themselves, they did permit Jews and Christians to print in their empire. Gershom ben Eliezer was the last known Soncino printer, and he printed this book, *Refu'ot ha-Talmud*, shortly before his death in 1562. Hebrew printing did not resume in Egypt in any substantial way for 300 years.[9]

Ca. 1562 CE

T-S Misc.17.8

Talmud Tractate Authorised by Suleiman the Magnificent

Fragmentary title page from Talmud tractate *Bava Mesi'a*, printed in Ottoman Salonika by Joseph ben Isaac Ya'bes during the reign of Suleiman the Magnificent (1520–1566). The paper was produced in Europe and bears a watermark similar to another attested in Parma and Padua around the same time. In the last two lines, Joseph pays respect to "our lord, the great and mighty King Sultan Suleiman, may his majesty rise and his kingdom be lifted up."

Ca. 1547–1566 CE

T-S Misc.19.108

The Venice Haggadah

This page comes from the Venice Haggadah, perhaps the most famous illustrated edition of the Passover Seder. Israel ha-Zifroni printed it at the Venetian press of Giovanni di Gara in 1609. In addition to the original Hebrew and Aramaic, this haggadah appealed to local Jews with a translation in 'Judaeo-Italian' (that is, Italian in Hebrew characters). Several other pages of the same imprint survive in the Genizah, as well as other books printed at Di Gara's press.

1609 CE

T-S Misc.17.107

T-S AS 197.305

T-S NS 270.167

Fragmented Bragadini Bible

One of Daniel Bomberg's successors in Venice was Alvise Bragadini. He died in 1575, but several generations of his descendants took advantage of his brand recognition and continued working as printers. Pietro and Lorenzo Bragadini printed this Hebrew Bible (specifically the *Ketuvim*) in Venice in 1619. The two fragments of the title page are in completely different sections of the collection that were conserved about 25 years apart.

1619 CE

A Jewish Printer in Istanbul

Beginning of a book of responsa called *Pnei Moshe*, printed by Abraham
Franco in Constantinople in 1669 CE. Abraham worked at a printing press that
his father, Solomon, founded several decades earlier. On the title page he
gives the common formula used by Hebrew publishers in the Ottoman Empire:
"Under the rule of our lord, the King Sultan Mehmed [the fourth]."

1669 CE

T-S Misc.16.118

T-S Misc.15.3

The Venetian Vendraminis

Hebrew printing in Italy gradually declined during the 17th century, but it didn't stop completely. In 1631, the Vendramini family founded a new Hebrew printing press in Venice, calling it *Stamparia Vendramina*. They printed short prayer books for use by Jews around the Mediterranean Sea, including this liturgical booklet, *Seder Ma'amadot*.

1686/87 CE

Mosseri Ia.36

Bavarian Edition of Mizrachi's Commentary on Rashi

Title page from Elijah Mizrachi's 'supercommentary' on Rashi and the Torah. Mizrachi was a Greek Jew, born in Istanbul, who studied in Italy during the 15th century. He was famous both as a religious scholar and as a mathematician, and he eventually became the Grand Rabbi of the Ottoman Empire. Isaac Itzik ben Leib printed this edition in Fuerth, Germany.[10]

1763 CE

Arabic Haggadah with Italian Engravings

Haggadah for the Passover Seder printed in Cairo in 1833/34. It comes from the printing press of Moshe Qastillo, one of only a handful of Hebrew printers known in Egyptian history. Typically in Hebrew and Aramaic, this haggadah includes a handwritten Judaeo-Arabic translation that was copied using the relatively new printing technology of 'lithography'. The images are reproductions of woodcuts originally produced for the Venice Haggadah of 1609 (☛ T-S Misc.17.107 above). Uniquely, however, this haggadah also included a woodcut illustration of enslaved Jewish labourers building the Egyptian pyramids. Although that page is lost from the Genizah copy, it reveals that, at least by the 19th century, some Egyptian Jews believed that their ancestors built the pyramids.[11]

1833/34 CE

T-S Misc.17.88

The Trieste Haggadah

The 19th century marked a golden age of Jewish culture in Trieste. In 1864, Jonah Cohen printed this elegant Passover Haggadah there, edited by Abraham Morburgo and illustrated by C. Kirchmayr (notice the *tiny* signature beneath the lower border). The book probably came to Egypt with Italian Jewish immigrants in the late 19th century.[12]

1864 CE

T-S NS 166.133

Ladino Haggadah with Dutch Engravings

Page from a 19th-century Passover Haggadah with translation in Ladino ('Judaeo-Spanish', or Spanish in Hebrew characters). It includes reproductions of elaborate woodcuts originally carved by the German Jewish engraver, Abraham ben Jacob, for the Amsterdam Haggadah of 1695. Jews around the Mediterranean recycled his woodcuts for new haggadot in the centuries after his death. The illustration depicts Moses striking an Egyptian in Exodus 2.

19th century

17 הגדה של פסח

אי מונגו קי אנסי דיזי איל פסוק מילאבראה קומו אירמוייו דיאיל
קאמפו עידי: אי מוג'יגואסטיטי אי אינגראנדיסיסטי איג'ינסטיס:
קון אפייטי די אפייטיס פיגוס פואירון קונפואיסטוס איטו קאג'יליייז
אירמולייסיו: איטו דיזנודה אי דיסקוג'יירטה: אי איכמאלייסיירון אנוס
לוס אג'יפסיאנוס אי אפריירונוס אי דייכון סוג'רי נוס סירג'ימייכטו דורו:
אי איכמאלייסיירון אנוס לוס אג'יפסיאנוס קי אנסי דיזי איל פסוק דאד
אסאג'יכטימוס נוס פור איל קיסאם סימוג'יגואם איסירה קואנדו נוס
אקונטיסירה פילייה אי איכייאדירה עאנביין איל סוג'רי נואיסטרוס
אבוריסייכטים אי פיליארה קון נוס אי סוג'ירה דילה טיירה: אי
אפריאירון נוס קי אנסי דיזי איל פסוק אי פוזיירון סוג'רי איל מאיורלאלים
די פינגאס פור אפריאירלוס אין סוס לאזירייאס איפראגו או סיג'דאדים די
איכקאסטילייאדוראס אה פרעה אה פיתום אי אה רעמסס:

משה מאטה אה איל מצרי

ויתנו עלינו עבדה קשה כמה שנאמר ויעבדו מצרים
את בני ישראל בפרך: ונצעק אל יהוה אלהי
אבתינו וישמע יהוה את קלנו וירא את ענינו ואת
עמלנו ואת לחצנו: ונצעק אל יהוה אלהי אבתינו כמה

Hagadah Sph.

T-S NS 25.275

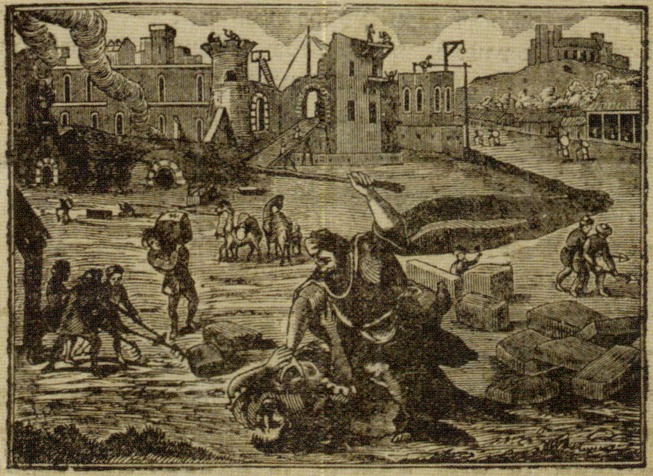

Alexandrian Amulets

After Gershom Soncino's press closed in 1562, no one in Egypt managed to start a successful Hebrew printing business until after 1860. Then in 1873, an Iranian Jewish immigrant named Faraj Mizrahi founded the most successful Hebrew printing press in Egyptian history. It stayed in business for more than 40 years. Working from Alexandria, Mizrahi and his assistant, Abraham Zaytuni, printed this amulet featuring the Ten Commandments sometime before 1897. More than a dozen fragments of amulets that Zaytuni and Mizrahi printed together survive in the Genizah, easily spctted by their characteristic blue ink.

1872–1897 CE

T-S NS 26.226

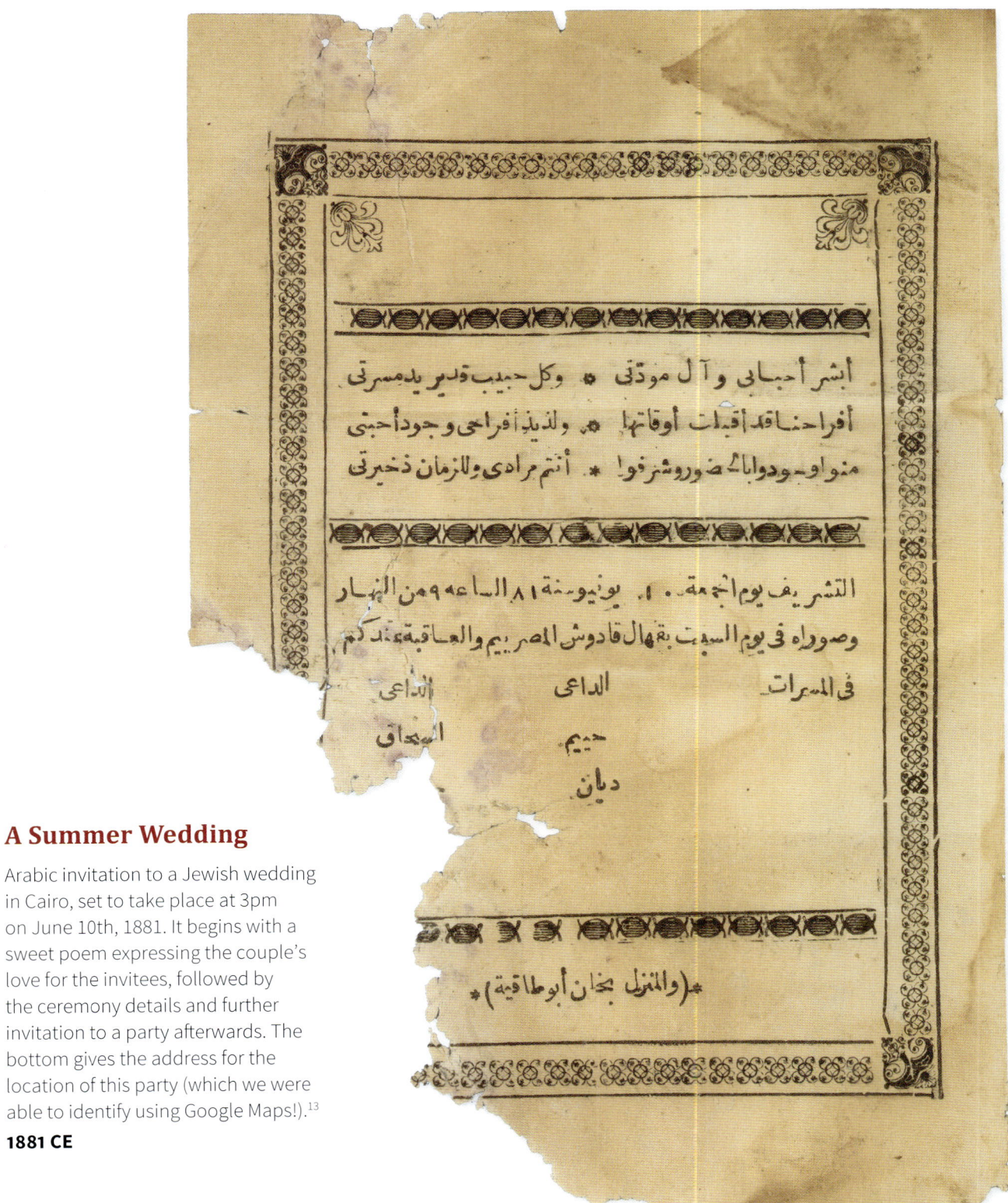

A Summer Wedding

Arabic invitation to a Jewish wedding in Cairo, set to take place at 3pm on June 10th, 1881. It begins with a sweet poem expressing the couple's love for the invitees, followed by the ceremony details and further invitation to a party afterwards. The bottom gives the address for the location of this party (which we were able to identify using Google Maps!).[13]

1881 CE

T-S NS 266.113

El Tiempo Newspaper

Fragment of the front page of *El Tiempo* from January 25th, 1881. *El Tiempo* (*The Time*) was the first Ladino newspaper published in Istanbul, mainly serving Jewish communities of the Ottoman Empire from 1872 until 1930. Some of these Jews were descendants of Iberian refugees who fled Spain and Portugal in the 1490s and continued speaking Ladino in their new homes.[14]

January 25th, 1881 CE

T-S AS 195.546

Q: When did Jews stop using the Cairo Genizah?

When we talk about 'The Cairo Genizah' it often sounds like a well-defined collection of papers that Cairo's Jews stored in a single location. The reality is a bit more complex. While it's true that the majority of Genizah fragments come from the genizah chamber of Fustat's Ben Ezra Synagogue, that is not the case for all fragments. In fact, when Solomon Schechter arrived in Cairo in 1896, the Cambridge University Library already had hundreds of fragments that we think came from the Genizah (in this book they are the classmarks starting with 'Or.' and 'Add.'). The University Library – advised by Schechter – purchased these fragments from private dealers on the Egyptian and Palestinian antiquities markets to expand Cambridge's small collection of Hebrew manuscripts. Many scholarly libraries were doing the same, and by the 1890s, other European collectors – most notably Adolf Neubauer of Oxford's Bodleian Library – had also acquired thousands of manuscript fragments that probably came from the Ben Ezra Synagogue. But we cannot be certain that they were all from there. Some manuscripts could have come from the Karaite Dar Simha Synagogue or from one of the other dozen or so synagogues in Egypt in the late 19th century.

We also know that Schechter and Cambridge University Library purchased additional manuscripts to add to the Taylor-Schechter Collection after 1897.

The number of fragments stored in the Ben Ezra Synagogue seems to have declined steeply in the 17th and 18th centuries as Fustat's Jews moved to other parts of the city, but they kept producing manuscripts and storing them in separate genizot. Even after Schechter and his 'hoard' left Egypt, other collectors found Jewish manuscripts buried at sites around Cairo. As late as 1912, a local Jewish collector named Jacques Mosseri dug up caches of old texts (now with classmarks beginning 'Mosseri') in the grounds of the Ben Ezra synagogue and the Basatin Cemetery. More recent discoveries in Egypt speak of a 'New Cairo Genizah' with texts from even later than 1912. In that sense, the Jews of Egypt never 'stopped' using the Cairo Genizah – they continued reading and writing and depositing their old papers in safe places for as long as they lived there. For our purposes though, practically everything from the 'Cairo Genizah' that resides in Cambridge was produced before 1912.

Viennese Genesis

Title page of Genesis that Josef Schlesinger printed at his Viennese *Buchhandlung* in 1882. It's only a few inches wide – easily small enough to carry in a pocket. At the time, Eastern Europe was the centre of Hebrew printing and Schlesinger was a leading publisher of Hebrew religious works. Although we don't know exactly who was selling them, many of his books ended up in Egypt and are now found in Cairo Genizah collections.

1882 CE

T-S NS 165.62

A French Invitation

One of our favourite fragments in the collection, this is a French invitation to an Italian Egyptian Jewish wedding between Raphael Lagnado and Bienvenue Eliakim. It's split down the middle so their parents could have separate messages. Dated February 9th, 1888, just *one week* before the wedding in Cairo.

February 9th, 1888 CE

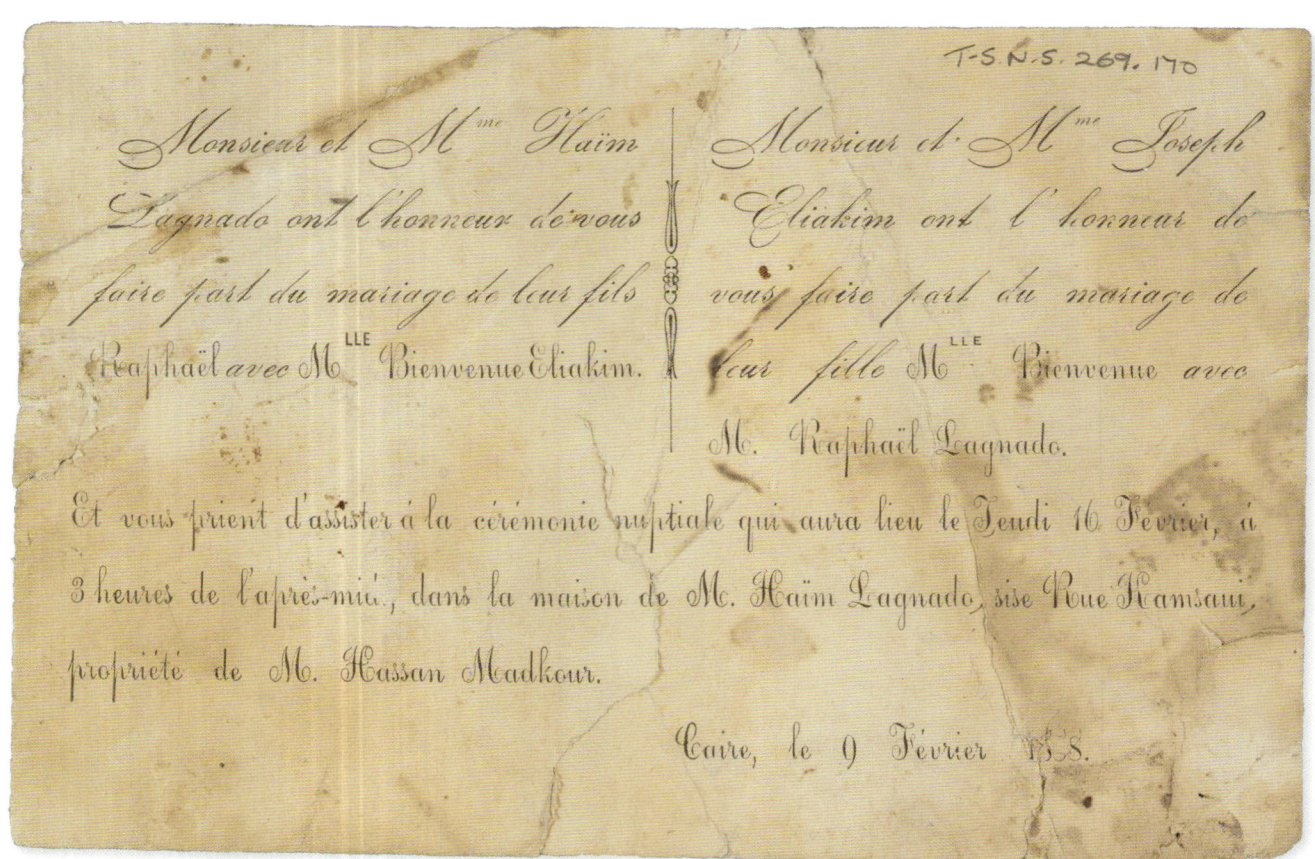

T-S NS 269.170

T-S AS 192.467

El-Falah Newspaper

The front page of Cairo's *El-Falah* newspaper from April 21st, 1888. Arabic newspapers operated in Egypt from the early 19th century onwards, and several have survived in Genizah collections. This paper gives its name in French and Arabic, the date in both Christian and Muslim formats, and even provides advertising rates (25 pence for a front-page ad!).[15]

April 21st, 1888 CE

Notes to Chapter XI

1   See Karl Schaefer, 'Eleven Medieval Arabic Block Prints in the Cambridge University Library', *Arabica* 48, no. 2 (2001): 210–39; Kristina Richardson, *Roma in the Medieval Islamic World: Literacy, Culture, and Migration* (London: I.B. Tauris, 2022), 103–126.

2   Thank you to Magdalen M. Connolly for directing us to this fragment. See Karl Schaefer, *Enigmatic Charms: Medieval Arabic Block Printed Amulets in American and European Libraries and Museums*, vol. 82, Handbook of Ottoman Studies (Leiden: Brill, 2006), 94–96.

3   Nick Posegay, 'Solving European Writer's Block in Jewish Cairo (T-S 20.188)', *Fragment of the Month (January)*, Cambridge University Library: Genizah Research Unit, 2023.

4   ISTC No. im00866160. Thank you to Michelle Margolis and David Selis for helping to identify this edition.

5   See Nick Posegay and Orietta Da Rold, "Following the Mediterranean Paper Trail: A Study of European Paper in Late Medieval Cairo (ca. 1350–1600)."

The Library (2024). T-S Misc.12.32.1–6 is another imprint that alternates between paper and parchment.

6   Eva Frojmovic, 'From Naples to Constantinople: The Aesop Workshop's Woodcuts in the Oldest Illustrated Printed Haggadah', *The Library* 18, no. 2 (1996): 91, 105–7.

7   Ronny Vollandt, 'The Constantinople Polyglot of 1546', *Genizah Fragments*, 2010.

8   Nick Posegay, 'Hebrew Printing and Printers' Colophons in the Cairo Genizah: Networking Book Trade in Europe and the Ottoman Empire', in *Literary Snippets: Colophons Across Space and Time*, eds. George A. Kiraz and Sabine Schmidtke (Piscataway, NJ: Gorgias Press, 2023), 85–86.

9   See Diana Rowland-Smith, 'The Beginnings of Hebrew Printing in Egypt', *British Library Journal*, 1989, 16–22.

10 Nick Posegay, 'Hebrew Printing and Printers' Colophons in the Cairo Genizah: Networking Book Trade in Europe and the Ottoman Empire', in

Literary Snippets: Colophons Across Space and Time, eds. George A. Kiraz and Sabine Schmidtke (Piscataway, NJ: Gorgias Press, 2023), 92–93.

11 Diana Rowland-Smith, 'The Beginnings of Hebrew Printing in Egypt', *British Library Journal*, 1989, 16–22.

12 See Shlomo Simonsohn and Samuele Rocca, 'Trieste', in *Encyclopedia Judaica* (Detroit: Macmillan Reference USA, 2007).

13 Nick Posegay, 'Searching for the Last Genizah Fragment in Late Ottoman Cairo: A Material Survey of Egyptian Jewish Literary Culture', *International Journal of Middle East Studies* 54, no. 3 (2022): 436–437.

14 Dov Cohen, 'Missing Treasures: Tracking Lost Ladino Books', *Zutot* 17, no. 1 (2020): 64.

15 Nick Posegay, 'Searching for the Last Genizah Fragment in Late Ottoman Cairo: A Material Survey of Egyptian Jewish Literary Culture', *International Journal of Middle East Studies* 54, no. 3 (2022): 436–437.

Further Reading

Abraham's Luggage: A Social Life of Things in the Medieval Indian Ocean World (Cambridge, 2018) by Elizabeth A. Lambourn

Arabic Legal and Administrative Documents in the Cambridge Genizah Collections (Cambridge, 1993) by Geoffrey Khan

The Cairo Genizah and the Age of Discovery in Egypt (London, 2022) by Rebecca J. W. Jefferson

Coming of Age in Medieval Egypt: Female Adolescence, Jewish Law, and Ordinary Culture (Princeton, 2018) by Eve Krakowski

Composing Egypt: Reading, Writing, and the Emergence of a Modern Nation 1870–1930 (Stanford, 2016) by Hoda A. Yousef

Composition Analysis of Writing Materials in Cairo Genizah Documents (Leiden, 2021) by Zina Cohen

Islamic Codicology (London, 2015) by François Déroche et al.

Fortifications and the Synagogue: the Fortress of Babylon and the Ben Ezra Synagogue, Cairo (Montreal, 1994) edited by Phyllis Lambert

From a Sacred Source: Genizah Studies in Honour of Professor Stefan C. Reif (Leiden, 2010) edited by Ben Outhwaite and Siam Bhayro

From the Battlefield of Books: Essays Celebrating 50 Years of the Taylor-Schechter Genizah Research Unit (Leiden, 2024) edited by Nick Posegay, Magdalen M. Connolly, and Ben Outhwaite

Hebrew Manuscripts of the Middle Ages (Cambridge, 2002) by Colette Sirat

Heresy and the Politics of Community: The Jews of the Fatimid Caliphate (Ithaca, 2008) by Marina Rustow

In an Antique Land (London, 1992) by Amitav Ghosh

A Jewish Archive from Old Cairo (London, 2000) by Stefan Reif

Jews in Nineteenth-Century Egypt (New York, 1969) by Philip M. Landau

The Last Watchman of Old Cairo (New York, 2018) by Michael David Lukas

The Lost Archive (Princeton, 2019) by Marina Rustow

Medical Prescriptions in the Cambridge Genizah Collections (Leiden, 2012) by Efraim Lev and Leigh Chipman

A Mediterranean Society (6 vols.) (Berkeley, 1967–1994) by Shelomo Dov Goitein

Sacred Trash (New York, 2011) by Adina Hoffman and Peter Cole

Sacred Treasure (Woodstock, 2011) by Mark Glickman

Sisters of Sinai (New York, 2009) by Janet Soskice

Solomon Schechter: A Biography (Philadelphia, 1938) by Norman Bentwich

Trade and Institutions in the Medieval Mediterranean: The Geniza Merchants and Their Business World (Cambridge, 2012) by Jessica L. Goldberg

La Vida Cotidiana de Los Judíos de Alandalús (Siglos X–XII) (Córdoba, 2021) by José Martínez Delgado and Amir Ashur